STOP
Flushing
Your Money
Down the Drain

by

David A. Thyfault

ATTRIBUTION

To my son, Adam, who attended one of my lectures and said, *You should write down some of that stuff.*

I did as he suggested, then took the next step.
This book is the result.

Thanks, Son.

DEDICATION

As a seasoned landlord, I have rented apartments to young tenants who are fresh out of high school and who have already abused a credit card. I have catered to old-timers who never could get on track. I have received countless bounced checks. I have watched adults cry like babies when bank representatives have visited our tenants to repossess their vehicles. I have known people who pay late fees month after month. I have had to evict too many families because they spent their rent money on other things they did not need.

I have observed their pain, first-hand, as their personal property was moved to the streets under the watchful eye of the sheriff and the courts. I have seen the fear in the eyes of their children as they wondered what would happen to them next.

Upon entering certain tenants' homes, I have witnessed the chaos in their lives. In the most extreme cases, they had not vacuumed their dwellings for months. Dirty dishes, trash and old clothes were frequently lying around. Empty cans of beer or pop spilled out of bags in the corner of the kitchen. The stench was disgusting. The bedrooms where the children slept were filthy. I have found mounds of fecal matter from pets in basements or bedrooms, as well as maggots, cockroaches, mouse tracks and signs of rats.

The saddest part is that, in most cases, the drama could have been avoided if only they had known how to use their resources more wisely. That is why this book is dedicated to anybody who has ever been evicted, or had the misfortune of foreclosure, job loss, poor money management practices or personal tragedy. My goal is to extract something positive from the disastrous experiences I have seen, and use that information to help other people prevent or eliminate financial misfortune so that they can lead happy, prosperous lives.

TABLE OF CONTENTS

SECTION ONE – THE DIM PAST

SECTION TWO – TAKING ACTION IN THE PRESENT

SECTION THREE – CREATING A BRIGHT FUTURE

ABOUT THE AUTHOR

This is supposed to be a section in which I take on the voice of a third person and impress you with my background. Ideally, it would sound something like this: Mr. Thyfault graduated first in his class from Harvard Business School at the age of ten. From there he found a dollar behind the 7-Eleven and bought a can of lemonade and sold it on the corner for a handsome profit. Before he knew it, the President of the United States called him, seeking financial advice . . .

It ain't gonna happen. Who can really relate to somebody like that?

Instead of my blowing my horn, why don't I just tell you, in a straightforward way, why a guy who was raised in the lower middle class might just be qualified to discuss financial matters with you.

For starters, nobody handed me a fortune. When my dad died, I got a couple of his shirts, and a few tools. That was about all he owned. My mom passed ten years later. Her house was sold, and each of us kids raked in about ten thousand dollars. So that wasn't it.

I wasn't overly smart either. I graduated just a couple spots below the middle of my high school class back in the sixties. Ah, the sixties—the hippie years. I explored those years with enthusiasm. Too much, in fact. I flunked out of two colleges. So that wasn't it.

I didn't hit the lottery either, although I did manage to wrangle up a very special wife, or life-partner, if you prefer. That was as close as I got to hitting the lottery.

Best job? For two years, I was a produce manager for a grocery store. Next?

Brilliant inventions? None.

There are no oil wells from a rich uncle, no miracles, no extraordinary breaks.

Do you see anything in that history that intimidates you or out-classes you? I doubt it.

Yet somehow I managed to accumulate millions of dollars. More than several millions. Enough of them to last me a lifetime and beyond. It was all done before I reached my 50s. I retired at age 49.

So how did I do it? What secrets propelled me to financial security?

I seemed to have a lot of common sense, including financial common sense. For instance, we all know that time passes every day and people grow old, but I wanted to figure out how I could make those dynamics work in my favor. So I paid attention to things that others tend to dismiss as boring.

One thing I did was figure out a formula that would serve me and others, whether we were smart or not, had top paying jobs or not, were lucky or not and, eventually, whether we worked or not.

I decided that I hated most debt, but not all of it. I decided to save consistently, even if I didn't have any money to save. And I decided to invest money wisely.

The key to it all boiled down to figuring out where to get the money to invest wisely. Once I knew where to get the money and what to do with it, everything fell into place over time.

The cool part is that nearly everybody has the exact same resources that I had. They just don't know it. It's right under their noses and within arms' length.

So who's better qualified to help them: some smarty pants professor with a bunch of letters behind his or her name and who's probably always on the financial edge himself, or somebody who knows, firsthand, how ordinary people can become financially secure or even wealthy if that's what they want? Give me the fellow with experience. You can keep your sheepskin.

The bottom line is I know why and how people should hate debt; I know how and why they can save money they don't even know that they have; and I know how to invest that money wisely.

And that's all that really matters.

Call it a biography if you want to.

FOREWORD

If you would like to get a better handle on your finances,
then this book is for you.
If you are a financial novice, you need this book.
If you want to avoid suffering through the pain
and discomfort of total financial collapse,
you should read this book.
If you are considering bankruptcy,
you should read this book.
If you are Bill Gates, Donald Trump, or Warren Buffet,
you are excused.

Too many smart people let their finances happen to them in a haphazard fashion. When they want to buy something, they examine their checkbook balance, and if there is a sufficient amount to cover the purchase, a few bucks quickly slip away. If the checkbook is devoid of sufficient resources, they revert to Plan B: pull out the plastic money. All of this happens with little regard for the fact that the future is fraught with money-hungry obligations and opportunities.

These misguided people have no idea why they are always broke. They may not even realize some of the ways they lose the money they make. As a result, they are destined to live in the proverbial "poorhouse," or at least well below their potential. It is a shame too, because it does not have to be that way.

There are all sorts of reasons why good people have financial problems. Unfortunately, their parents and schools don't usually take the time to teach them what they need to know . . . frequently because those leaders suffer from the same lack of knowledge.

Other reasons include the following. They seek instant gratification. They cannot distinguish between wants vs. needs. They become addicted to spending and consuming. They borrow money from their credit cards or home equity to subsidize their bad money habits. They have never experienced the gratification of saving or investing. They don't mind living with monthly payments. They do not understand basic financial principles like compound interest. They justify unnecessary purchases with sentiment like, "I deserve this." They only make minimum payments on their credit cards. They like to have the same toys others have. And, they do not understand risk management. There are many more, but you get the point. Obviously those folks just do not know how to manage money and that is what this book is all about.

I am not talking about worshiping dollars, exploiting people, lying on your taxes or working two full-time jobs to get ahead. There is no need to do those things. Instead, my objective is to show you how to do a better job of using the money you already receive, and to help you attract new income in new ways. By adopting prudent money management practices you can improve your own life as well as the lives of those around you.

One of the most important things you can do is to become more proactive in determining how your money should be earned and spent. Oh, sure, you know how much money the boss pays you, and how much the car payment is, but how long has it been since you obtained a hard copy of your credit report or reviewed your auto insurance policy? Yawn! Who wants to do that? Right? Well, those are the kinds of habits that determine whether you get to use your money for things that matter to you, or whether you allow somebody else to decide how to spend it for you.

The point of all this is that you need to control your money or it will control you. This book will show you how to do that.

How Do People Face Their Finances?

One person told me that the people who need this information most are the ones who are least likely to read it. I suppose there is some truth to his point because a fair number of people don't read much of anything. It is unfortunate that many of those people respond to their financial woes by getting a part-time job or living beneath their potential. They would not have to do that if they would put a fraction of that effort into learning good financial habits.

Aside from those folks, I have discovered there are many other people who seek financial advice for various reasons. Perhaps you are one of them. Regardless of your motives, I am glad you dropped by.

I hope to reduce the bulk of this information to common sense because that should make it easier to retain and employ in the future. I believe that, by lending structure to some of the knowledge you already have and adding plenty of fresh information, this book will be both informative and profitable for you.

This book is comprised of three distinct sections. The first one is about the PAST. In it we review some of the unwise decisions you may have been making in your day-to-day life, sometimes without even knowing it. The second section is about the PRESENT. We will explore the actions you need to take right away in order to set your life on a prudent economic course. Finally, there is a section for the FUTURE. It addresses the financial decisions that come up from time to time as life unfolds. The objective is to provide some specific information, in advance of when you need it, so you will be better prepared when these choices do actually confront you.

You will get the most out of your time if you slow down and spread the reading out over multiple sittings, rather than to skim over the ideas in a flurry. The goal here should be gaining knowledge, not adding another finished book to a bookshelf.

Okay, then, let's see what this book is all about.

SECTION ONE

THE DIM PAST

THE WORST THINGS ON WHICH WE WASTE OUR MONEY

What is the most you would pay for a cup of coffee?

By seven o'clock this morning, I was at the local grocery store. There is a Starbucks inside and several people were already in line, including a few regulars.

Even though I have never bought coffee there before, I decided to get the biggest, best, most expensive cup of coffee they had. It was a large pumpkin spice Frappuccino with four shots of espresso. It had a healthy dose of whipped cream and some cinnamon sprinkled on top. It was chilled, like a fantastic malt. For the next forty-five minutes, I savored every sip.

Since I have only bought one other cup of gourmet coffee in my lifetime, I wanted to discover the very best experience somebody could have with such a purchase. For $7.75 I spent 45 minutes in coffee heaven. But now the coffee is gone and so is the $7.75. And I can say without any doubt, it was NOT worth it. To compound my misfortune, I will be paying interest on that money forever. That is because . . .

Every single purchase we make in life brings with it a lifetime of interest expenses, even if we pay cash for the items.

Let me use food to illustrate my point. Since you have to eat, some of the money you spend for this purpose is justified, but a lot of the money we spend on food is wasted. When you pay

3

somebody else to prepare your meal for you, some of your cost is a convenience fee.

For example, if you could grill a burger at home for $1 but instead you drop by your favorite fast-food restaurant and buy a nice burger for $3, you are paying them $2 to do the work for you. From that moment on you will have an interest cost on your wasted $2... FOREVER!

That is because you could have used that $2 to pay off other debt you have. Let's suppose you have a credit card on which you typically carry an unpaid balance of $500. For our purposes, we shall assign an interest cost of 12 percent to that card's debt.

Now, every dollar that you waste on some other frivolous purchase or some other expense that you could reasonably avoid (whether you know about it or not) is denying you the opportunity to pay off that high interest cost on your credit card. Therefore, if you flush $2 down the drain on a burger or $100 on the wrong insurance policy or a few bucks in ATM fees, etc., that is money you could have used to pay off that debt and thereby save the interest expense that is attached to it. But since you did not pay off that debt, the interest lives on and can never be recovered.

So every purchase you make also costs you 12 percent in a different pocket, even if you paid cash for the item in question. In this example, twelve percent of $2 is twenty-four cents. Therefore every year after that fast-food burger is consumed, you will have to pay an extra twenty-four cents in interest costs.

That does not seem like much, but when we add that purchase to thousands of others just like it, we quickly get to an enormous annual expense. Two or three such choices a day for ten years will add up to an annual hit to your budget in the thousands of dollars.

Unfortunately, most of us do not restrict our poor choices to the ones that cost a couple of bucks. Sometimes we are talking about wasting hundreds or even thousands of dollars on ill-advised purchases, and that raises our annual interest losses to tens of thousands of dollars. If you can afford to ignore losses like that you probably don't need this book.

When I share this concept with students, there is usually somebody in the room who suggests that he pays off his credit card every month, thereby implying that he has no such ongoing interest expense. At that point I respond by asking if the person has a car loan or a home loan. Typically, he does and that ends the discussion.

Students then realize that they could be paying off those debts with the money they waste on other things, and, by paying off debts rather than spending the money, they save the interest expense of those loans.

Furthermore, even if they have no loans whatsoever, there is still an interest expense attached to any frivolous spending or misspent funds. The consumer who has no debt can invest his cash in various ways.

Savings accounts pay a small percentage and other investments can be more lucrative. Any dollars that are flushed down the drain could be used to generate that interest, so, if that opportunity is lost, there is an interest expense attached to the loss.

To simplify, any outstanding debt has an ongoing interest expense that you could reduce or avoid by paying down the loan; and, even if you are completely debt-free, you could invest wasted dollars and receive interest income . . . forever. But, by foregoing that opportunity, there is a FOREVER INTEREST expense to all of your purchases.

The Payoff

If we are only talking about one cup of gourmet coffee a month that may not be a very big deal, but people who buy impulsive and convenient coffee or hamburgers don't ordinarily do it just once. They do it day after day. They justify their purchases with self-assuring comments like, "I deserve this" or "It is only a few dollars" or "I can always cut back tomorrow."

These are the kinds of justifications that lead otherwise smart people into financial ruin. Their habit or laziness costs them a cash

5

register full of money every month. And, in the worst cases, they finance their extravagant purchases with credit cards, which they do not pay off at the end of the month. That is financial suicide.

Here is why this is all so important: If you only buy one Frappuccino per lifetime (or occasionally), I can assure you that it really is special; but if you can find just $4 per day that you are wasting on such things and if you can redirect that money to pay off debts or make investments, you can accumulate $465,000 in buying power in one adult lifetime (more on that later). Even a complete idiot would know that a daily cup of gourmet coffee is not worth that.

In this section we will discuss things like gourmet coffee, pets, alcohol, transportation, children and more. These are some of the worst things on which we waste our money. I am not suggesting that it is a waste of money for you to buy a cup of coffee or to have a child. That is for you to decide. What I am trying to illustrate is how much these things are going to cost in the long run. Once you understand this, you can redirect your resources more wisely if and when you want to.

CONVENIENCES

Americans pay through the nose for convenience. I know because a whole bunch of them pay me.

For years I have owned and operated one single vending machine, which dispenses soda pop at a 100-unit apartment building. I am constantly amazed because that one machine generates about $2,600 in gross profit per year.

That machine is a constant reminder of all the people who struggle financially. Most of them fail to comprehend simple money priorities like how expensive "convenience" really is. Instead of buying their soft drinks at the grocery store, just like I do, they pay me to go get them for them. Eight thousand times a year, somebody in that building steps up to that machine and hands me 50 cents, of which 30 cents is gross profit for me . . . just for doing something they could easily do for themselves.

Sadly, these same people, and others like them, pay handsomely for conveniences in other areas of their lives too. When they go to the gas station, they pick up a pack of cigarettes because it is convenient. In so doing, they disregard the enormous mark-up they are paying for not buying their smokes by the carton at one of the giant food warehouses.

Later on, they get their dinner at a drive-through food chain or have a pizza delivered.

The "convenience factor" governs nearly every phase of their lives. They pay $15 for a carwash even though they could get a bucket of hot water from the tap and perform that duty themselves practically for free. In another example, every year millions of Americans pay tax penalties to the IRS because it is more convenient to put off filing their returns than get them completed on time.

I must admit that I also fall into the convenience trap. My weakness raises its head when the Girl Scouts sell their cookies. I like to be nice to youngsters and they come right to my doorstep to charge me for the privilege. I am a sucker for their little smiles and leprechaun-like uniforms. I am amused when they say, with a straight face, that they charge $4.00 for each box of what amounts to a half-bag of cookies.

But before they leave I usually buy a box or two of Thin Mints for the freezer, plus a couple of boxes of Trefoils and several boxes of Do-Si-Dos. Ironically, I always thank them for "coming by" as they walk away with my cash stuffed in their little pockets. And I join the ranks of those who pay through the nose for conveniences.

I am not suggesting that we should always do things the hard way just to save a few coins. But unfortunately, the folks who ignore the high price of convenience are frequently the ones who can least afford to be so cavalier. Over a lifetime they would pocket many tens of thousands of dollars in savings if they would stop flushing their money away like they do.

How much are you willing to pay for convenience?

There are countless examples of entrepreneurs taking advantage of the convenience seekers. At a recent trip to the grocery store I noticed two containers of soup. They each held the same quantity of clam chowder. One container was a typical can and the other was a microwaveable, disposable bowl. The latter cost more than twice as much, so the consumer pays double to avoid a dirty dish.

The grocery stores are packed with other examples of the high cost of convenience. Have you ever strolled past the deli and noticed how good those salads look? YUM! I like the three-bean salad, but it is so easy to make, it is nearly sinful to pay them to put it together in a bowl. The same holds true for macaroni salad, potato salad and Jell-O. These dishes are all made with simple ingredients and can be made at home fairly quickly.

The dairy case has a half-quart sized carton of "real egg," What? Packaged real eggs! Are you kidding me? Eggs are already real and already packaged (in shells). Who the heck wants to pay for the convenience of somebody else cracking eggs and putting them in a carton? To be fair, the carton actually says egg whites and I will acknowledge that some people prefer them, so I will cut that group some slack, but common sense says that plenty of other people pick up that carton just because it is so convenient.

The frozen food aisle is packed with opportunities to flush your money on conveniences. On a recent stroll there I noted frozen pancakes and frozen sandwiches. Good grief! Is there any dish on the planet that is easier to prepare than a sandwich? A ten-year old can do that. It defies logic to pay somebody else to make a sandwich or a pancake for you. If you want to buy frozen vegetables to serve when they are out of season that is one thing, but pancakes and sandwiches are never out of season.

Perhaps the greatest example of people over-paying for convenience at grocery stores is single servings of microwaveable popcorn. You can buy a big bag of loose popcorn for $2 and you can get a hot air popper at Wal-Mart, or similar places, for $20 or less. The cost of a serving of popcorn made this way is less than 10 cents. But the microwave packages are five times as much. Now here is the surprise. The hot air popper actually cooks at a slightly faster rate than the "convenient" microwave. There is one other benefit to the do-it-yourself technique: You can control what ingredients go into your snack. There are only a couple of very minor drawbacks: You have to have a place to keep the popper and you have to wipe it off when you are done. That might take 15 seconds. The bottom line is you pay a forty-cent penalty for saving fifteen seconds of your time. That means you are paying $96/hr. for somebody to clean up your popcorn popper.

That seems like a ridiculous price to me.

The last time I went to the grocery store I looked at the various ways to acquire a pepperoni pizza. One can buy the basic ingredients for a large pie at a cost below $3.00. But you do have to take the time to find them in the store and make the pizza yourself. As an alternative, the customer can visit the spaghetti aisle and find a nice prepackaged box with all of the right ingredients to make that same pizza. You save some of the shopping time, but the price nearly doubles. There are still more options.

The same basic pizza can be picked up from the frozen food aisle for about $8. You pay two dollars extra because you don't have to do all of the preparation. You just pop it in your oven. But the highest cost of all is via home delivery. Add a couple more dollars for the company to prepare your pizza and throw in a few more bucks for the delivery fee. Kick in an extra dollar for sales tax and about $4 for a tip, and you are up to $15 or so–five times the cheapest route. But there is still one more very expensive thing to consider.

A consumer who willingly pays $15 to get a pizza delivered is severely penalized by the government. Before that person can pull $15 out of her purse, she must first earn about $20 at work. Then there are income taxes deducted from her check. What she has leftover is called "after-tax" dollars and that is what she uses to buy her pizza (and everything else). Therefore, the government is charging her something like $5 for her pizza. The bottom line is this: the more convenient, the higher the cost.

The most frivolous food costs are borne at your favorite restaurant. In addition to the usual convenience costs (preparation, clean atmosphere, cooking and clean up) you must add 40-60 percent to any price on the menu. The sales tax is 5-8 percent and there is an 18 percent gratuity (even though we usually compute the tip based on the total ticket, which includes the sales tax). Then throw in the fact that you had to earn extra money at work and pay the income tax out of that and you might as well stop by the poorhouse for a donation on your way home.

Two days ago, I ate just such a lunch. I had a salad that would have cost about 75 cents to assemble at home. I also ate about eight mushroom-stuffed ravioli that I could have made for less than two dollars. I paid $10 for my lunch; then I compounded my problem by picking up the tab for my two friends. The taxes alone were more than I would have had to pay for my meal, if I had made it at home. The lost $30 will cost me $3 per year . . . FOREVER. All of that was with after-tax dollars. There is no doubt that I paid through the nose for convenience.

I really enjoyed the experience because I had not seen my friends for a couple of years, but it is not the kind of thing I do on a habitual, thoughtless basis. I know to save those frivolous moments for special occasions. Being lazy is not a special occasion.

Food is not the only way that we pay for our desire to take the easy way out.

The Trap of Credit Cards

Credit cards are among our worst enemies. We will have a nice discussion about this "funny money" a little later on, but for now we cannot overlook the convenience factor. Too many of us submit to the temptation of instant gratification. If there is no cash in the purse, grab the plastic money and get that new shade of lipstick before it gets away. If there is no money in the checkbook, call upon that credit card and drop by the sports bar for a good time. Who cares if the next paycheck is spent well before it is earned, as long as we can enjoy ourselves now?

Sometimes the financial considerations represent only one part of the cost for convenience. For example, environmental types are obsessed with disposable diapers. They say that such products take a long time to break down and the messy stuff attracts pests and diseases. Then, there are all of those Styrofoam containers we get from fast food restaurants. When we look at the combined costs of such convenience, we have to admit they are very high.

As I said earlier, I am not suggesting that we worship every dime. It is okay to order a pizza once in a while; but if you ordered a pizza last night and you go out to dinner tonight, then you microwave some soup in a disposable bowl tomorrow night, you are addicted to convenience and that is one of the worst things to waste your money on. A person who spends money like that instead of using it for necessities and investments might as well use a paycheck as toilet paper, because its greatest potential is flushed down the drain . . . precisely what we are trying to avoid.

ADULT INDULGENCES

This chapter is devoted to observing traditional "vices" and anything else that might take on an expensive and habitual role in our lives. I am not passing judgment on your choices; I am primarily focused on the long-term financial consequences. We will start out with smoking.

Smoking

When we think of smoking in daily terms, it seems financially manageable, but when we look at the cumulative effect, the cost is astronomical. If we assume that a person is going to smoke a carton of cigs each week for 40 years, and if the cost of that carton is $40, the smoker will spend over $80,000, but that is just the tip of the proverbial iceberg. If prevailing interest rates are 7 percent, and if the smoker would have paid off debt or invested the money instead of wasting it on this adult indulgence, he would have accumulated nearly a half-million dollars in buying power (I will explain this later). But that opportunity goes up in smoke . . . literally. Then there are the peripheral expenses. For example, we have made no allowance for the rising prices of the product or health care costs. What about all of those trips to the store, other impulsive purchases that are made at the store as a result of going there, plus lighters, burned clothes and burned furniture or similar expenses? It all adds up.

The smoker mentioned above winds up losing hundreds of

thousands of dollars over a lifetime and all of that is the product of a habit that costs a little more than $5 per day.

Drinking

A six-pack of beer or a few glasses of wine can easily cost as much as the daily expense of the smoker's habit. But what about the person who goes to a bar on some sort of regular basis? It is nearly impossible to get out of there without dropping twenty dollars or more. If a drinker were to spend an average of $10 per day over an adult lifetime and if we add in the compounded interest on all of that money, a young drinker would lose nearly a million dollars in buying power before retirement. We should all get on our knees and weep for the person who cannot drink at home, in moderation.

The following are some true drinking stories in which the cost of the "refreshments" was only part of the problem. The real cost to the consumer came in the complications that ensued.

True Story #1

A 21-year-old woman worked as a waitress in a bar. One night she served several drinks to an under-aged friend of hers and they both got caught. The bar owner threw them both out and fired the waitress. She was out of work for several weeks, losing nearly $3,000 in salary and tips. The ongoing interest loss is going to cost her $25 PER MONTH . . . FOREVER. She was lucky she didn't have legal problems, on top of that.

True Story #2

A few years ago a bunch of local high school students, ages 15-16, were having a big party. There were so many of them they quickly ran out of beer, so they decided to pile into several cars to go to the liquor store together (the drinking age is 21 in this state).

Three vehicles came upon a train track and the red lights were flashing because a train was coming. The first car hurried to beat the train at the intersection. The second car quickly accelerated with the same objective, but the outcome was different. Five teenagers were killed instantly as the unforgiving train ripped their car to pieces. Meanwhile the third car full of teenagers had a front row seat to a grim horror show they will never forget. The total loss is incalculable.

True Story #3

On the first day of my second year of college, I witnessed an alcohol-induced drag race in which one of my classmates was killed and several others were injured. They had just come from a bar. One of the cars was brand-new and going nearly 100 miles an hour when the driver lost control. His car turned end-over-end and eventually rolled down the mountain. I was about a quarter mile behind them when it all happened. The crashed car was totaled and cost thousands of dollars, and the medical costs had to be monumental. The driver of the other car had his license revoked.

There are many other examples: One of my college buddies had too much beer and drove his car into a guardrail; it cost him his foot. My dad's good friend was a heavy drinker for many years; he died on a bar stool and his children lost their father and a much-needed income. One of my uncles wrestled with alcohol addiction all of his life; he drank up every spare dollar and died in an alley on his way home from his favorite bar. I know several young people who have been arrested and convicted of DUI. The legal process adds up to $8,000 for each conviction ($60 per month, forever).

I would not want the reader to conclude that I am a complete fuddy-duddy. I see nothing wrong with a cold beer after mowing the lawn or a hot buttered rum by the fireplace at a ski lodge. A nice glass of wine can easily enhance a fine meal and a glass of spiked punch at a friend's wedding can complement the mood very nicely. In all those examples the alcohol enhances the social experience and the financial impact is essentially insignificant. Therefore, a few dollars spent in this way, once in a while, is no big deal, but when social drinking takes on a more prominent role in a person's life, the cost can be catastrophic.

Gambling: Lottery Tickets and Other Forms of Playing the Odds

Many years ago I recognized that gambling can be a lot of fun but I also realized it is nearly impossible to beat the odds in the long run. We all have heard the idea that they don't build those fancy casinos by losing to the common folks. Still, I believed that if I studied the industry I could at least keep my losses to a minimum and even win from time to time. I checked out all the library books on the subject and soaked up the information better than Sponge Bob Square Pants would absorb a bathroom accident. Eventually, I became a very good amateur gambler.

I could expand on many of the lessons I have learned, but the most important one is this: There are only a few ways you can beat the odds and here are the ones I know about.

The best one is to buy your own casino and be on the other side of the table.

Become a card counter at 21. There are rare occasions when the deck will favor the player. In essence, you bet small amounts while you study the remaining cards in the deck. Then, when the deck finally has a sufficiently disproportionate number of face cards, you increase your bet substantially. There was a mathematics professor at MIT named Ed Thorp who developed and proved this theory in the '60s. But, the casino bosses caught on and made some adjustments which make it a lot harder to duplicate his success.

Become a highly skilled poker player. In the long run all players get essentially the same cards, but a few players (less than 20 percent of them) grow their purses consistently while weaker players serve as their prey. But regardless of how good you become, there are odds working against you in poker games too. The house takes a piece of every pot, known as rake, and most players tip the dealer with each winning hand. All this overhead makes it very difficult to overcome the daunting odds, so the biggest winner is still the house.

Get incredibly lucky. I know one lady who hit a Vegas slot machine for just under one million dollars. Her payout is $47,000/year for 20 years. The problem was that she did not really understand how lucky she was. Millions of dollars have to be lost by other players in order to build the jackpot to that amount. In the meantime the machine had to cover all of the other smaller payouts along the way and earn a profit for the casino. Considering she was playing a quarter machine and it only keeps about one cent per quarter, that is an astronomical number of losses. The first year, after she received her annual check, she tried to duplicate the feat, but she soon lost all of the money. The same thing happened the next year and the next. After that I lost touch with her, but I suspect she may eventually give all of the winnings back, and end up a loser like everybody else.

Manage wins and losses. The trick here is to observe streaks and bet a lot more when you are in winning streaks and a minimum when you are losing. The problem is the dice or cards have no way of knowing they are falling in any particular sequence and they have no obligation to continue in the pattern. Therefore, any new roll of the dice or set of cards has the exact same odds as any other. Your streak is just as likely to end as it is to continue. Still, anybody who has gambled a fair amount can tell you there are those occasions when the cards are especially cold or hot. If the gambler is astute enough to take advantage of the trends he can exaggerate his winnings and subdue his losses. This technique can be very successful in spurts, but it too is mostly a matter of luck and doomed to failure in the long run.

Cheat. We have all heard stories about somebody who

bought off an athlete, a coach or referee in a sporting event. Other rascals have put doggie downers in the food of a lightning-fast greyhound and swayed the outcome of a race. People have been known to shave the dice, so that one number is more likely to come up. Black jack dealers have formed partnerships with other cheaters to skim money. Others put invisible ink on the back of cards, and so on. This all sounds fascinating, but . . . I "bet" I don't have to finish this sentence for you.

Everybody else is a net loser. The more you play the more you lose. The best you can hope for is an occasional good session and a lot of fun for your entertainment dollar. So dump the gambling bug unless you can accept those facts.

The lottery is your very worst gambling value. If you listen to the radio ads in Colorado and other places you will frequently hear this phrase: "Prizes equal 50 percent of sales." Put another way, the house (the State) keeps 50 percent of all the prize money. The most ruthless casinos give you much better odds than that. As if giving up half the lottery money is not bad enough, the "lucky" winner gets screwed even worse because the Feds and the State take another big chunk of the winnings in the form of income taxes—potentially more than 40 percent. Good God, even the Mafia wouldn't charge you that much. Still the State preys on the many lottery addicts who buy tickets week after week. Sadly, many of the people who live in this dream world are the ones who can least afford it.

As far as I am concerned, there is nothing wrong with an occasional visit to Las Vegas or playing poker with friends a couple of nights a year. However, when the topic is wasting money, compulsive gambling is as bad as any other addiction. The hard-core gambler cannot get enough action, win or lose. In the worst cases, these people are known to lose everything they own and to destroy loving relationships. I have known three such addicts personally; two of them went broke and the third person could not get through the day without betting on all sorts of things. Obviously, anybody who has problems like these people needs to consult with qualified counselors before all is lost.

To close out this topic, let's see if we can agree on something: Occasional small losses (let's say $50 or so, a few times per year) can be a reasonable price to pay for entertainment at the gaming tables, and going to Vegas or Atlantic City can really be a lot of fun. It is okay to occasionally earmark a reasonable amount of money for this entertainment, but doing so more than once per year, or losing regularly or losing large amounts, or buying any lottery tickets, are among the worst things on which we waste our money.

Sporting Events

Sports fans can also flush a lot of money down the drain. Among the most exploited souls are the season ticket holders. For starters, there is the cost of the ticket. Add to that the time and expense to get to the games and back. Then there are the refreshments. A fan can easily spend $7 for a few beers, and he'll probably grab a hot dog or two. Chances are good he will buy an occasional souvenir, as well.

Add all of that up, and double it, because he usually has two seats (or more) and so he takes a partner, thereby compounding all of the expenses. Finally, there is the lost time, which could have been spent on something more productive. In a few short hours this sports fan has easily consumed $200 or more of his net worth by indulging his adult activities. And, he will do it many more times before the season is over. Once again, there is nothing wrong with enjoying sports, but the people in this situation can easily flush thousands of dollars per year and we have already observed that $2,000 per year, compounded at 7 percent for 40 years adds up to an incredible $465,000. Good grief! No wonder athletes get such huge salaries.

Other fans visit sports bars on a routine basis where the volume is turned up, expensive drinks flow freely, and salty munchies are compounding it all. Many of these customers gamble on the outcome of the games or in fantasy sports leagues. Other fans have parties at home and spend just as much. When we consider the sum of these sports fans' expenses and allow for the interest costs as previously noted, these people also lose hundreds of thousands of dollars in opportunity costs over time.

The above categories are not the only downfalls of self-indulgent adults. Nearly any activity that can dominate large blocks of time and money can lead to financial problems. Other such activities include illicit drugs, hobbies, habitual shopping, the daily Red Bull or latte, excessive dining out, elaborate wardrobes, extravagant traveling, recreational toys or pricey jewelry.

Most of these activities or purchases are acceptable in moderation. It is all just a matter of degree. You might think of it as a typical ham and egg breakfast: The chicken has an interest in it, but the pig is committed. Which one are you? If you find yourself committed like the pig, adult indulgences are among the worst things on which you waste your money.

LEGAL MATTERS

*In Kentucky, the law says a person must
take a bath at least once a year.
In Tennessee, it is against the law to drive a car while sleeping.
In Utah, birds have the right of way on any public highway.
In Virginia, the Code of 1930 prohibits corrupt practices or
bribery by any person other than political candidates.
In Colorado, a pet cat, if loose, must have a tail light.*

These silly laws were observed on http://www.strangefacts.com. A quick Google search of "weird laws" will find many more. I am not certain of the consequences that might be imposed upon those who flout the above laws, but ordinarily when we misbehave in the eyes of law, the price tag is momentous.

Have you ever gotten a traffic ticket? If you get a speeding ticket today for going 10 miles over the speed limit, you are likely to pay a fine of $100 or so, but that is only the beginning. The consequences of that infraction are compounded. The next time you get a bill for your auto insurance, there is a good chance your premiums will go up quite a bit, perhaps for as much as five years or longer. When we realize the total cost of that activity we ask ourselves questions like, "Is all this expense really worth getting there a few minutes earlier?" The answer is nearly always "no."

So traffic tickets are very expensive, but if you combine drinking with driving, you might as well drive straight to the poorhouse. I will leave it to the courts to lecture you on the evils of drunk driving, but that still leaves room for me to focus on the financial penalties of this action.

Court costs, attorney's fees, required classes and treatments can easily run into the thousands. One friend of mine got caught driving drunk so many times he had to go to jail for a year, which cost him his salary and all his work benefits, such as paid insurance and opportunities for advancement. When he got out, he was not allowed to drive for another four years. So he had to accept low-paying jobs near the bus line. His new lifestyle was so demeaning it wasn't long before he fell back into the bottle.

About a year went by and he still did not "get" it. One day he called me and asked for a loan to buy a car. He did not have his license back, he did not have insurance and he was still drinking heavily. Naturally, I had to turn him down. Sadly, I never heard from him after that, but somebody else told me he drank so much he was diagnosed with alcohol poisoning. His health suffered greatly, costing him more money that he could not afford.

As you would expect, he ruined several good relationships along the way. His college education and a lot of potential were reduced to sweeping floors in a hardware store and begging on street corners for money to buy his next drink. But the focus of this story is his financial losses, which were catastrophic. His failure to separate the bottle from the automobile cost him a generation of income.

It might surprise the reader to learn that I have also lost a lot of money because of my own brush with the authorities. When I was a teenager I was arrested and convicted on a ten-dollar marijuana charge. It was the '60s and I was like many others in the hippie era. Generally, we considered the marijuana laws to be ridiculous. I openly smoked pot and thought I was doing my part to promote the legalization of the substance.

As I worked my way through the judicial system I tried to educate the "ignorant" authorities that their laws were needlessly harsh. But the town where this all took place was a bit like Mayberry on the Andy Griffith Show and "Andy and Barney" were not to be persuaded. In fact, the judge referred to me, in court, as "the scum of the earth." I don't know if he really thought a teenager with $10 worth of marijuana was the scum of the earth, or if he was merely trying to knock some sense into me, but he did cause me to rethink my behavior. Eventually, I was found guilty and sentenced to 60 days in the county jail and 5 years of probation.

Disregarding the drama and aggravation of my indiscretion, there was still a high economic price to pay. The least of my problems was the cost of the drugs. There was also the lost income because all the court hearings were held on weekdays, when I should have been working. Other expenses included bail bonds, court costs and attorney fees. Even a complete idiot can think of better uses for hard-earned dollars. I am still paying FOREVER interest for that event.

Fortunately, I began to phase out of that lifestyle. I didn't want to fight the system anymore, but I was still young and in search of a good time, so I shifted my attention to beer drinking. After a couple years of that I realized drinking was just as destructive and I gave them both up. That was more than thirty years ago.

There are many other good examples of how the legal system can steal away your assets. One of them has to do with bail bonds. If you have never been asked to bail somebody out of jail, count your blessings. It is a dramatic and costly exercise. Here is how it works.

If the accused party does not have all the money needed for bail, someone contacts a bonding company. Its fee is frequently 10 percent of the bond amount. The bondsman will then pay the full bond (or provide its own preapproved bond) to get the person out of jail. Eventually, when the case is settled, the bonding company gets its money back but whoever paid the 10 percent fee to the bonding company forfeits all the money paid.

In one case, I put up $2,500 for a fellow who was genuinely innocent of the charges. After the authorities realized they made a mistake they dropped all the charges. He was a man of honor and paid me back a little at a time, but it was very difficult for him. Regardless of his innocence, my friend lost a lot of money, which he can never recover. By now, you can probably figure the FOREVER interest expense to him.

One of my in-laws has a relative who was at the wrong place at the wrong time and his loss is immeasurable. One day, the young fellow went to a party. An older guy had a knock-out drug and spiked the drinks of some young women who were with them. There was no sexual assault or rape, but two of the women passed out and one of them ended up dead. The courts threw all of the fellows in jail. The one we are talking about was sentenced to eight years in prison for not helping the women. He spent nearly all of his 20s behind bars. What monetary value do you place on that?

Count me among those who believe that the judicial system preys on citizens. Creating laws and wrangling in the "wrong-doers" creates a lot of jobs for police, sheriff departments, district attorneys, court clerks, bonding companies, people who build and maintain jails and others, whether particular laws are necessary or not. They all have job security as long as there are plenty of laws to enforce. When the courtrooms and jails get overcrowded there is more emphasis on enlarging the system than there is on reducing the laws. If you are like me, you do not want to subsidize that madness any more than you already have to via your taxes.

My son, Adam, once lived on the corner of a semi-busy street which was designated as a snow route. Whenever there were large snowstorms, the city quickly plowed that street to keep the buses running. The only thing they could do with the volumes of snow was push it to the side of the road and on the sidewalks.

One year, a big storm rolled in so Adam got up early and shoveled his sidewalks before the plows came by, then he went to work. When he got home that night, he saw several feet of snow piled back on his walks from the plows and a citation was on his door because the sidewalks were not cleared. He had the option of paying a fine or going to court. It was a matter of principle for him, so he went to court to explain the situation. The judge dismissed the case, but that did not discourage the plows or the sidewalk inspectors. Adam moved after a couple repeat episodes, but could not replace the lost time and money going to court, missing work and dealing with the system.

Even if you are innocent, your purse is doomed whenever you get dragged into the judicial system (unless you are the plaintiff in a successful lawsuit) so it is painfully clear that this is one of the worst places we can waste our money.

It may be a little boring to seek a designated driver when you have been drinking, or to file your income taxes on time, or to drive within the speed limit, or pay attention to the traffic laws and parking rules, or the height of your weeds or any of the hundreds of other government rules and laws, but it is a big waste of your money (and time) to misbehave in the eyes of the law. The benefits of unruly behavior just don't justify throwing your valuable resources away.

At the very least, I hope you will have enough sense to avoid Kentucky if you think that bathing once a year is unnecessary.

DEPRECIATING ASSETS

Practically everybody knows that an automobile loses more value when you drive it off the lot than at any other time. However, that is not the end of it. Most vehicles lose half their value within a few years. To make matters worse, some consumers obtain loans of five years, or longer. That requires interest payments and whatever insurance the lender might require. Consumers who accept that loan start out upside-down (they owe more for the car than it is worth) and many of them never get caught up because the payments outlive the vehicle. I had to learn that lesson the hard way like so many others have had to do.

At this very moment, I am losing approximately $350 per month in FOREVER interest because I bought several new cars when I was a young man and each one of them cost me about $10,000 in depreciation. If I would have paid off debt instead, I would have more than $150,000 extra in my pocket right now, and that does not even include investing the money for additional returns. I hope you won't make that same mistake.

One time my nephew and I were discussing how quickly cars depreciate. We devised a simple formula to determine which vehicles were the worst. We came up with the idea of "miles per dollar." It is useful for any car you might be thinking of buying as well as those that you already own. Here is how it works. Let's say a woman bought a new Jeep for $32,000 and put 106,000 miles on it over 6 years, after which it was still worth about $4,000. We can see that her 106,000 miles cost her

$28,000 ($32,000 - $4,000). Conclusion: She got nearly 4 miles per dollar.

In another example, my nephew bought a used minivan, at an auction, for $2,000 and he put 35,000 miles on it going back and forth to work for three years. When we did the analysis on the van, it was still worth a salvage value of $500; so it cost him $1,500 for 35,000 miles, which is well over 20 miles per dollar. Comparing those two situations makes it ridiculously clear how costly depreciation actually is.

Our formula is very simple so it would be easy to improve on it. One could factor in gasoline costs, maintenance, and insurance rates to get a more precise number, but we thought the basic message was clear enough without the extra calculations. In the above comparison, the person who bought a new vehicle spent five times as much for transportation, which nearly everybody can understand.

One of the best ways to avoid *flushing* your money down the drain on automobiles is to buy good quality used vehicles. In the third section of this book there is a chapter on how to effectively buy new and used cars. Be sure to read the section about buying vehicles at auctions. Once you do that you may never buy another new vehicle.

When it comes to fun vehicles like motor homes, boats, motorcycles, camping trailers, snowmobiles, jet skis and similar items, I suggest you rent them on an "as needed" basis. At first the idea of owning these items offers a certain excitement, but most of us don't use them enough to justify all the money we lose as they depreciate right under our noses. Then there is the nuisance factor along with storage, insurance, maintenance and licensing. They all demand our time, effort and money. In fact, you may have heard about the fellow who said the best two days of his life were the day he bought his boat and the day he sold it.

If you still wish to buy items like these, I suggest you wait until the off-season and buy them from private parties. Look for some sucker who is still making payments while his toy is taking up space in his garage. Chances are he will have learned his lesson the hard way and will give you a great deal because nobody else wants his mistake at any reasonable price, especially in the off-season.

My own father made a lot of great deals this way, buying boats at Christmas time and snowmobiles on Memorial Day. We had a lot of fun with his toys but they were a pain in the neck for him. Unless you use these items a lot, and buy them in the off-season from private parties, they just depreciate too much to justify pouring your money into them.

The big-ticket items are not the only ones that depreciate and lend us opportunities to throw our money away. New televisions, household furniture, exercise equipment, computers, appliances and new clothes are just as bad. And jewelry may be the worst culprit of them all. If you ever try to sell a diamond ring, you are destined to lose most of its original value, even if you bought it at a 50 percent discount.

There are dozens of items that you can buy used to avoid paying depreciation. Consider this group: furniture, paintings and rugs, exercise equipment, sporting equipment, children's clothes, toys, books, cameras, computers, software and printers, cell phones, musical instruments, video games, DVDs and CDs, televisions, appliances, designer clothing and, of course, jewelry.

I buy lots of things like these on eBay and have a fun time doing it. If I get tired of them I can simply resell them on eBay and get most or all of my money back. Sometimes I just donate them to charities. Other good sources for used stuff include Craigslist, surplus dealers, auction houses, second-hand stores, garage sales, flea markets and pawn shops. Bargain hunting can be a wonderful source of entertainment but the bigger benefit lies in the fact you avoid *flushing* precious dollars down the drain in the form of depreciation.

Finally, there is an exception to every rule and so it is with depreciating assets. There are a couple of situations in which it is perfectly acceptable to buy certain items that wear out, and naturally, one of them involves real estate. The IRS allows very friendly tax breaks for real estate investors, as well as other business owners who need equipment for their trade. Examples of these situations would be a farmer who needs a tractor, a saleswoman who buys a cell phone for her work or a machine-shop operator who acquires a new lathe. In effect, the government reimburses these people for some of the losses they incur in the pursuit of a profit. By transferring some of their loss to the taxman these entrepreneurs easily justify the purchase of such depreciating assets.

The next time a friend offers to take you for a ride in a new car, compliment him on how pleasant it smells, but remember that your friend is wasting his money on a major depreciating asset. You may smile knowing you will never do that yourself again.

RENTING AND LEASING

I don't know if women chat with strangers in the stalls of public restrooms but it is not rare in the men's room. If you make enough visits to urinals in sports bars, sooner or later a tipsy fellow will assume the standard position at the twin porcelain fixture next to you. After attending to the necessary prep-work he will break the awkward silence with the familiar quip: "You only rent beer." You will know exactly what he means: Even though you pay for it, you don't get to keep it very long.

Beer isn't the only odd thing you can rent. If you are so inclined, you can rent an elephant, priceless jewelry, a clown, a tree house in the tropics or a luxury yacht.

It also makes perfect sense to rent moving vans, meeting halls, specialty tools, movies, jet skis or anything else for which you have limited need. On one occasion we were hosting a family reunion, so we rented one of those portable outhouses for relatives who wanted to dispose of their rented beer.

Unfortunately, many consumers have trouble recognizing when renting is a bad idea. Even I have screwed up in this regard. One summer I rented a slip (parking space) in a marina for a pontoon boat. The boat was fairly large so I didn't want to wrestle with putting it in the lake and taking it out over and over again. I paid $1,000 to keep my boat in the lake all season; however, we only used the boat three times. The next year I did the exact same thing. What a dummy! It would have been smarter to sell the boat and rent one from the marina manager on those few occasions. The next year, I got rid of the boat.

In another example, people often pay health clubs for the use of their equipment only to learn they are time-poor and don't go to the club as much as they expected. In such cases, their membership fees are *flushed*.

Tenants are among the people who most need to know when it is time to rent, and more importantly, when it is time to buy.

Dan and Mary Ann were renters for many years while they went to college and started their family. By the time they entered the workforce they had grown accustomed to living on a tight budget and renting. They thought they had to have a big down payment and a long employment history to qualify for a home loan. But they were thrilled to learn they qualified for a special government program and they bought a fine entry-level home in the San Diego area.

To be fair, I should point out that there are circumstances that justify renting housing. Most new high school graduates lack the resources, wisdom and stability that are necessary to buy a home, so renting is a worthy idea until they figure out their career paths.

In another example, Bob wanted to live in a new town, so he rented for a while, until he gained the information he needed to determine which neighborhoods he liked. Major life changes, such as a divorce or a death in the family, can also force people to become temporary tenants. Nonetheless, in general it is usually better to purchase property than to rent it. After all, regardless of where you live you are paying off somebody's property, so it might as well be your own. Furthermore, real estate generally tends to increase in value. In a later chapter I will tell you how and why the government implements policies to maintain a modest inflation rate. As long as that continues, real estate values are generally guaranteed to go up with the inflation rate. From there, it follows that the sooner we buy, the less we pay. Contrast that to what happens if we keep renting: That same inflation rate is constantly putting upward pressure on rents.

As a seasoned landlord, I am grateful for all the tenants who share their paychecks with me, so that I can pay off my buildings. I am especially fond of the long-term renters. One of our tenants has been in the same apartment for eighteen years. She brags to our other renters about her tenure there. But if she would have purchased a small condominium when she moved into our building, she would have paid off her own place by now. As an owner, her monthly payment would have been capped when she bought her condo, but instead she has endured countless rent increases over the years, which she could have used to pay off her own property.

This mistake is not peculiar to less educated folks, either. Joey retired after many years as an engineer. He was a perpetual renter. After he retired, he obtained a real estate license and decided to work part-time in the same office in which I worked. After learning his situation I asked why he never bought his own home. With conviction, he boasted, "Because I want to have the ability to pack up and leave anytime I want to." I was dumbfounded because he was in the middle of his sixteenth year, renting the same townhouse. As in the previous example, he could have paid off a similar property in that time. Oh, by the way, the property he was renting doubled in value along the way while he watched his rent go up time after time. It is no surprise Joey's landlord thought Joey was an excellent tenant.

If that isn't enough incentive to make you stop renting, you might need to be reminded that the government provides great income tax benefits to homeowners that are not available to renters. This can add up to an additional profit or savings of several thousand dollars EVERY YEAR for owners.

And finally, there is a certain pride in owning your own home and not having to look over your shoulder for a landlord who is watching your every move.

In extreme cases, a particular market can be especially hot and home values rise much faster than standard inflation rates. On a two hundred thousand dollar home, the price might increase by seven percent a year or more for several consecutive years. That would be $14,000 per year, which provides the owner with a very handsome "back-pocket" income. What do you suppose happens to the tenant's housing expenses in those circumstances? We can conclude from all of this that standard inflation usually works for homeowners and against tenants.

In previous chapters we suggested that wasting $120/mo. for 40 years can add up to $465,000 after you consider the power of compound interest. But we are not talking about a mere $120/month when we are talking about lost rent dollars. The losses are much bigger than that. Given all of this information, it amazes me how many people fail to buy their own properties. No wonder renting takes such a prominent position on the list of the worst things on which we waste our money.

So, just to be certain there is no doubt, most renters should buy a home as soon as it is practical, but it is always okay to rent your beer.

ENERGY

Nobody would call me a whacked-out "greenie" but I am certainly tuned in to the fact that we waste a lot of energy and that seems like something worth correcting for economic reasons alone.

Cars

In these times of four-dollar gasoline and a struggling economy, everybody is looking for ways to cut their energy costs. Some people are running out and buying new energy-efficient cars and that may indeed cut their gasoline bill, but they still need some sort of energy to move the vehicle. In those cases that energy comes from large electric batteries. According to a report by CNNMoney.com it will take slightly less than $1 in electricity to recharge the battery for the Chevy Volt that will then take the vehicle about 40 miles. Since it would take slightly less than a gallon of gas to move the vehicle the same distance the savings is 2-3 dollars, depending on gasoline prices.

However, before you run out and buy one of those vehicles, that same article suggests the car will cost somewhere around $40,000. The article also points out some energy credits that the IRS allows for buying such a vehicle, but the adjusted price is still well into the thirties. At that rate, it will take a very long time to recover the excess purchase price compared to similar gasoline-powered vehicles. Then there is the inconvenience of plugging in and unplugging your car every time you use it.

Beyond that, batteries are in their infancy and they are expensive to replace. If you need a new set of batteries every 25,000 miles, you will never get ahead. Somebody has to make those batteries and deliver them to a retail outlet. Therefore, the "energy-efficient" vehicle will actually use more energy than the gasoline-powered one that it replaced.

Finally, you can color me skeptical for this one, but I think politicians have grown so accustomed to spending the tax dollars they receive from each gallon of gas (roughly 20 cents to the Feds and 20 cents to the states) they will find some way to offset that loss. If they merely add a new tax to the electricity at a similar cost per mile, the energy-conscious consumer is a big net loser. The bottom line is the buyer of these vehicles may be a good citizen, but the economics are currently worse than horrible.

Homes

Most of our other energy costs originate in our buildings. You may not have much say-so regarding what goes on at the local grocery store or your dentist's office, but your voice ought to count for something in your own home. There are dozens of things you can do around the house to cut your expenses.

Naturally, you can take action "for the planet" if you want to, but I am more focused on the economics of the matter. As an example I would not throw away a functioning light bulb just to replace it with a $3 feel-good bulb. I don't think the planet is going to shrivel up and blow away if I wait until the original bulb has exhausted its useful life. Besides, throwing away useful products like light bulbs just adds trash to landfills, and it takes extra energy to make replacement bulbs and distribute them so any environmental impact of converting to energy-efficient bulbs is minimal until the old bulb actually needs to be replaced.

One of the best things you can do is conduct your own in-home evaluation. It is not difficult. Closely inspect the entire property. Take thorough notes. Examine each room, one at a time, looking for ways you can make an immediate financial difference. Here are some of the things to consider:

Air Flow

When it comes to wasting energy, one of the most important categories to think about is air leaks. Obviously, you can just run out and buy the best triple-pane windows, but that could easily be too costly to justify the expense. Before you buy windows, or any similar big-ticket products, I suggest you do some research and determine if you can recover any investment in energy savings in less than 10 years. If not, I would not make the change. In other words, if it costs you $10,000 for new windows, you would need to save $1,000 per year in energy costs to get your money back in ten years, and thereby justify the investment.

A prudent person could make the argument that adding such windows increases the value of a home and that therefore a consumer recovers some of the investment in another pocket. I would go along with that, but do not get roped into buying windows for that reason, because there is not ordinarily a dollar for dollar return. There needs to be some significant, ongoing savings in the equation.

For less industrious enterprises, begin on the outside of the property. Look for daylight around doors and windows. Jiggle them to verify they always close tightly. Make sure storm windows are still sealed and there are no cracks in any of the glass. Examine old caulking for cracks that might need to be repaired or replaced. Check for any gaps around the foundation, and any incoming pipes, faucets, electrical wires or cable. Make sure there are good seals where dissimilar building materials meet, such as where the chimney abuts to siding, or the garage door meets the floor, or vent pipes come through the roof.

Once that is completed, make an inspection of the interior of the property. If you have a fireplace, make certain the flu closes properly. After that, get a small lighter or candle (or a cigarette or stick of incense) and close all doors and windows; then do a little sleuthing. Hold the flame near the baseboard and see if it flickers and dances for you. Do the same thing around the door frames, window frames, light fixtures, electrical outlets, air conditioning units, heating vents, attic or crawl space access points or any other place where the walls, ceilings or floors have been disrupted. If there are air leaks around door frames or window frames, you may need to remove them to see if insulation is needed.

After you have completed your examination, make any needed repairs. Then suffocate that moving air with caulking, weather stripping or insulation, as the situation warrants. This exercise can save 20 percent or more on your energy bill.

There is one final note for those of you who live in large communities (100 units or more) with common heating systems. Ask an officer of your homeowners association where the group buys natural gas for heating. If they are buying natural gas direct from the local utility service there is a good chance you can lower the cost by 10 percent or so by contracting with the importers at the point of origin, such as Houston. The importers use the same infrastructure (pipes) to deliver the gas as your utility company does. You will have sales people to help you with the details and you will usually place one order per year at a predetermined price, rather than float with the market as you do with the utility company. Perhaps you can get the building owner to slip you a month's free rent for the tip.

Insulation

When your home was new, the contractor probably provided the amount of insulation that was required at the time. But energy costs rise and insulation settles over time; therefore, an inspection would be prudent, and more product may be in order.

First off, make sure there is some sort of vapor control. This keeps humidity from the attic area from penetrating the home.

Frequently on the roll-type of insulation you will find one side that has a thick paper attached to it for this purpose. Other times you will find plastic sheets or tar paper. If there is nothing there for that purpose you can get special paint for your ceiling that will help.

Be sure to check all of the areas where the insulation might have been improperly installed or moved, for instance, around pipes, the access area, and near light fixtures and the chimney. Likewise, check all of the air vents to make sure air flow is not obstructed.

It is fairly difficult for the average person to get an accurate assessment of the insulation in the exterior walls. You can cut holes in your sheetrock and do some probing through them as well as through the outlet areas, but this is fairly inexact. For more accurate information, you may need to employ a thermographic inspector. They use infrared scanning to get a good reading.

If you have a heated basement, the exterior walls should be insulated. If you do not have a heated basement you will want insulation under the floorboards. Once again, inspect any of the exposed pipes and foreign objects for good seals.

The effectiveness of insulation is measured in "R" value. You can check with your local utility company or home improvement center to discover the recommended R-value for attics, walls and floors in your area. Since heat rises, more heat heads to your ceiling than anywhere else. I recommend you spend the money to upgrade the R-value if you can expect to recover your investment within 10 years.

Furnace and Air Conditioner

These two systems are often combined into one unit. They have equal but opposite purposes. To control the climate in our homes in an economical way, we need to maintain the systems properly. That means reading and abiding by the manufacturer's recommendations regarding changing filters and obtaining regular inspections.

A furnace can seem to be working just fine but have a cracked heat exchanger. When that happens, it can be inefficient and dangerous. Cracked heat exchangers leak carbon monoxide, which has no noticeable odor, unlike natural gas. I have known people who have lived with unexplained headaches for years, only to discover it was the fault of a defective heat exchanger.

Furnaces tend to have a useful life of about 15 years but they can last longer with good care. Oddly, it can be financially prudent to replace them even if they are working properly. That is because new and better products have hit the market over the last ten years. Some of them can easily pay for themselves in energy savings within 5 to 7 years.

Overall, I am a big fan of heating with boiler systems and radiators. These systems can last for decades and they distribute the heat fairly evenly, without blowing dust all around. Furthermore, once the radiators get warm they hold their heat for a fair amount of time before the system has to be reactivated. Maintenance is also affordable. The primary downside to boilers is they cost quite a bit more to install in the first place.

Air conditioning units are frequently tied into the heating system in order to take advantage of the ductwork for distribution of the cool air. Therefore, if you have a joint system, you should change the filters at the beginning of each season.

There are two primary concerns regarding air conditioners. The first one is an environmental issue. Until recently, air conditioners used a Freon product that is not especially friendly to the ozone. However, newer units use a different refrigerant that is more environmentally friendly.

Next, in more humid areas, these units can be subject to mold problems, which can affect people with allergies. Mold is relatively easy to remove by cleaning the unit thoroughly once each year.

It is not usually cost-effective to replace an air conditioner unless it is rusted out or the compressor dies. They lose some efficiency over time but they can be recharged and most of the other repairs are fairly affordable compared to replacing the entire unit.

Therefore, it can be cost-effective to replace a furnace, even if it is still working, but it is generally better to repair air conditioners than replace them.

Hot Water Heaters

This simple device consumes up to 20 percent of your home energy costs. It seems unwise to heat 40 gallons of water just to get a small amount from time to time; unfortunately, this is still the best bang for your buck. To maximize the life of tank-type hot water heaters drain off a half-gallon of water once every year. Most tanks have a faucet for this purpose near the bottom on the outside of the tank. If you see a lot of rust in the water, your tank is near the end of its useful life. Consider yourself lucky if your hot water heater lasts for ten years.

From an economics perspective, tankless heaters are not yet cost-effective. They will likely save you about $75-100/year in heating costs, but the purchase price is so high it takes nearly 20 years to recover your investment. When that number comes down to 10 years, they will become popular.

Fireplace

If you use a fireplace for heating, even occasionally, remember that warm air moves toward cold air, especially when the cold air is straight up. Therefore the fireplace not only sends the heat from your fire up the chimney, but it also draws warm air from other areas of the home. When that happens, cold air from outside is drawn through any leaky areas to replace the departing warm air. That is why some rooms in older, poorly insulated homes get so cold in spite of the heat in the fireplace. Therefore, do not use a fireplace unless you have sealed the home as we discussed earlier.

As we have observed, there are lots of ways to *flush* money on energy costs. One way is to waste energy unnecessarily. Another is to buy new products when you do not need them or cannot recover your money in a reasonable period of time. If you elect to make environmentally friendly adjustments, even when the rate of return is not there, I am among those who admire your motives. That is an excellent topic for some other book.

DEPENDENTS

This chapter is touchy. The title of this book is S*top flushing Your Money Down the Drain*. Then we find ourselves in a section called "The Worst Things on Which We Waste Our Money"...and now I want to talk about dependents, including children and pets. I can see how somebody might put all of that together and assume I am actually saying that our kids and animals are one of the worst things we can spend our money on, but that is not my perspective.

I realize I have no business telling anybody how big their family ought to be; however, I can shed light on the true costs of having children and pets so that the reader can make more informed decisions.

Children

Unless you have bottomless pockets, each new family member reduces how much is available for the other members of your family. If two families earn the same amount of money but one family has two children and the other family has five children, they will have different lifestyles. Let me show you what I mean.

I happen to come from a large, lower middle class family. I had six sisters. We never had many material things, so when we wanted something to do we played cards or went outside and played games like hide-and-seek, tag or basketball. That was all our parents could afford. If we wanted anything more than that we had to get a job. Only two of us ever saw the inside of a college. But we had great holidays and I became a fairly good athlete because of all of that outdoor activity. Our family reunions are cool and there are all sorts of cousins, nieces and nephews.

On the other hand, my wife comes from a home of similar means but she has only one sister. They could afford to live in a better neighborhood because there were not so many mouths to feed. Their home was smaller but much nicer. Their parents provided a great deal of stimulation for them. They traveled quite a bit, they had horses, they were involved in neighborhood and school activities, and both of them graduated from college. Decades later, they are usually under control. They don't take risks but they have had long, stable and rewarding careers. Overall, they don't have to struggle financially and their adult lives are less stressful than the lives of my sisters.

So you see, your family size can determine where you live, what kind of cars you drive, whether you have to work a part-time job or whether your children get to go to college. You will have to decide for yourself if you would rather take two children on exciting vacations or have a larger family with less glamorous options. Each has its benefits. I like my large family and my wife is equally fond of her roots.

Obviously, once parents have one child, they can review their circumstances and decide if another child is their own best choice, but once a family elects to use its resources to raise more children, they leave fewer dollars and opportunities for everybody else. There is no going back, no "do-overs."

If we can agree that the economic implications for families who plan for their new children are serious, we ought to recognize that the financial burden for many parents of unplanned children is nearly catastrophic. And do not suppose that we are talking about small numbers here. One study revealed that 25 percent of white babies are born out of wedlock. More than 40 percent of Hispanic babies and 70 percent of African American babies fall into this category.

As I am certain you would imagine, a high percentage of these babies are born to mothers of limited means. In many cases the parents do not finish high school, so they are not likely to secure high-paying jobs. Even if they can earn a reasonable wage, who is going to watch the kiddies while a single mom or dad is off at work? If a single parent has nobody to help out, he or she can consider day care, but that frequently chews up an entire paycheck, so why bother? Many single parents have to get government aid just to provide the basics. Frequently they find that if they need more money the quickest solution is to have another baby, and the problem is compounded.

One of the charities, which our family supports, caters to single parents like those just mentioned. Over ninety percent of the children in the community live with their mothers, which means only a few of the households have a father. In many cases, the mothers have several children.

The reason I like to support this group is the parents (usually moms) came to a decision that they needed to take responsibility for their own actions and the futures of their children. The community offers them a dignified alternative to a life of poverty. The parents make a sincere commitment to turning their lives around. They must submit to regular drug tests, they must do something to improve their employment opportunities like get a GED or go to college or enroll in a trade school. They are also required to participate in some sort of spiritual endeavor. Nobody is trying to convert them to any particular religion. The goal is simply to help them discover their value and self-esteem.

In exchange for their commitment to a life of responsibility, they are given a two-year lease at one-third of market rents. Day care is provided for their children. Counselors work with them to help accomplish their goals. The outside community (that's where we come in) makes financial and other contributions, including food, clothing, field trips and all sorts of support. After their two years are up, they are better prepared to provide for themselves and to set good examples for their children. The counselors stay in touch and try to provide ongoing encouragement and support wherever they are needed. The program is so successful there is a long waiting list to get in. But the screening is tough, because the leaders only want the parents who really want to do their part, not the ones who are simply looking to milk an easy gig.

I cannot speak for everybody else, but I really admire these parents. It takes a lot of courage and character to make difficult life changes like they do.

As difficult as life must be for parents like these, other parents are not so lucky. Sometimes they are just too naïve to understand their plight. One fourteen-year-old girl told a friend of mine that she was anxiously trying to get pregnant. My friend inquired why she was in such a hurry. The youngster responded, "because then somebody will have to love me." This sentiment suggests that teenage pregnancy is not always an accident, but can also be a naïve plot of immature minds.

There are many other reasons our citizens get stuck in these situations and the problem is not peculiar to unwed parents. In fact, a recent study revealed that about half of all pregnancies are not planned. Some people do not use protection and just assume that "it" will not happen to them. Others simply rely upon abortion as a means of birth control. Others do not realize the likelihood of getting pregnant with any particular encounter. Many people are wholly willing to just take their chances. I guess they are subtly seeking a "surprise."

My own suspicion is that a lot of these people would have taken a different tack if they really understood the long-term monetary effects of their choices. It does not take long before a stark reality visits parents: Having a baby is a life-long commitment with incredible financial obligations. First, there are the prenatal costs. Then there are the delivery room and hospital expenses. As far as I am concerned anybody who cannot afford to pay for those things has already started on the wrong foot, because somebody else has to pick up the tab for them.

After that, the diaper parade begins, then formula and

pajamas and baby food and car seats and more diapers and bathing supplies and clothes and toys and food and more diapers, and child-care and additional medical costs and tennis shoes and books and Scouts and soccer leagues and band and art class and lunch money and transportation and better clothes. WHEW! That is an incredible financial burden compared to the cost of a single condom.

Furthermore, we have only identified the basics. What about vacations or college? What happens if the child has special needs or disabilities or has a horrible accident? Who is going to pay for all of that?

If the parents do not have the resources, they must rely upon somebody else. Grandma or other relatives may be willing to pitch in, and they would probably not consider their money to be "wasted," but what if the grandparents are using money that they themselves need for a dignified retirement or their own health?

If no such relatives are available, the rest of society has to pay higher taxes to subsidize the social programs that end up paying for these children. The bottom line is this: Unplanned children come with substantial monetary burdens and any money that is seized from others to pay for them is money that could have been used for other purposes.

In Section Three there is a chapter that breaks down the actual costs of raising children to age 18. You might be shocked at the numbers. But for now, we can agree that cavalier attitudes, ignorance and hasty actions can be big mistakes. While few people would consider the money they spend on their children to be wasted or *flushed*, there is no doubt when parents have to spread their resources around, each family member has to make sacrifices. I will leave it up to you to decide what is best for you.

Pets

Similar consideration should be given to the acquisition of pets. Every dollar that we spend on them is a dollar that could have gone to something else. That is why it is so important to think things through and avoid impulsive commitments. If somebody has the money needed to care for a pet and is willing to forgo other items, then I wish them and their pets all of the blessings that life has to offer. But is it really fair to your children or other pets or even yourself to stretch a budget to the limit, just because puppies are so darn cute?

One family I know has three boys and more than two dozen pets. They have all sorts of critters: four-legged ones, some with shells on their backs, others that slither and some that eat bugs. All of them require food and shelter. And of course there are the acquisition costs and other financial responsibilities. It just so happens that the parents are responsible people. They are far from wealthy, but they can provide a good life for them all.

Even so, all of that responsibility takes away from other possibilities. For example, it reduces what they can do for vacations; it might restrict how many of the children get to go to college or limit which colleges they might attend; it limits which vehicles they can buy and what home they can afford. It reduces their savings account and eventually their quality of life upon retirement. In this family's case, they have made their choice and they handle it well, so I think their money is well spent. But one kitty in the wrong hands can be a waste of money that is needed for more urgent matters.

FINANCIAL INSTITUTIONS

Banks

The last time I wrote a check that bounced my bank charged me $12. I had a very good relationship with my banker, so I called him to see what happened. I learned that their computer is in charge of these situations. It is not programmed to "care" who is involved or what happened; it just sends the notice and creates an opportunity for the bank to grow its revenues. My banker immediately waived the fee.

Nowadays a bounced check charge is much higher, sometimes $25 or so. That seems a bit on the sleazy side to me. Ordinarily the bank doesn't have to do anything extra for that money. Oh sure, they invested in a computer that automatically spits out the notice, but it is not as if that is the only purpose of the computer. And it costs them a little bit for an envelope and a stamp.

Furthermore, the entire procedure tends to prey on the people who are the most vulnerable because it is usually the people who struggle financially who get stuck paying these fees. I will admit that some customers need a little incentive to make sure they don't write bad checks, but these fees seem excessive to me. For the customers who ask, many banks will erase one such penalty per year as a courtesy, even if the customer really did screw up. But on the flip side, banks make enormous amounts of money off the people who simply won't ask them to waive the onerous charges.

These institutions have created countless other opportunities

49

to profit from their relationship with you. Some of the ways are wholly appropriate but other ways are as dubious as the bounced check fee. Banks are known to penalize certain customers if they don't use their accounts enough and other customers who use their account too often. They charge you a fee if they have to count your change. One bank wanted to charge me a fee because I deposited a hundred one dollar bills from my piggybank. They said it takes them too long to count that many items (it takes about one minute). They charge a fee if you use the wrong ATM machines. There is a fee for copies of checks and a charge to verify account information. Expect to pay up if you need a duplicate statement or a cashier's check. And on, and on, and on.

Another very profitable technique, which banks regularly use, is called "float." It is not uncommon for them to put a hold on the funds from any new check a customer deposits (even if you deposited a cashier's check) just so they can use the money for as long as possible without paying much for the privilege.

Note: To avoid or reduce this fee, have your larger deposits wired directly into your account in the morning because the bank will usually clear the funds later that afternoon and you can begin collecting the maximum interest on your funds right away. But it should not surprise you to discover that some banks have wire fees. In this case, you can compare the wiring charge to the interest savings and determine which is your best bet.

Banks are frequently under investigation by the Federal Reserve. Recently, they were busted for charging outrageous fees for overdraft protection. This is different from the bounced check fees mentioned earlier. In this case the customer has "protection" that, if there are not sufficient funds in the account when a check arrives, even for one cent, the bank will cover the check, rather than bounce it, but their kindness comes with a stiff cost—sometimes $25-35. Once again, nobody at the bank has to do anything extra. It is usually just a computer-driven revenue stream. In addition, there may be a daily fee for every day that the customer does not bring the account to a positive balance.

In some cases, customers have found themselves taking it in the shorts to the tune of $100 or more in fees for an account that was only short by a small amount.

Another way banks have been making excess profits lately has to do with the order in which they pay out checks. Traditionally, banks paid checks in the order in which they were received, but some of these money-grubbers have modified that practice, and guess who benefits? These more aggressive banks now pay out larger checks first in hopes that the customer runs short of funds. In that event, there will be a slew of smaller checks that bounce and multiple bounced check charges can be deducted from the customer's account. But if the bank had paid the checks in the order they were received, there may have been only one such fee charged to the customer.

If you complain about the tactic, the bank may make a feigned attempt at reasonableness by waiving one such bounced check fee, but usually "bank policy" will forbid the teller or bank officer from forfeiting any more of their ill-gotten booty.

Another sleazy banking practice has to do with debit cards. In some cases when consumers use a debit card to make a minor purchase, let's say a modest lunch, the bank puts a hold on a larger sum of money from that account. So if the consumer thinks he has $70 in his account and spends $25 on that lunch, the bank could put most or all of the remaining money in the account on hold for a couple of days. Then, if the innocent consumer goes to the gas station to fuel up, he may find insufficient funds available in the account and, to add insult to his injury, he can owe overdraft fees, even though he had enough money in his account all along.

If you are not aware of all the ways the bank has to profit from their relationship with you, ask them for a copy of their fee schedule. It is likely to include several pages of fine print. They consider some of these fees as sacred cows and others as negotiable. Clearly, you should learn the difference. If you are charged an unexpected fee, ask your banker if it is firm. Unless you are a particularly seedy character, chances are good they want to keep your business and will try to accommodate you. Don't be afraid to change banks if you believe the relationship has gotten one-sided.

Mortgage Companies

Banks aren't the only financial institutions that have creative ways to get us to waste our money. Mortgage companies also have some artistic ways to invade your purse. For starters, there are the outrageous late fees if you make your payment after the designated date. Usually this fee is clearly identified in your loan documents, but that doesn't make it any less painful to pay. A common penalty is 5 percent after the payment is 15 days late. On a $1,200 monthly payment the borrower will owe $60 extra if she makes her payment on the 16th instead of the 15th of the month. That is an astronomical penalty for such a minor indiscretion.

Most people know that mortgage companies charge fees if we pay our payments late, but did you know there can also be a penalty if you pay too much or too soon? Sometimes these prepayment penalties can be thousands of dollars. In fact, if you pay off your mortgage loan on the 20th of the month, it is very possible that you will owe both a late fee and a prepayment penalty—at the same time. To find out if your loan has a prepayment penalty review the loan documents or ask your mortgage company.

Mortgage companies also love to set up escrow accounts for your funds. Each month you send in a portion of your anticipated property taxes and annual hazard insurance premium and they pay the respective bills when they eventually come due. They pay you no interest on your escrow account so you are a big loser because you could have used that same money to pay other debt you might have somewhere else, thereby saving the interest you have to pay on that alternate debt.

One of the most audacious parts of the mortgage company's escrow activities has to do with their responsibility to pay the taxes for you. Many new loans levy a charge against the borrower called a Realty Tax Service Fee or something similar. In essence, the lender charges you another $100 or so to set up an account with some neutral third party, who in turn processes the payment of your taxes from your escrow account on behalf of the lender.

It is my belief that if lenders are going to keep our money, interest-free, in their escrow account all year, the least they can do is program their computer to write the checks when the taxes are due. Charging customers an additional fee for a service the bank ought to perform in the first place is really pouring salt into our collective monetary wounds. Fortunately, there are some loans that do not require escrow accounts. Naturally, I suggest you always take those loans when they are available.

Another recent creation of mortgage companies involves the extra fees they charge to originate their loans. Anybody who has taken out a new home loan in the last few years knows what I mean. Front-end fees are outrageous. Many of those fees did not exist just 10 years ago. But, somebody in a smoke-filled backroom figured out they could charge Document Preparation fees and Underwriting charges and more. In the old days, mortgage companies charged a loan origination fee and they expected to prepare the documents and have their underwriters review the file as part of the approval process. But now the borrower is likely to pay all three of these expenses and a few others as well.

The best way to keep these fees under control when obtaining a new loan is to ask a successful Realtor which lender he or she recommends. These agents send their lenders a chain of business and those lenders know it is foolish to abuse the relationship by charging excessive fees. Finally, it is usually acceptable to pay these itemized costs if the Loan Origination charge is less than one percent or the interest rate being offered is ¼ percent lower than that of other lenders.

Credit Card Companies

Credit card companies (CCCs) are another type of financial institution that preys on our monetary ignorance. Their products include bank cards as well as cards issued by other merchants, like department stores, oil companies and the like.

The CCCs have several ways to help you waste your money. A common one is annual fees. There are many companies that do not charge annual fees, so if you are paying such an expense, be certain you have a good reason or consider transferring that debt to some other card with no such fees. In a quintessential example of "damned if you do and damned if you don't," one of the built-in rackets is if you close out credit card accounts, your credit score may actually go down. So if you keep the card, you have to pay annual fees, but if you close out the account, you see a temporary drop in your credit score.

The CCCs also charge you very high late payment fees. Whenever you find yourself faced with the possibility of owing late fees to any of these banks, I strongly urge you to borrow from somebody else, including a private party, so you can pay your card or debt on time, avoid the financial penalty and preserve your credit score. Then promptly repay the new lender in case you might need them again. Then, take the money you would have paid as a late fee and pay down your balance a little more.

Next, there is the over-limit fee. There are several reasons it is crazy for you to pay this penalty. First, you ought to have a better handle on your available credit than that. Second, most banks will raise your limit if you ask them to.

Then there is this tricky ploy with credit card checks. Many banks will send you a group of checks from time to time and tell you that in the name of "convenience" you can simply use one of their checks. That sounds okay until we get into the fine print.

They frequently charge a higher interest rate for the money they advance to cover checks than the rate they charge to cover your purchases. Credit card checks are frequently treated as typical cash advances. There can be a charge of 2 percent or more just for using the "convenient" service. But wait, there is more.

If your payment is not enough to pay the unpaid balance on your account, in full, the banks are known to pay off the charges for purchases (the lower rate) before they apply the payments to the high interest charges on the cash advances. Is it any wonder new credit card companies are always sending you teaser rates to get you to transfer your balance to their bank at an appealing introductory rate? The hope is that you still have plenty of unpaid balance when the introductory period expires.

One other underhanded practice kicks in when you use your credit card overseas. In the fine print of your Credit Card Fee Schedule you may find that your CCC has the right to add on 1-2 percent for any transactions that you complete in foreign lands. They charge more than a cash advance and throw in a conversion fee, even though they don't have to do anything to convert the money. Before you embark on international journeys be sure to find out what kind of extra fees your CCC has for this purpose. And we're not done yet.

Another tactic you need to know is that if you borrow more than 35 percent of your credit limit at any time, the banks might raise your interest rate. Furthermore the credit reporting agencies will lower your credit score, which will also cost you more money on some of your other accounts. Generally speaking, it is better to have your debt spread over several cards than to owe more than 35 percent of your credit limit on any one card.

Finally, one of the CCCs' best gimmicks is the Payment Protection Plan. In essence, if you are stricken by some disaster, like you fall ill or lose your job, they will make your credit card payments for you. Unless you have some reason to believe you are likely to have your income disrupted this is nearly always a waste of money. I am amazed at how many people fail to see this as a form of insurance. If you want insurance, go to an insurance company, not a credit card company – but first, read the information in the section of this book about insurance companies and then don't buy it from them either.

As unpleasant as you may find it, you might as well face the truth: You are going to be doing a lot of business with lending institutions like banks, mortgage companies and credit card companies. If you don't take the time to learn the inner workings of these organizations you are going to get fleeced, perhaps costing you thousands of dollars annually. The biggest issue is excessive interest rates but you should also make certain you never pay late fees, bounced check fees or other penalties and always avoid escrow accounts if you can.

None of us begrudge lenders a reasonable profit for legitimate services, but one of the worst things we waste our money on is the extraneous charges these institutions seek to impose. If you know the rules of the game, you can make smart choices.

INTEREST

One day, my elderly Aunt Beverly, whom I call "Tantie," told me a story about my mother and her, when they were little girls. As the story goes, a relative gave them each a new buffalo nickel to buy an ice-cream cone. Since money was so scarce in those days, this was a special treat. But my aunt, who was the younger of the two girls, had an idea how she could utilize her new-found coin in a wiser way than my mom was likely to use hers.

Tantie's plan began by allowing my mom to buy the first cone. Once that was accomplished, Tantie elected to save her nickel rather than spend it. Naturally, a short time later my mom's ice-cream cone was gone along with her shiny nickel. After that, my aunt was delighted by the fact that she still had her new coin, effectively outsmarting her elder sibling.

So, the question is: What did this little girl instinctively know that so many "smarter" people never quite understand? Simply put, whenever we buy things that we don't need, we are stealing from our own better choices.

One of the more obvious examples of this common mistake is on our highways, where millions of consumers chase each other around in flashy vehicles, most of which are financed. The value of most of these cars drops faster than gravity itself while many of the drivers wonder why they have such a difficult time making ends meet. Similar indulgences are common for other high-priced purchases. A quick stroll through the local shopping mall will reveal dozens of stores offering opulent furniture, extravagant jewelry, and exciting vacation packages. Still, other people find it difficult to get into their own driveway because of the boats and motor homes they own, but rarely use.

Whenever we submit to such frivolous purchases, the cost of our nonchalance is enormous. However, as bad as that is, the consequences are intensified further when consumers lack sufficient funds to pay cash for their hasty acquisitions. When they then borrow funds to complete these unwise transactions, they only cause further hemorrhaging of their already bleeding budgets.

In an earlier chapter titled "Adult Indulgences," I introduced the concept of "buying power." In that chapter we observed that a smoker who spends $28 per week on cigarettes for 40 years loses nearly a half million dollars in buying power. That is because of compound interest.

In the cigarette example, the actual cost of the smokes is $58,240 in money spent ($28 per week times 52 weeks per year times 40 years). But when we factor in the lost interest on other debt that could have been paid off or the interest that could have been earned, the actual cost to the smoker is about $465,000. You might be asking yourself, "What interest?"

As we have discussed, whenever we make any purchase including cigarettes or anything else, there is an interest fee which goes along with the purchase. That is because we could have used that money to pay off some credit card debt, but since we did not do that the interest charge on the card lives on as an expense in our lives. If you don't have a credit card, you could have paid down a car loan or a mortgage loan and saved some interest on those loans. Even if you have no loans at all there is an interest cost to all of your purchases because you could have invested the money in some way and received interest for your investment, but since you spent the money rather than investing it, you have lost that interest income and it becomes a FOREVER cost of your purchase.

Another way to look at it is if our smoker would have taken the same $28 per week that he spent on the cigarettes and put that money in an investment that was paying 7 percent interest, by the time 40 years passed he would have a whopping $465,000 in his account. That is the "buying power" he has lost . . . all from just $4 per day.

All of this suggests I am saying never spend any money on anything because the interest charges will eat you alive, but obviously that would be ridiculous. We have to have the necessities of life and most of us want a few frivolities along the way. After all, what fun can a life be if it is only about saving and never about actual living? It all comes down to balance. It is one thing for a millionaire to buy a ticket to a baseball game, but it is different for a young working couple to run out and buy season tickets with their credit cards.

If you already have interest expenses that you are paying out of your own efforts (car loans, credit card debt, etc.) you should consider getting those debts out of your life as quickly as possible. But for everybody else you might want to adopt the philosophy of my father-in-law. Lyman regularly said, "Save a little, spend a little." He lived a great life and he was always financially secure, but he never had a car payment or unpaid credit cards.

Regardless of whether we are talking about a car loan or a credit card purchase, the added burden of repaying the inevitable interest charges is an ongoing penalty for living beyond our means. Think about it this way: If you had an extra $100 per month, would you rather donate it to a bank in the form of interest payments or treat your friends and family to a string of fabulous backyard barbeques? Which of those options really adds quality to your life? If you want to have more barbeques, don't throw your money at unnecessary interest.

Consumers are faced with buying decisions like these all the time, but those who avoid paying interest, and even get interest to work for them, get a lot more "stuff" out of their money. The people who truly understand the cost of debt don't carelessly run out and buy new cars and such things. For those who are already burdened with debt and the painful interest that goes along with it,

I suggest you adopt a new philosophy: "If you can't pay cash, you can't afford it."

Acceptable Debt and Interest

There are only a few circumstances that justify taking on debt and the interest expense that goes along with it. The common thread among these cases lies in the fact we can transfer the responsibility of repaying the debt and interest to somebody else. The examples mirror those we discussed in the chapter about depreciating assets.

The first situation is when you buy your own home. In this case, the debt and interest are acceptable burdens for several reasons. For starters, we have to live somewhere and most of us have to pay rent if we don't buy our own place. Since we have a housing expense in either event, we can take away the money we would otherwise pay to some theoretical landlord and use that money to buy our own property. Another reason that this is acceptable debt is that the tax man will help you pay off your home. Both the interest on your home loan and your property taxes are deductible, which translates into income tax savings for you. Money saved on taxes can be used to pay off the home quicker.

Similar benefits are afforded landlords. If you own rental property, you can use the rent you receive to pay the interest on your loan and end up with property that is paid off. Obviously, debt and interest are helping you in such situations.

Our final example of acceptable debt involves the purchase of tools used in trade. Naturally, a carpenter needs a hammer to go to work. If he borrows the money to buy that simple tool he can use it to generate money to pay back the debt and any interest. The same can be said of a tractor, a stethoscope, a vending machine, a computer program or many other items. Naturally, this writer suggests you try to pay for these items with cash, but I understand that most of us don't have enough loose change lying around to pay cash for a front-loader, so in a situation like that, new debt is tolerable.

So there it is: a very small group of circumstances that justify debt and interest.

As we conclude this chapter about interest, a quick review reveals three primary lessons were offered for consideration. First, any time we buy things we don't need, we waste opportunities to save and invest that money for something more important, like income. Second, we established that monthly payments and interest expenses are an ongoing penalty for making hasty purchases. And third, the only times we should take on debt and interest is when we can get somebody else (a theoretical landlord, a tenant or an employer) to pay it back for us.

It has been approximately 75 years since that fateful day when my aunt socked away her humble buffalo nickel. It would not surprise me if she still has it because that shrewd little girl accumulated an abundance of resources over her lifetime. Many other folks have lived by similar principles and accomplished just as much and more. YOU can do it, too. That is why it amazes me that so many intelligent people fail to understand that impulsive or unnecessary purchases, along with any related debt and interest, are among the worst things on which they waste their money.

INSURANCE

Insurance companies have realized that many people think "insurance" is a dirty word, so they use synonyms to sell their products. If a company offers a "warranty" or "protection" or "security" from some problem, they mean "insurance."

Almost everybody misunderstands insurance. Sometimes they have too little or too much life insurance. They may buy home warranties they don't need, or have too low a deductible on their auto insurance or too high a deductible on their home hazard insurance. Generally speaking, insurance is a racket and the insurance companies have figured out that people will pay to insure practically anything.

You can insure your kids, your pets and your jewelry. You can insure you won't make a mistake at work. You can protect yourself against snow, wind or floods. You can get kidnapping insurance or identity theft insurance. There is protection against your computer losing information. Consumers buy extended warranties on their TV and insurance for their credit card payment. Renters may insure their furniture. Your mortgage company may require you to buy insurance on your home loan. You can insure that your travel plans won't be disrupted.

You can buy insurance for your teeth or your fingers. Farmers can insure against crop failure. The Mafia has been known to "insure" that certain businesses do not suddenly and mysteriously blow up. The social security system is designed to insure a minimum lifestyle for the elderly. Heck, you can even buy insurance on your cards at a blackjack table in Las Vegas. If all that is not enough, call Lloyds of London. They will insure practically anything. By now, you ought to be able to guess why there are so many types of insurance: The insurance companies win, and nearly every consumer loses.

Ask yourself this question: Why would insurance companies take on so much risk for such small premiums? The answer is obvious. They take in more money than they pay out. After they pay their own rent, their utilities, their taxes, all their payroll and other employee expenses, commissions on all the policies that their agents sell, interest on their loans, and all their other costs, they still have enough money left over to pay all the claims, and still make a profit. They do all of that without setting up a warehouse or manufacturing anything. It is as simple as that. It makes financial sense for them to take on your risks—provided you are willing to "overpay" them for the privilege. Is it any surprise that insurance companies are among our largest and most profitable corporations?

In spite of my sweeping generalizations that insurance usually should be avoided, and it is a big "net loser" for consumers in the long run, there are a few occasions when it is barely justifiable. But even in those situations, you will most likely end up being another victim to the insurance system. You will probably overpay or have the wrong deductible or simply fail to collect as much as you pay in. So, how do we wade through these murky waters and come out fairly clean?

In order to decide if any given insurance policy is worth our money, we must first define what insurance really is and what it is not. Insurance is a way to transfer the risk of a specific negative event happening and nothing more. Insurance should not be a means to gather enrichment, or to prove our love, or be treated as some sort of magic pill to protect us from minor losses. So, now that we have established what insurance "is" and what it "is not," we can form a good Rule of Thumb to guide us whenever we are considering handing our money over to insurance companies:

Except in unusual circumstances, we only need insurance to protect us against major losses.

Given the above philosophy, consider the following examples of risk to determine if you would rather pay the insurance company to take the risk or take on the financial threat yourself and save the premiums.

Situation 1: *Your house might burn down and you have a big mortgage to pay.*

Question: *Is avoiding a potential $200,000 loss worth a premium of $70 per month?*

Situation 2: *Your cell phone might break two months after the warranty expires.*

Question: *Would you rather pay a one-time extended warranty fee of $45 or accept the risk yourself and save the fee?*

Situation 3: *Someone might steal your brand-new car, then crash and destroy it.*

Question: *Is avoiding a potential loss of $30,000 worth an extra $70 per month for full coverage auto insurance, or should you take your chances?*

Situation 4: *Bad guys might break into your garage and steal $500 worth of power tools.*

Question: *Is it worth $39 per year for protection in case it happens to you?*

Situation 5: *A spouse might have a stroke and medical expenses could be $400,000 over a 5-year period.*

Question: *Is avoiding a potential loss of $400,000 worth $360 per month in health insurance premiums?*

Situation 6: *Some people have accidents on ski slopes and need a helicopter ride to the emergency room, which costs $4,000.*

Question: *Is it worth an extra $5 per month on your health insurance policy to get the insurance company to pay for any emergency helicopter ride you need?*

Situation 7: *Some dads die at a young age and leave school-age children behind.*

Question: *Is a half-million dollar life insurance policy worth $35 per month or is this risk so small it does not justify paying the premiums?*

Situation 8: *A single woman, with no dependents and a net-worth of $20,000 is considering buying a $50,000 life insurance policy to cover funeral costs upon her demise.*

Question: *Is such a policy worth $22 per month or should she save her money?*

If we apply what we learned in our Rule Of Thumb we can see that the big risks include the odd numbered examples and the even numbers are low risk or not necessary. Therefore, average people should protect themselves against major losses to expensive assets like homes and new cars (not a $3,000 truck) plus serious medical problems and death if there are dependents whose lives would be substantially disrupted.

Even though the insurance companies make big profits on these policies too, the potential losses are so enormous when they do occur, consumers can get wiped out. Consequently, it is okay to shift the risk to the companies that can afford it, but insurance is generally not worth the cost unless the consumer's exposure could become life-altering.

In addition to buying insurance to cover less serious risks, consumers also buy the wrong type of insurance, or overpay for their deductibles. In Section Three, there are thorough guidelines to consider when you are faced with specific insurance decisions.

For now, we should be able to recognize that buying the wrong type of insurance or insurance we don't need in the first place is flushing our money down the drain, and that any money that we spend in that way is among the worst things on which we waste our money.

TAXES

I have asked dozens of people what they believe is the single biggest expense in their lifetime. When my wife heard the question, she suggested she should be my biggest expense. I was too cowardly to tell her the answer is really taxes.

Nearly everybody says their homes cost them more than anything else. That supposition is reasonable. Somebody who makes $4,000 per month could easily pay one-quarter of that amount in rent or mortgage payments. That would definitely become a substantial sum over time, but that is not the biggest expense. Other people suspect their cars, college educations or groceries constitute their greatest expense but those aren't it either.

When you consider all of the necessary purchases that we make just to get by, and then add up all the taxes we pay for them, it is enough to make you cry. We all pay dozens of taxes that citizens of 100 years ago never even heard of. For example, let's peek at basic transportation. You have to get to and from work so you buy a car. Before you take possession, there are sales taxes and license plates fees. Money from toll roads is a tax. High taxes are built into your insurance premiums and all of the parts and maintenance costs. You pay approximately forty cents in taxes (half for the state and half for the Feds) for every gallon of gas you buy.

Then there are all of the other hidden taxes that we pay every day. Property taxes on our homes, a seat tax at a sporting event or concert, a tourist tax if you rent a car or hotel room, sales taxes on all of your purchases. Smokers and drinkers pay a fortune in taxes.

Take a close look at your utility bills, cable bills and phone bills. Taxes, taxes, taxes!

Finally, throw in the income taxes and we are paying half of every dollar we make on one form of tax or another.

According to census figures, there are slightly more than 110 million households in the USA. The median income per household is about $50,000 and the average household pays more than $26,000 in taxes. One-quarter of that is Federal Income Tax and the remainder is paid to the feds, state, county and local governments, in various ways.

Another way to look at the total US tax burden is to consider the annual Tax Freedom Day. This is the day on which all of our combined taxes for the year would be paid in full if we all paid 100 percent of our income into a giant tax fund. After that, any money we earn is ours to keep. Usually that day is sometime in the month of May. Regardless of how you measure it, taxes consume an enormous percentage of our resources.

The IRS takes the biggest bite out of our tax dollars. It collects more than 1.2 TRILLION dollars from the income taxes of individual tax payers every year, Take a different look at that staggering number, which is $1,200,000,000,000. To better understand exactly how much that is, imagine you were sitting at a table and receiving one dollar per second. In that exercise, you will earn $3,600 per hour or a whopping $86,400 per day, and you will receive that amount each and every day for nearly 32,000 years, before you finally get your last dollar. WHEW!

So, the IRS takes 1.2 trillion dollars from the public every year for income taxes, but that is not the end of their money grab. They also collect that much again from employment taxes (mostly social security taxes, known as FICA) and corporate income taxes. Then they confiscate another hundred billion or so from the combination of estate taxes, excise taxes and gift taxes. They also peel off 18 cents per gallon from our gasoline purchases (the "greedy" oil companies only get half that much). Then there is rental of government resources, park fees, fishing and hunting licenses and a lot more. Amazingly, that is not enough for them. They are always looking for ways to get more. One politician recently recommended a tax on the wind.

As stated earlier, the IRS is only responsible for one-quarter of all our taxes, but it is the primary area where taxpayers can actually fight back. In mid-April, and in an attempt to reduce their income tax burden as much as possible, approximately one-third of those who file tax returns actually itemize their deductions. But, many of them are at least partly intimidated by the tax system and fail to take full advantage of their available write-offs, perhaps because they hope they are less likely to get audited.

Then there are the other two-thirds of the tax filers who merely take the standard deductions and make no attempt to itemize. There can be no doubt many of them would save money if they took the more laborious route. Perhaps they are frightened by the forms or too lazy to do the work or unaware of how much money they could save with a little effort.

Another group of taxpayers who lose their money unnecessarily each year are those who file their returns late. In that event there are penalties and interest and it piles up quickly. The Federal government will charge you up to 25 percent for filing just 5 months late. The mob does not even charge rates like that. Then there is the Failure to Pay Penalty. It seems to me that filing late and failing to pay ought to be the same thing, but this penalty is .05 percent per month for each and every month you file late. That can add up to a lot of money. Finally, there is the interest they charge. This is a percentage that has been anywhere between 4-8 percent per year over the past ten years. If it is foolish to pay taxes that we can legally avoid, it is insanity to pay penalties and interest.

Naturally, some people pay more taxes than others. Since you are reading this, it is safe to assume you wish to earn higher than normal income, even though you realize it means you will be obligated to pay higher than normal taxes. Therefore, you have plenty of incentive to reduce your tax responsibility as much as possible, and thereby keep a higher percentage of your earnings.

Since I do not know your personal circumstances, I can only give you general guidelines. First, I suggest you secure the services of a qualified tax expert to review your situation and make specific recommendations. If you can't afford that at the moment, go to the Internet and get familiar with the common deductions other people take. Talk to some people whom you believe are informed on the topic.

I suggest you get serious about digging for all legitimate deductions to which you might be entitled. Be aggressive about your claims, but don't cheat. If you are in doubt whether a deduction qualifies, ask yourself if it is "reasonable." That is a common measure that is used by the IRS. For example it would probably be reasonable to take a young couple (even if you are related to them) to lunch to discuss opening a day care center with them, but a reasonable person would not take them on a Mediterranean cruise for that purpose.

The worst thing to do is nothing. Ask yourself how many hours you would work on a part-time job for a sum such as $1,500, and then devote that much time to learning how you can save that amount of money in the next year by employing what you have learned. Each year thereafter you will be positioned to gain from that knowledge.

Next, if you do not already own your own home, look into buying one because you have to live somewhere and the tax laws favor owners over tenants by a mile. All of the homeowner's interest payments and property taxes are deductible, but no similar benefit is afforded tenants. That purchase alone can save thousands of tax dollars.

You should also consider starting your own business or begin writing a book or do something else that you could consider a home business. There are substantial benefits for doing so. For example, you can buy surplus goods and sell them on eBay or mow lawns or design Web pages. If you need ideas, ask your friends what they think you might be good at.

You do not need to set any records in the beginning; you just need to be working with the "intent" to make a profit. Once you have established that, you will be able to write off all sorts of expenses that you do not get to deduct now. For example, if you plan on writing a book for profit about the best lakes for bass fishing in Texas, a lot of your fishing expenses could qualify as deductions. Or, if you want to repair automobiles on weekends for extra money, chances are good you can write off any new tools you buy for that purpose and probably a percentage of the tools you already have that will be used in that endeavor. Or, if you are babysitting for additional income you might be able to deduct baby furniture or toys needed for the work.

One of the best options is to buy rental real estate. You not only gain all the same deductions as you would for buying a home but you can write off all your real costs like insurance and utility costs. And, there is also a depreciation allowance and all of the daily costs to maintain the property, including things like cell phone costs or auto expenses to drive by and inspect it. If you take a trip to Las Vegas and look at properties, some of your travel costs could be deductible.

If you start your own business you just might get lucky, like Craig Newmark, who sent out notices about meetings at work. People liked his notices so they encouraged him to do more. Before long, Craigslist was born and a humble man made it big.

Next, there are estate taxes. People whom I consider to be responsible constantly surprise because they have never prepared a will or done anything to prepare their finances for the day of their demise. Most people don't have to worry about estate taxes (the death tax) because their estates are not big enough. But for those who have larger estates, this tax may be the most ruthless one of them all, sometimes taking half of the deceased person's possessions. Prudent tax planning can usually eliminate a lot, if not all, of that. Someone with a five million dollar estate might save a million dollars or more by utilizing trusts and other planning tools.

As I stated earlier, it is wise to talk with a tax expert who knows your situation before you get into these things, but if you are like many others, there are countless deductions available to you. But don't ignore the urgency. You need those dollars a lot more than the IRS does. Based on the income they take from us all, we are over-governed, not under-taxed.

Finally, there is an issue with your employer withholding money from your paycheck for income tax purposes. I have known lots of people who like to give the government their money as the year progresses because they like to get a refund at tax time. Quite honestly, that is not very smart.

The government does not pay you anything to park your money there but your credit card company is charging high rates that you could pay off. Therefore you can get 15 percent or so by paying that instead. If you have no loans that you can pay down, then put the money in the bank and collect some modest interest.

All you have to do is visit the payroll department at work and have them adjust your withholding so that less money is taken out of your paycheck; then, make automatic payments to the best alternative place. The bottom line is this: The various governments get enough of your money in one way or another, but you should be using the maximum possible amount of your money yourself.

If you rethink all of the ways that you pay taxes and seek to reduce them honestly but substantially, you might easily save $120 per month and that happens to be the same amount our smoker saved in a previous chapter, which ended up producing $465,000 in "buying power" over his lifetime. It is easily worth the effort.

OVER-IMPROVING HOMES

One of my son's high school classmates hit upon a technology goldmine and suddenly found himself making $100,000/mo. while he was a mere 19 years old. Suddenly, he had so much money he did not know what to do with it all. One of his first choices was to move out of his parent's house and into one of his own.

He bought a very nice residence with an approximate value of $350,000. He immediately started to throw money at it. He bought all of the things he and his buddies could enjoy. One of his choices was to convert the large garage into a fantastic disco-type lounge.

Since he and his visitors never had much responsibility before, they did not respect much of anything. They were always breaking things but nobody cared because the fellow had so much money he would just get new stuff. He bought a $130,000 classic car and promptly wrecked it. The attitude was, "Oh well, I will just get something else." One contractor performed a $1,000 job for the young man; then for his compensation he was given a motorcycle that had only been driven for a couple of months.

Eventually, the young fellow spent more in ridiculous upgrades to the home than he had spent for the dwelling itself. Then the paradigm changed. The gold mine of income that he discovered began to dry up because competitors moved into his part of the business world. His income steadily declined. By the time it was over the young fellow had made a couple million dollars, but then it was over, just as quickly as it began.

Naturally, he went broke because he spent all his money.

Eventually, he had to sell his home. That is when we got called in. We were asked to make an offer for the property. Unfortunately we could not pay as much for it as the young man paid in the first place because we had to remove most of the specialty items he had installed. He might have gotten some of his money back if he had done that same work to a home in a million dollar neighborhood but people who want to buy million dollar homes don't want to live in a $350,000 neighborhood.

The bottom line was he lost nearly a half million dollars by over-improving a home, and that is a pool-sized flush.

Another example of a big *flush* involved a woman and a fireplace. I got the story from a contractor friend. Keith has a Scottish accent that resembles that of the Geico gecko. It seems his client inherited an incredible amount of money and so she bought a home in the mountains. Like the fellow above, she immediately started making expensive changes to it. Keith is very talented so he was called in to serve as her general contractor.

The wealthy lady wanted her moss-rock fireplace moved to one side by two feet so one of the areas adjacent to it would be bigger. My friend has a famous quote that he uses whenever a homeowner comes up with offbeat ideas like that. His accent is very charming when he says, "We can do that." He is very positive, because he has found that he makes a lot of money off of such whims, but he is also highly ethical so a polite education usually follows. He went on to tell this particular lady that moving such a fireplace would be an incredible undertaking.

First, he would have to cover everything up because a project like that is very messy, causing dust to get everywhere. Then, it would take two men a couple weeks to remove the old fireplace stone by stone, so as not to have a catastrophic collapse from all of the weight. After that, a talented crew would have to fix the ceiling where the chimney kisses it. Then the building inspectors would require that the foundation be modified to deal with the new distribution of the weight. Then a new floor would be needed to hide the old hole. Of course she would have to order new stone. A new hole in the roof would be necessary to receive the new chimney. Finally, a new custom-made fireplace could indeed be constructed right where she wanted it. He went on to give her a six-figure estimate and suggested the entire project could easily take a month. But Keith was not done.

He went on to explain that even if they did all of that work, she might not like the finished product because the new fireplace, as she had envisioned it, would disrupt the natural flow of traffic within the central part of the home. In other words it would be in the way when guests moved from the foyer on their way to the main living quarters. She barely considered his input and quickly suggested that the new fireplace would be such a masterpiece that it would actually be nice to walk around and take in its beauty. She measured my friend's comments, but she was excited about her idea, she gave him the "go ahead" anyway. He responded once more, in his gecko voice, "We can do that."

A month later, her fantastic fireplace was standing tall. Keith said it was one of the finest fireplaces he had ever seen. A couple of days later, the wealthy lady called my friend into the main room to look at that fireplace just one more time. She said she was observing what he meant when he said it would disrupt the flow of the room. She then apologized to him for not listening in the first place and sheepishly asked him if he could remove it and build a new one, right back where the old one was. You know his response. And so it was. The final cost to remove a fireplace and then move it back to where it started was nearly a quarter of a million dollars. In the end they were all happy, and I guess that is what matters.

The above two examples are certainly extreme cases, but the projects do not have to be so drastic to negatively affect a family's monetary situation. An elderly gentleman I know is a good example, and he is like many others who are always tweaking their property. I guess they think that "because they can, they should." Sure you can put wallpaper over there, but does it really matter? He was always adding rooms to his old house and then decorating in all sorts of odd combinations.

He eventually expanded the home to twice the size of others in the area and decided to move on. He bought a new property in a nicer area and did the same thing. The pattern goes something like this: Move in and paint everything; add a new porch, then enclose it, then remodel the kitchen and bathroom. Finish off the basement; heat the garage, put up a shed. It never ends. The sad thing is his projects do not enhance the property value on a dollar-for-dollar basis. Therefore, he is a net loser financially, not to mention the time he has lost.

I have backyard neighbors with the same addiction. They are constantly throwing money at their home. In the last five years they have completely transformed their property, both inside and out. I have never been inside their home, but I can tell you they have built a spectacular outdoor paradise, complete with several tiers, a sitting area, fountains, a fine trellis, a stone walkway, a sitting area, BBQ pit, plush flowers and the like. They have added the very best storm windows and a wonderful ground-level patio plus a new deck off the master bedroom. The front yard has also become the finest on the block.

This week they dropped by to ask if we would allow them to walk on our yard a bit as they construct a new eight-foot brick enclosure around their entire back yard. They were very proud of the incredible, custom fence-to-be. There will be two colors of brick plus a stone cap as well as pillars and gargoyles. They gushed at their guilty pleasure when they suggested it is going to cost more than $15,000. We have always liked them, so naturally we were supportive.

If their work on the inside matches their performance on the outside they have probably spent $100,000 in improvements; but practically all of that money is *flushed*. No matter how much money they spend on the home, it is still in a neighborhood of $250,000 homes. A future buyer of this property will like all of those things, but they won't pay much of a premium for them. Buyers who want a $250,000 home tend to shop in neighborhoods of that value rather than look in cheaper areas for overbuilt homes. Besides, the home would not appraise for a high value because other homes in the area just don't sell for that much.

The old guy up the street offers another example of over-improving a home. In his case it was a timing issue. He waited for his kids to grow up and then he removed the roof from the house and added a whole new story on top. I don't know what he and his wife do in all of that new space, but it seems to me if the home was big enough to raise their family, it ought to be big enough for the two of them. Anyway, the home is bigger now with new stairs and elderly people who probably don't really like climbing them all that much. Furthermore, it has not increased in value on a dollar-for-dollar basis for the same reasons as in the previous examples. Throw in higher utility bills, higher insurance premiums and higher property taxes for good measure. If he had made those improvements when his children lived there, he would have still have lost money, but at least the space would have been used a lot more.

Many smaller projects also qualify as *flushing* money down the drain. I know all sorts of people who spend $25,000 or more to remodel a kitchen or put an addition on their home. New carpet, new windows, landscaping and an endless list of home improvement lure their dollars away. But in many cases they will never recover their money.

One woman put a $25,000 pool in the yard of a $75,000 home. She only stayed in the home for a few years and could not recover her money because of the neighborhood. Her son bought the house from her and did not maintain the pool. When he died, we had to fill in the hole with new dirt and sod so the home would match the others in the area. A modest estate lost an enormous amount of money because of the pool.

Since I am a retired Realtor, I have literally been in thousands of homes. I have seen every type of over-improvement you can imagine. The sad but common thread is that these people never get much of their money back. The smarter thing is to buy a below-average home in a nicer area and bring it up to average or just slightly above average. But do not install amenities that are extravagant for the neighborhood. If your home blends in with those around it, you have a much better chance of recapturing your money, or even making a nice profit when you sell.

Over-improving homes is one of the worst things on which we waste our money, and as these examples illustrate—the *flushing* is substantial.

HONORABLE MENTION

When it comes to wasting money, there are a few other topics worth a brief mention. These items are not as substantial as the ones mentioned earlier, but they still consume ongoing funds that could be diverted to more productive endeavors.

Gift Buying/Holidays

If you are like me, you think gift giving has taken on an excessive role in our finances. Perhaps it is the fault of the greeting card industry. There is a holiday nearly every month on top of all of our personal obligations.

If I were as responsible as Hallmark says I ought to be I would buy my wife a bottle of Champagne in January, a box of chocolates for Valentine's Day, a lily for Easter, flowers for Mother's Day, a night out for her birthday in July, an anniversary gift in December, and a Christmas gift. In addition, experience tells me I had better buy a couple of gifts or cards "for no reason" once in a while and take her out to dinner with some regularity to show appreciation for all of the things she does. Although I do actually enjoy acknowledging her, I have to admit I reject some of the obligations that retailers attempt to thrust on me.

When our boys were growing up the craziness extended to them. In addition to all of the parental obligations we had birthday parties, 4th of July celebrations and active Christmas holidays. At the same time, our kids had young cousins who were of similar ages. For a few years we bought birthday and Christmas gifts for all of them, but eventually we drew names out of a hat so each person only had to shop for one present.

The problem is not restricted to the home front. The stores barely finish with their promotions for one holiday before they are building displays for the next one. Christmas ads begin earlier every year. They might as well just make it perpetual.

Other symbols of excessive gift giving are all around us. Some of them include toy boxes that are over-stuffed and grandparents who spoil the youngsters.

In addition to our relatives, we have a half dozen special friends and coworkers to whom we direct our money into wedding gifts, baby showers, Tupperware parties, birthday presents, random cards, parties, and going out to dinner. You are probably the same way.

It is nice to recognize the important people in our lives, but it seems we could do that without a perpetual carousel of financial obligations.

I suggest you look for ways to cut this expense. Meet with key family members and find ways to recognize each other without all of the commercialism attached to it. Most of us appreciate a heart-felt hug or kind word just as much as a gift. Can you write a poem or bake a cake? When was the last time you went on a picnic? Have you ever given anybody a foot massage? Perhaps you could wash your brother's car for him. Mom might need her bathroom painted. In many cases your kind deeds will mean a lot more than another pair of slippers.

Creature Comforts

Some people justify impulse purchases of unnecessary products and services by telling themselves that they "deserve" them. Everything from a regular trip to the ice-cream store to a luxury vacation is justified in this way.

Treating ourselves to goodies is probably okay when we really fulfill a goal and the reward was tied to the project from the beginning. For example if you were to tell yourself, "I am going to lose ten pounds and when I do, I am going to visit the museum," that reward is earned. There was a justification to indulge rather than an indulgence looking for justification. It is well thought out, not impulsive.

The point is to avoid whimsical purchases. Constantly making up reasons to buy new things is a sign of low self-esteem and a path to financial disaster. You see it in hoarders and in people who keep refinancing their homes. They run up their credit card balances with unneeded purchases and then tell themselves, "Let's refinance our home and pay off our debts, then we will tighten our belts." They get the refinance accomplished and then forget the rest of the message. One of my pals was just like that.

One time I went on a weekend fishing trip with Ed, who was always using credit cards to treat himself to various purchases. Most of his credit cards were maxed out and he was forever struggling to make minimum payments, which were almost exclusively interest. I talked with him about the kinds of things mentioned in this book. We agreed that when we returned, I would help him refinance his home one last time if he would agree to use the monthly savings to pay down other bills and eventually climb out of debt. He observed that it would take three years to become debt-free and from then on he would be able to begin saving and investing his money.

The ink was barely dry on his new loan documents when he received a letter from a bank offering him a brand new credit card. He went right out and bought a $200 fly rod on the grounds that his old rod was too short. I don't know why he thought that; he constantly caught more fish than any of us. Then he bought a big screen TV because he "wouldn't have to go to sports bars anymore." All of a sudden he owed more than before the refinancing and could still only make minimum payments. In an odd twist, Ed died a few months later from cancer and never did have to pay the money back. The TV was returned and the bank holding his credit card got a small percentage of its money back.

All of his other creditors were left high and dry because Ed had no other valuable assets.

I guess somebody could say that Ed's self-indulgent practices worked out because he beat the system, but if that is what it takes for creature comforts to make sense, I say, no thanks.

Phone frills are another area where you can waste a lot of money. When you make a phone call and the line is busy you sometimes get a very friendly voice saying, "For only ninety-five cents, we will keep trying that number and let you know when the line is clear." In this day of redial, I cannot imagine very many situations that would justify *flushing* a dollar that way. If you can't remember to try again later, the call was probably not that important in the first place.

What is it with our obsession with phone calls? We pay for caller ID, call waiting and recording devices all for our landline phone at home. Then we buy cell phones so we won't miss calls between home and the office. I can understand this attitude if you use the phone to make a living. After all, a customer might just call a competitor if they cannot reach you quickly. But the rest of the time the phone should be the slave to us, not the other way around. If you usually have a cell phone with you, I suggest you consider disconnecting the hard-line phone and function exclusively off of the cell phone.

Clothes

One day I performed a simple survey of my Facebook friends wherein I asked what they wasted their money on. I was surprised how many people (all women) said they waste a lot of money on clothes and especially shoes. Michelle said, "Shoes, my weakness has always been shoes. However, I am much better now and am recovering nicely. The black boots I purchased on Friday were a necessity, I swear it!" Nicky said, "Books, clothing sales and travel. Those have always been my three vices."

Another woman I know had more than 50 pairs of shoes

that she never wore. They were stuffed under her bed and in her closets when she died. This was not a "high-society" lady. In fact, the price tags were still on most of the shoes and she rarely paid more than $10 a pair of them. She just could not pass up a good shoe deal when she found one. Clothes are one of three necessities (food, clothing, shelter) but it is easy to get carried away. If you are one of the lunatics who have to have a drawer full of jewelry, or 10 different pairs of tennis shoes, you may have a self-esteem problem. Going broke buying clothes you do not need is not going to solve it.

Health Clubs

Many of us tend to wrestle with our weight. We end up with two or more wardrobes: the fat one and the skinny one. We buy all sorts of things to get rid of pounds. One lady I know actually bought "exercise" pills. I guess she thought they would go jogging for her. There are plenty of other ways to lose weight instantly. You can see all sorts of examples in magazine articles at the grocery store checkout lines . . . right next to the magazines about cooking fantastic pastries. I do not know what your ideal weight is, but trying to buy a thin figure seems a bit misguided to me. Just consume fewer calories and get out one of those extra pairs of tennis shoes we were just talking about and then go for a walk.

Brain Candy

Books

Most of us buy books that we never get around to reading. There are many millions of them sitting on dusty shelves. I just took a look at my own bookcase and I have several of them waiting for me to follow through on a previous impulse when I bought them. That is obviously a waste of money. Over the last seven years or so, I have purchased most of my books from eBay. The majority of those were used. My wife has recently been employing a more novel concept: going to the library.

Technology

Do you have to get the newest cell phone or laptop or iPad? There are new techno toys on TV every week. If you have to get them all, you are like a dog chasing its own tail only the dog isn't going to go broke in the process. Besides, the brand-new lap top, or any other computer-related toy is obsolete before you buy it. Get something that works and stick with it for a few years. So what if somebody else can watch more movies in more creative ways than you can. Let them *flush* their money, while you use yours in more productive ways.

Music and Movies

I am amazed that people pay for upgraded cable TV packages with all sorts of movie channels and they also buy DVDs and slip in a pay-per-view movie from time to time. I have nothing against watching movies but if you can't find an acceptable movie on cable TV, you are too picky . . . and paying handsomely for your problem. I suggest you find some other way to fill your time.

Payday Loans/Pawnshops

I have never used the services of the industries noted, but I know people who have. I suppose I can make sense of it in certain situations. For example it is important to keep a credit report fairly clean, so it would probably be better to borrow money from these sources and pay your loans on time than to bounce checks or pay late fees and damage a good credit rating. However, I would suggest if these outlets see you more than a couple of times in your entire lifetime, you are probably living on the financial edge and ought to look at other areas of your life for ways to cut back on the distractions that go along with these transactions.

One of my friends had an alcohol problem and pawned off a lot of fine music equipment to subsidize his problem. Regular high-interest payments were required to retain ownership of his property. The store contained a wall full of such equipment from other customers who never did get back in time to pay their ounce of flesh for their former equipment. Eventually, my buddy's stuff was on the wall right along with the other merchandise. The pawnshop preys on people like that.

It is not uncommon to pay $50 in fees and interest for a 30-day payday loan. Since that is roughly comparable to a bounced check fee or a late fee on a loan, I guess it is manageable, but this amount, expressed as an annual interest rate, comes in at just under 300 percent. Paying interest rates like that is among the worst things on which we spend our money.

SECTION ONE CONCLUSION

When discussing the worst things on which we waste our money, it is common to see two or more of the previous items together. For instance, drinking and gambling losses frequently go together. Bad habits with credit cards lead to lower credit scores and higher interest rates on all our loans. When we obtain extended warranties, we are probably buying a wide-screen TV or something else we don't really need.

A well-known offender is the leased automobile. The consumer who leases a car loses in four ways: depreciation, interest that cannot be shifted to somebody else, new taxes and higher insurance rates. If we find ourselves trapped with clustered losses like these, we will usually enjoy a compound benefit by fixing just one of the problems.

I encourage you to write down any other items on which you think you waste your money. Explain to yourself why those purchases are important to you and how to improve your decisions when faced with those choices again. Add that information to what we have discussed so far and make a list of the things you wish to improve on. Then choose that one item that would offer you the greatest benefit if you were to fix it. Put that item at the top of your list and vow to work on it immediately. Once you have completed all you can do on that item go to the next most beneficial choice and do the same with it, and so on. You will be surprised how quickly some of these situations can be repaired.

Once you gain a little momentum, you will want to do more.

Review the list regularly until better choices become second nature to you. Before long your list of the worst things on which you waste your money will become a very short one and your life will become accordingly enriched.

A good way to summarize this section is to share with you a lesson that my father taught me. It goes something like this: We all make mistakes, but it is how we deal with those mistakes that determines how successful we will become. Naturally, he was correct. When it comes to wasting money, we have all fallen victim to the wasteful ways mentioned earlier—and many others. But some of us learn from our mistakes and take action to cut our losses.

One of the keys to financial security or wealth is understanding and redirecting where your money goes. The bottom line is, for every $120 you can find in ongoing monthly savings (or new ongoing income) you can accumulate $465,000 in buying power, over time. That ought to be worth your time and energy.

As the book progresses I will show you ways to round up some precious resources, but a good first step is to stop wasting money wherever possible. In many cases, this one simple adjustment can make a huge difference in how you spend your golden years.

Now that we have successfully examined the mistakes of the past, we can learn about the things you should implement right away. Just turn the page.

SECTION TWO

TAKING ACTION
IN THE PRESENT

THE MULLIGAN

When an amateur golfer wants to ignore a bad shot, he can resort to a common tactic called "taking a Mulligan." In essence, he gets to try it over again. He gets a second chance. That is what we are going to do. We are going to take our financial "Mulligan," and start over.

Simple But Not Easy

In my previous book, I promoted a constant theme: The real estate business is very simple, but not particularly easy. The objective of real estate agents is to find people to work with, but the Realtor who expects people to miraculously walk in the door by themselves is doomed. It took more than 200 pages to explain how to successfully find clients.

In our financial lives, the guiding principle is the same: simple but not easy. In this case, we want to have enough money to acquire all of the things we need (food, clothing and shelter) and a few creature comforts along the way, and we would like to have all of that without a bunch of stress. That is very simple, but the people who have achieved that objective on their own would tell you it was not particularly easy.

For starters, they had to gain specific information. Sometimes they had a mentor, such as a wise family member, to guide them. Others sought formal education. Still others figured it out the hard way, via trial and error. Once they learned what it takes, they had to develop new habits and employ them over a long period of time. That is the hard part because most people want instant gratification.

Clean Up and Avoid Repeating Past Mistakes

If you are going to take your financial Mulligan, you need to quickly fix any of the problems identified in the first section of this book (The Worst Things on Which We Waste Our Money). Among those is to eliminate bad habits, including instant gratification. For example, stop shopping at convenience stores. You may still have a latte from time to time if it is part of your budget, but you won't be indulging wild impulses that lead to bulging credit card balances, painful debt, burdensome interest charges, and worst of all, crippling payments.

I am not going to ask you to stop living and begin worshiping money. Money is not the objective; a stress-free lifestyle is. Therefore, all we need to do is attract enough money, and use it wisely, so that it will fulfill our needs.

The Financial Puzzle

If your financial life is all jumbled up you might just think of it as a child's puzzle. There are all sorts of pieces randomly living together in a box, but it needs structure to fulfill its potential. That is what you are going to do: put together a financial puzzle. That will become a nice long-term plan. Once that is done, you will make your day-to-day decisions according to how they fit within your puzzle/plan.

We are going to discuss how you can achieve financial freedom and reward yourself. You will establish objectives. You are going to learn enough about financial planning, credit scores, credit reports, budgeting, debt, saving, investing, frugality and risky relationships to make wise and deliberate choices from here on out.

I promise you that none of this is very complicated. Nearly anybody can understand it. The biggest obstacle is breaking old habits and we will deal with that, too: simple, but not easy.

Clean Up Your Desk

In order to make any sense out of a puzzle, a person would find a clean place to work and begin putting the pieces together, one at a time. The same is true with your finances. You need a clean work area and some blank file folders and an in-basket. You must schedule time to regularly attend your responsibilities in a smart and timely way. I suggest you pay your bills and attend to monetary matters on the 14th and the 28th of every month. That way your payments arrive at your creditors' desks right on time or a little early. Take this step seriously and you will be off to a great start.

Assembling the Pieces

Once you have your work area under control and a basic schedule, it is time to bring structure to your finances rather than just living with a box of jumbled pieces. Just like when you attack a new puzzle, the first thing to do is locate the corner pieces. Then make up the borders. Then fill in with interior sections. Near the end there are just a few odds and ends left over and it is not too difficult to figure out where they go. Every piece fits in somewhere.

That is what this next section is all about: putting pieces of your finances together, one-by-one, in a nice orderly way that will make a clear picture. Once that is done, you will always know what you are trying to do and why and how. So let's get going. Let's just start over.

This is your second chance. It is your "Mulligan."

THE FOUR CORNERS OF STABILITY

We just discussed that setting up a successful financial plan is a lot like putting a puzzle together. Everybody knows that the best way to assemble a puzzle is to begin with the corners, so that is what we are going to do. The four corners to your monetary puzzle include: 1) self-honesty; 2) establish realistic goals; 3) get organized; and 4) take action.

Self-Honesty

The first corner is like a surveyor's stake. It is not especially complicated, but it is very important because it is the starting point for any construction that follows. That all-important first corner is self-honesty.

If you have ever read or seen the play *Hamlet*, you are probably familiar with the well-known line of Polonius, "To thine own self be true." It seems odd that we would have to encourage ourselves to be honest with the person in the mirror but sometimes that is the easiest person for us to fool.

Many fine people go broke because they cannot face the reality that their debts exceed their income. Whenever their homes go up in value they refinance them to get additional cash to pay off excessive bills and to buy more new stuff. They do whatever they can to maintain their image. One asset after the other is consumed trying to keep up with the bills that their instant gratification demands. They tap their savings accounts and their retirement plans. They sell their stocks and anything else of value to avoid cutting back their spending. Their entire lives would run much smoother if they would only be realistic with themselves in the first place, and live within their means.

To avoid such a plight, you must be informed and realistic in all of your assessments. If you are acting on good information you will make good choices, but if you mislead yourself, you are just setting yourself up for more disappointments. So, self-honesty was a good idea when Polonius advised it, and it is a good idea now.

Establish Realistic Goals

Successful people, like athletes or CEOs of major companies, share the common practice of establishing goals. They usually have their objectives written down and refer to them regularly. If you do that, remember to keep them realistic. If you make them too demanding, you may not be able to attain them and that may give you a sense of failure. It is like going to a buffet and putting too much food on your plate. It does not take long to realize your expectations were unrealistic.

Perhaps you are like me. I have found that formal goal setting leads to frustration. If I do not reach my objectives I get disappointed, even if I did fairly well. On the other extreme, if I attain my goal, I have a tendency to be complacent, in which case I have to wonder if the goal was too low and I could have accomplished even more without it. So, I do better without rigid structure.

However, most of the people who know me well would say that I have accomplished quite a bit. I think that is because I usually instinctively know what I am trying to do. In financial matters I have always understood that my future depends on present-day decisions. I realized as a young man that time was going to pass by whether I did anything about it or not, but I could make it work for me if I made smart long-term investments. That is why I was drawn to a career in real estate.

I also learned the consequences of wasting money that I could otherwise invest. I found out the importance of maintaining good credit and paying my bills on time. All of these things have served me well, without writing them down. In spite of the above, I still make lists for daily matters because I have found that simple things are easy to forget. I prioritize them and I work on them because I understand that procrastination is the enemy of success.

If you are a detail person, you will probably do best if you write down your objectives and refer to them regularly. Some people call that "planning your work and working your plan." If you are more like me, you may do better with some solid objectives but a less rigid format. Either way is fine, provided you have a good idea what you are trying to do and you actually follow through.

Regardless of whether you work best with rigid structure or simple lists, you need to consider what you wish to accomplish or change about your financial life, and why. Pay special attention to the big-ticket items like your job, your housing, your transportation and health care. There are complete chapters on each of those topics later in this book, but for now here is a basic overview of what to consider.

First, review your employment situation. Are you satisfied or is a change in order? If you do not like things as they are, can you force your employer to accommodate you (for example, my sister's employer allowed her to work from home three days per week) or are you the one who needs to make an adjustment? Is change realistic? If this is something you think you ought to correct, write it down and identify why you think it is important. If you are satisfied with your job, move on to the next category.

Housing is the next thing to consider. If buying a home is in your near future (less than one year out) then do not take on car payments or other debt. Could you benefit from downsizing your housing expenses? What, if anything, do you want to do about your housing arrangements? When? Why?

Do not go buy a brand-new car. They are accompanied with high payments, high sales taxes, expensive licensing fees, lots of depreciation, loan costs, interest and high insurance rates. Instead buy something used. It is better to pay cash if you can swing it; then save up some money for an upgrade.

Shop for the best health care prices. If you have to pay for health care out of your own pocket, be sure to shop around so that you are getting excellent value. Do not renew policies without verifying that you still have a very good deal.

After you consider the big-ticket items, identify any other areas that are ripe for improvement. For example, you may wish to be debt-free in five years or you might want to sell a boat or reduce clutter in your life. You may want to control impulse purchases or begin a college fund for your children or get a part-time job. Include long-term and short-term goals.

After you have examined all of these items, place them in priority order based on urgency or ease of accomplishment. Once you do that, you have a reasonable long-term financial plan. Make all of your day-to-day financial decisions based on how they help you achieve your long-term goals. If you need a new refrigerator, you are not going to jump in your car and go get a new one on store credit. You are going to ask yourself what makes the most sense based on your goals. Review your plan regularly to keep it current. Now, you will always know what your priorities are and what to do next.

Get Organized

The disorganized people whom I have known are interesting characters indeed. Perhaps you are a lot like them. These people have fertile minds and a broad range of interests. They see all sorts of books they want to read. They own broken things that they intend to fix. They have many unfinished projects.

They are usually late because they are so busy. They put off preparing their income taxes until the very last moment. Their cars are messy, and so are their purses, closets, garages, basements, desks and counter tops. They have stacks of paperwork and old mail piled up, usually in plain sight. Their trash cans and their minds are full to capacity. These complicated people fail to fulfill their potential because they lack focus. They cannot distinguish between what to do first, what to do later, and what to avoid altogether.

Disorganization is a curse to those people and it can be just as disruptive to you and your monetary matters. One of the easiest ways for you to get your finances organized is to purge any clutter around the house that represents previous unwise financial choices. Get rid of the items that are symbols of your attraction to things you don't need or don't even want. For example, if you have a stack of books you have purchased but have not read, return them to the bookstore or sell most of them on eBay or at a secondhand book store. Vow not to get any new books until you read the ones you already have; then get your new books from libraries or online so that you do not accumulate clutter.

If you have purchased items that you do not use such as a boat, snow skis, a time-share, lawn furniture, jet skis, a motor home, etc., sell them, donate them or give them away. If you have too many fishing rods, or houseplants, or anything else then simplify your life so that you feel like it is under control.

The point of this exercise is to dispose of things that consume your resources and bog you down mentally and physically. Do not lend artificial importance to material goods. Money and time that you spend on these things can be redirected into more productive endeavors. Reduce the clutter in your mind and your life.

What about those other financial matters? Do you have several checkbooks, too many credit cards, multiple car loans, unpaid bills, late notices, bounced check fees, overdraft notices, and mounds of incomplete paperwork?

Organizing finances requires some effort. Take emotion out of it and do this logically. Set up an office, get a file cabinet and gather all of your bills and credit card statements, as well as the last four years of your tax returns. File them away so you can get to them when you need them. Consolidate and simplify. Designate a specific time for bill paying and financial planning. And remember that it is easier to do a little bit consistently than it is to do it all at once. Eat your elephant one bite at a time.

Take Action

All of the great thoughts and planning in the world are wasted without action. There is a big difference between reading a book about gardening and actually growing your own vegetables. You can imagine what it would be like to be in love, but nothing will teach you the pain and joy of romance like a real loving relationship. You can watch TV programs about training a dog, but your dog is not going to learn how to properly walk on a leash until you take the time to train her. In all of these examples, action is required.

One of the primary differences between the people who have accidental financial problems and those who enjoy deliberate economic rewards comes down to taking action. The procrastinators may know the "theories" of success, but the doers know the "reality" of accomplishment because of their experiences, borne of effort. You can get inspiration, wisdom, ideas and assistance from all sorts of sources, but the momentum needs to come from your effort.

The First Step

The affable Homer Simpson of television fame once said, "Trying is the first step on the road to failure." Technically, Homer is correct; most failure is indeed the result of trying something. But the antithesis is also true; that is, trying is also the first step on the road to success. However, most worthwhile undertakings require more than that single first step.

You cannot do everything first, and major undertakings can

appear so overwhelming as to discourage action in the first place, so start off with something basic. Do something simple, like empty the trashcan in your office. Just getting one little thing out of the way will enable you to turn a symbolic page. Then you can do another small thing, like replace that burned-out light bulb.

Speaking for myself, whenever I take on a new project, such as writing a book like this, I begin by doing something simple. I might just write down the basic idea, or why I think there is a need for the information. Or I might call a friend to find out what he or she thinks of my idea.

From there, it takes time. I usually just work on it for an hour or so per day. I develop the work over 6-10 months and refine it constantly. Eventually, I have a completed project. The same thing holds true for your new financial objectives. At first, it may seem like the task is impossible, but all you need to do is follow Homer's advice and take that important first step.

Momentum

Once the first step is taken, each one thereafter becomes easier, and before long momentum will seem to be an invisible force that propels you all by itself. Momentum plays a key role in many phases of our lives. Sometimes it is negative and sometimes it is positive. For example, if you have ever gained an extra ten pounds, you probably did not try to do that. It just happened. Once it got going, it just kept on going until you intervened and changed the momentum.

Momentum also works for positive experiences. In fact, psychologists tell us that once we do something for 21 days, that activity becomes a habit and is easier to continue after that. Once you get a few steps into your new financial plan, you will gain momentum and once that happens, you will benefit from an all-new set of good habits.

Choose the Best Time

I tend to be most productive during the first couple of hours in the morning. It is quiet and my mind is clear. I also concentrate on financial matters twice each month: once in the middle and once at the end. I know of other people who find energy late at night. They like to tidy up loose ends just before they go to bed. They put the kids to bed, clean up the kitchen, do some exercises, take a shower and pay their bills. Then they hit the rack.

You should find a time that works for you. You might like to take a few hours on Saturday mornings, or use some of your lunchhour. Find a time that you can concentrate for a while, schedule the time and take action as your own internal clock requires.

Perhaps you want to become a millionaire or your goals might be more modest, but either way the path is the same. You must get a reliable financial plan and stick to it. To get it all started, find the corners: be honest with yourself, establish realistic goals, get organized and take action. Then you will be ready to put the edges of your puzzle together and that will form a complete framework for your future financial decisions.

THE FRAMEWORK OF SUCCESS

There is a natural progression to assembling a puzzle. After the corners are in place, the edges need to be established. They lend structure to the project. People with a strong sense of fiscal responsibility rely on the same practice. All of their monetary decisions are contained within four principles: 1) clean up messes, 2) make a budget, 3) employ discipline, and 4) keep score.

Clean Up Your Messes

It will be much easier to attend to the monetary items that are yet to be discussed if you clean up the messes that are already holding you back. Therefore, it is time to review and "fix" the issues we discussed in the first section of this book. Many of those topics have full chapters and more information a little later on, but at this point we are focused on what changes you can make RIGHT NOW, so let's see what we can do to repair any damage caused by poor choices in the past.

Conveniences

In this category, the only action needed from you is "inaction." That's right, stop buying these things, or at least cut way back. Convenience spending is lazy spending. Possibilities include goods from vending machine, packaged foods, microwaveable items like popcorn, disposable items such as diapers, car washes, anything in convenience stores, fast food, home delivered dinners like pizza and, especially, dining out. Instead, budget for two nights out per month and then you really will deserve and enjoy them.

Adult Indulgences

Once again, this is a category that can reward you handsomely just for exercising a little restraint. Practically everybody I meet can find an extra $100 per month by eliminating or cutting back on this group of money-eaters: smoking, drinking, illicit drugs, lottery tickets, perpetual shopping, season-tickets to nearly anything, travel, top-of-the-line cable TV packages, pay per view programs, fancy coffee, nice cars, extravagant vacations, travel, too many pets, etc. I am not talking about eliminating all of these things all of the time. I am more concerned about breaking costly habits.

Legal Matters

If you provide the people who are employed in the criminal justice system with a reason to hassle you, they are prepared to do so. Why give them opportunities? They may not win, but you will definitely lose. So obey all laws and stay out of court. It is as simple as that!

Depreciating Assets

Eliminate or reduce your exposure to any depreciating assets like cars, boats, motor homes, motorcycles and recreational toys like jet skis that you rarely use, especially if you have monthly payments on them. The sooner you sell these items, the better because they generally keep dropping in value and you have much better ways to use that money.

Renting and Leasing

The best way to get out of a costly housing lease is to buy your own property. If you have a car lease, I suggest you get out of it immediately, even if you have to take a modest loss. Cut the snake's head off. Then buy a modest used car and start saving the money you will need for your next upgrade.

Energy

You cannot really recapture money you have already lost, but you can avoid repeating your mistakes by implementing the recommendations in the third section of this book. There is a complete chapter on this topic.

Dependents

One of the best things you can do to cut the costs of raising your children is encourage them to work for the things they want. You will save money and they will build character.

If you already have several pets, perhaps you can find somebody else who would like to take one off your hands. As a minimum, you should realize you cannot afford to take in every little critter with pathetic eyes. If your heart is that big, I suggest you volunteer to help a local animal shelter. Those animals need your love too, but you won't go broke in the process.

Note: If you want to get a sneak peek at the actual cost of raising children or pets there are chapters to that effect in the third section of this book.

Banking

This is an especially important category. Take the time to know all of these items inside and out. Make changes whenever it will help you. Do not put it off, because these fees can come up again and again.

Commercial Banks - Order a copy of your bank's Fee Schedule. Read it and know what its fees are. Compare it to at least two other banks and change banks if you find a better deal for your needs. Avoid any ATM advances (especially any that carry fees) because it is too hard to keep track of where the money goes. If you are charged any surprise fees, make the bank officer explain them and ask him to waive them.

Mortgage Companies - If you have to refinance your home to pay off your debts you are living beyond your means. You have to adjust your spending habits or get a cheaper home, or both. Refinancing is so expensive it should only be done to lower payments or to get money to invest. Avoid escrow accounts if you can.

Credit Card Companies - If you can't afford to pay off your cards every month, you can't afford to charge additional items. Get a copy of the fee schedule and read it. Do not take on cards that come with annual fees unless you get other valuable benefits such as frequent flier miles. Pay your bill on time. Do not allow your account balance to exceed 35 percent of your credit limit. Do not carry balances on cards with high interest rates. Do not use checks drawn on your credit card account unless you verify there is no financial penalty for doing so. Do not use your credit card in foreign countries if there is any penalty for doing so. Avoid protection plans. Even though you should close out certain accounts, be sure to read the upcoming chapters about credit cards because closing out accounts (even bad accounts) might hurt your credit score for a few months.

Interest

Cut interest costs in every way you can. Refinance your home if you can lower the interest rate by one percent or more and recover your closing costs, through lower payments, within two years. Use a line of credit to pay off an auto loan with a higher rate. Check your credit card rate against those offered at creditcard.com. You may be able to lower your rate substantially or get zero interest for transferring your balance to a new card. If you are still carrying a balance, once every six months ask your cardholder to lower your rate. Do not take on any additional long-term debt. Do not charge items unless you can pay them off on time and in full when the first statement comes in.

Insurance

This may be the single most important category for you to understand and work on because any effort expended in this regard will pay you dividends over and over again. Even if you have made sound decisions in the past, it is prudent to review existing policies once per year to verify that your protection matches your needs. Remember that "warranty" or "protection" also means "insurance."

Get out all of your existing policies NOW. Examine your credit card statement for any words that suggest you have "payment protection." Eliminate any extended warranties on appliances, automobiles, cell phones, or electronic equipment that you can (unless you have some compelling reason to think you are more likely than a normal person to need these services).

Now go to the chapter about insurance in the final section of this book. Read any category that applies to policies you already have. Cancel any insurance you do not need. Downsize or modify policies where appropriate. Get refunds wherever possible.

Taxes

Call a tax expert to discuss your options. Consider claiming more dependents and using the extra take-home pay for any debt that carries interest charges. Buy your own home as soon as it makes sense because the tax savings are substantial.

Look into opening your own business or writing a book. A lot of the money you are spending now might become deductible and save you tax dollars. Consider buying rental property. The tax breaks are incredible. Finally, reduce or eliminate estate taxes. This is especially important with larger estates (more than five million dollars) or when there are extended families with step-children or half-brothers and half-sisters.

Over-Improving Homes

Once again, it is difficult to recoup money from past exuberance, so your focus should be on restraining any additional impulses. It is okay to paint and maintain your property as needed, but do not take on expensive upgrades unless you plan on using the items for at least ten years or you can verify that you will enjoy at least a dollar in increased value for every dollar you spend.

Make a Budget

The next important step to assembling the framework of a financial puzzle is to make a budget. Being financially responsible is not some whimsical idea that is practiced on an "as needed" basis. It is a lifestyle that requires some sort of perpetual budget.

Things may look bleak the first time you do this, but do not get discouraged. You are doing exactly what you need to do. It will be a lot easier to regain control if you really understand precisely what problems you are trying to solve.

A good first step is to visit the Internet and download one of many good budgeting spreadsheets. Excel has a good one that is free.

Review your checkbook and credit card statements for the previous year to find out what your expenses are. If you have a tendency to drop by the ATM or to cash your checks, then you need to start keeping track of where your cash goes. Better yet, make your purchases with checks or credit cards, so you can monitor your behavior.

Mvelopes Personal System

Long before accounting software, there was the old-school Envelope System, which operated as follows: You set up marked envelopes for all bills, savings and investments, and miscellaneous expenses, each marked with the amount of money that needed to be budgeted for that expense, and the date it was due. Then when you got paid, you cashed your paycheck, and divvied up the necessary cash among the marked envelopes. That way, when the expenses came due, the money was already there. And, if there was no money left over, you were simply kept from making any extra purchases until the next pay period, thereby avoiding going into debt.

The Mvelopes Personal System is an excellent online spending management program that is designed to imitate the Envelope System. It ties into any online accounts and banks that the customer has and wishes to include. The customer sets up virtual envelopes. When a deposit is made, the program places the appropriate amount of money into each envelope. When a bill is due, it can either pay the bill from the designated envelope or notify the customer via email.

Anytime the customer makes a credit card purchase, the program will transfer the amount from the appropriate envelope to one designated to pay the credit card, then the card will be paid in full every month because the money is already set aside. If you have an Mvelope account, you always have a great overview of how much is in any particular envelope and you can even transfer money from one envelope to the other if you deem it appropriate.

You will be able to track all of your loans, as well as any stocks, IRAs or investment accounts you may have. You will always know your net worth. They have perpetual online support. You can use your cell phone for mobile access to your account so that you can review the contents of an "envelope" whenever you are considering a purchase.

You no longer have to keep multiple checkbooks. You save postage and brain damage because so much of it is automatic. Say goodbye to late fees and reclaim your time. You can even try it out for free at www.mvelopes.com. If you decide you like the program, there is a fee of about $6 per month. The postage savings alone will frequently cover that. There are other cheaper envelope programs such as www.NeoBudget.com, which is about half as much. Whichever program you choose will almost certainly pay for itself if you use it as intended.

YNAB

"You Need A Budget" is another money management program that works off of the envelope concept. What makes it different is you buy the software (about $50) and download it. If you are apprehensive about handling financial matters online, you might like this better. The one-time cost of the software might be cheaper in the long run than a monthly fee, but eventually your software will become outdated. They offer some online classes and you can find them at www. YouNeedABudget.com.

Quicken

At the present moment it appears that Quicken is attempting to corner the money management market. They have recently converted to a FREE system. Since they have been a leader in this industry for a long time, their work is always among the best. If you want a good system and don't want to have new monthly overhead (a good idea) this may be the best choice for you.

Also Ran

I advise you to search the net for "budgeting programs" that offer the depth or simplicity that fits your situation. In the end the specific program you choose is less important than the underlying objective: Make a sound budget and stick to it.

The bottom line is you need to know exactly what your financial situation is and what you are trying to do. You will be surprised by how quickly your net worth will grow by making your savings account your highest priority.

Discipline

The best budget plan in the world won't overcome the person with poor discipline, but the most disciplined person can overcome almost anything. Discipline trumps intelligence, knowledge, good fortune, high earning power and practically everything else. It is a powerful force that has enabled ordinary people to accomplish extraordinary goals. There are two critical elements to discipline: getting started and perseverance.

Getting Started

Procrastination is the enemy of success, but sometimes people put things off because they really don't know what to do. In your case, your own experiences and frustrations have driven you to this book, so you are already in the process of gathering the knowledge you need and implementing it. By the time you turn the final page you should have more information about personal finances than nearly everybody you meet.

Perseverance

If you are like me, sometimes you get bogged down. I have found a good technique to deal with that. Imagine you are going on a cross-county drive, from New York to San Diego. You cannot drive all that way in one continuous effort. But you can break the trip into manageable pieces.

The same situation is in play when it comes to acting on other major projects, such as your financial situation. You cannot solve everything at once, so break your project down into manageable pieces. Whenever I take on new projects, I like to strive to get halfway. Then, I try to bite off half of what is left, and then, half of that. Before long the ending is in sight and nothing can stop me.

Interestingly, I am near the halfway point of this book. I am getting a little excited because now I know I will finish it. My enthusiasm is high and I get up each morning and look forward to working on some part of it. Perseverance has gotten me this far and I know it is just a matter of time until I have a finished product. I already know what my next project will be. The halfway point is a powerful milestone.

Fixing your financial situation and building a dynamic future is a marathon, not a sprint. So, use any little tricks that you can, like perseverance and halfway points, to help you stick with your objective.

Keep Score

A few years ago, when Microsoft was growing so quickly, somebody said if Bill Gates dropped a five hundred dollar bill, he could not afford to stop and pick it up because his business was making him even more than that. Whoever discovered that little fact was "keeping score."

Every worthwhile business and sophisticated financial institution keeps score. I suppose they could just make deposits and write checks then wait to see if they run out of money, but that would be foolhardy. By constantly keeping track of where they stand they are in a position to make monetary detours before their minor obstacles grow into insurmountable roadblocks.

It is important for you to keep score for the same reasons. One of the main ways to do this is through financial statements. If you utilize one of the budgetary software programs discussed earlier, a lot of this will become automatic. If you have elected to run a budget from a less structured approach, you can obtain blank financial statement forms from your bank. I suggest you update them at least once every three months, although once per month would be even better.

Regardless of which approach you take, it is important to know where you stand at all times. Each time you see your net worth climb, you will realize that your minor sacrifices are worth it. If you should take an occasional step backwards, you will quickly know why. If it is a one-time occurrence, you will be at ease, but if you see a pattern you can correct it before it does any significant damage. By keeping score you will quickly discover that cutting your losses is just another way to increase your profits.

Neither you nor I are going to attain the incredible wealth of Mr. Gates, but we do not have to. We can accumulate all of the money we will ever need if we just keep track of what we do with the money we already receive.

Hey, what do you know! Your puzzle is really taking shape. You have tied your four corners together with four solid edges and now you have the framework for your financial success. All we have to do now is work on a few other key sections of the puzzle and then fill in with some odds and ends.

RETHINKING CREDIT

Do you have car payments or a student loan? When you use your credit cards, do you get benefits such as frequent flier miles? How often have you refinanced your home? Do you pay off your credit cards every month? These are the types of questions that make up a very significant section of your monetary puzzle: It all has to do with how you perceive and manage credit.

Naturally, most people never give much thought to credit until they are confronted with an opportunity to buy something for which they do not have the money. Credit cards for department stores, gas stations or cell phones can be the starting point. The new consumer jumps in without much guidance. The first payments are relatively small compared to the benefits. It all seems so easy and painless, and before long the little card is like a Christmas present that just keeps on giving. But, there is a flip side to that coin: Credit can be a best friend or a worst enemy.

Credit allows you to take advantage of bargains, and thereby pay less for goods and services that you already buy. But credit can also be a curse, stalking you, tempting you and stealing away your resources and your future. Credit and the thrill of spending can be an addiction, just as damning as alcohol or drugs or gambling. It is similar to a powerful saw. In the right hands it can build an empire, but when used improperly, it can cut off the hand of the operator. One thing is for sure: Credit is not "free money."

How It Ought to Be

117

Nobody ever asked me, but if I had my way, I would require that all consumers take some sort of preliminary credit-awareness course, and a test, before they are granted credit in the first place. It would be similar to the driver's license procedure. I suppose if the idea was presented to the Congress or a local governor, one might hear something like, "There is a big difference, because automobile drivers can hurt other people and their property, but credit does not pose the same risk to the public." As you would expect, I do not agree with such a statement.

When adults get into credit problems, families are destroyed. It is often stated that half of all marriages end in divorce and the number one cause is financial hardships. Inevitably, the children are forced to change schools, abandon their friends, adapt to more humble surroundings and live in unexpected single-parent situations.

All of this leads to bankruptcies and foreclosures, which in turn, mean more vacant homes. Basic economics tell us that when the supply of bank-owned houses is increased, the prices come down, and that affects everybody in the neighborhood. Foreclosures also cause lenders to charge everybody else higher interest rates and loan fees to offset their losses.

On a grander scale, the entire country was brought to its collective knees when the housing market crumbled recently. Nearly every one of us suffered as housing prices dropped. Trillions of dollars were lost. Some banks closed and countless Americans saw their stock portfolios wither away. The federal government took on record levels of debt as additional trillions of dollars were created out of thin air for bailouts. All of the new national debt will be thrust upon future citizens who are not even born yet. Higher interest rates and hyper-inflation threaten us. We have had a very severe recession. To add more fuel to the already raging fire, many other nations are worried about the financial strength of once-strong America, and there is even talk of a worldwide depression.

All of that was because government officials and consumers themselves did not understand how easy it is to abuse credit. So I say it again, "If we require a test and a license for drivers because they might hurt somebody else, we should also require consumers to have some basic understanding of credit for the same reasons." The first class should be reserved for members of Congress and other government officials.

History

Credit, in one form or another, has been around for many centuries. It has always been in the US. We even had a debtors' prison up until 1800. The first indications of credit as we evaluate it today appeared in 1958 when Bill Fair and Earl Isaac started working on credit models. Then in the early nineties, a version of their idea was implemented in what we now know as the Fair Isaac Corporation (FICO). Today, our entire society uses FICO scores, ranging from 300-850, to evaluate a consumer's credit worthiness.

The entire credit reporting system, and the information on the credit reports, was a big mystery until 2003. But new laws granted consumers access to their credit scores and some of the information that goes into them. Now that we know more about the entire reporting process, we can take action to improve our credit scores.

The New Paradigm

Consumers and their creditors are no longer the only ones who are using our credit reports. Employers frequently check credit scores to decide if they want to hire us or offer us promotions. Our own Air Force and Coast Guard use credit scores as a means to evaluate the level of responsibility of potential recruits. Utility companies examine our reports to decide what deposit, if any, we must pay. Cell phone providers can deny services if they don't like our credit habits.

Insurance companies use the scores to determine a customer's sense of responsibility. Armed with that information they decide if they want to insure the customer at all, and if so, what the rates ought to be. In extreme cases, people who have great driving records might see their auto insurance premiums triple just because they had a bankruptcy or foreclosure.

As we have seen, credit has a rippling effect throughout our lives whether we pay any attention to it or not. It just makes sense to do what we can to improve it and avoid the activities that diminish it. That leads us to the next chapter, which is about obtaining a copy of your credit reports(s).

YOUR CREDIT REPORTS

It is time to make a transition from the "philosophy" of credit to the "mechanics" of it. In a previous chapter, we observed the importance of keeping score, and credit reports are a good place to do so. Fortunately, somebody else will assemble all of the information for you, but it is still up to you to constantly review those reports and make effective changes as needed.

The next few chapters have the potential to change your financial life. This information is vital to your monetary success. It is simple but not easy. It takes knowledge and effort. Please believe me when I tell you that the people who employ these lessons enjoy very productive and satisfying economic lives.

The Guts

By understanding some of the specifics that lead to our credit score, we can make this dynamic tool serve us for all the rest of our lives, rather than the other way around. To begin with, let's observe how much emphasis is lent to the various aspects of the reports themselves.

Recent Payment History - 35 Percent

The single most important factor in determining your score is Recent Payment History. Any recent late payments or on-time payments are weighted more heavily than those of years gone by.

One fellow I know recently missed a payment on a credit card. It was a complete accident, but his score dropped nearly 100 points overnight. He has so much other good credit he will recover fairly well within a few months, but his situation reveals just how important recent activity is.

Length of History - 15 Percent

This category is concerned with how long this person has been managing his/her credit. Obviously longer is better. When combined with the previous category, we can see that fully one-half of our reports are based on our history, in one way or another.

Amount of Actual Debt - 30 Percent

Oddly, a lack of debt can actually lower a person's credit score. That is because it is difficult to determine if this person actually knows how to handle credit at all. On the other hand, the person who rings up a bunch of new debt also appears risky. The trick is to accumulate available credit slowly and consistently without ever owing more than 30 percent of the available amount.

New Credit - 10 Percent

It is an ironic fact that new credit helps your score and hurts it at the same time. When you take on new credit you might run out and buy a whole bunch of new things, so you pose more risk to creditors. Therefore, that diminishes your credit score. At the same time, when you have more credit, your ratio of debt compared to your available credit decreases. If you do not take on a lot of additional debt, you have more financial breathing room, so you become a better credit risk than you were before. Consequently, new credit will hurt your score slightly for six months or so, but if you do not take on a lot of new debt your score should return to, and surpass, its previous level.

Type of Credit - 10 Percent

This part of the score is based on types of credit in use (retail, finance company, mortgage, and auto). Short-term, unsecured debt generally carries more risk than secured loans like real estate mortgages.

Who Are Those Guys?

One of the all-time classic movies is "Butch Cassidy and the Sundance Kid." In it, Paul Newman and Robert Redford play a couple of lovable bad guys who just can't get away from the grasp of the relentless authorities. After all sorts of running and frustrations, an exasperated Butch (Newman) turns to Sundance (Redford) and gasps, "Who are those guys?"

In a similar way, you and I are to be forever pursued by a gang of determined credit reporting agencies. The primary gang members are Equifax, TransUnion and Experian. They aren't affiliated with the government and they operate to make a profit by selling their products and services. There are many other members in the gang who also gather and sell information on credit matters. There is even a company called Payment Reporting Builds Credit, Inc., which allows the public to report their own payments for items that are not customarily included on the reports of the better-known credit bureaus (phone, cable, rent).

All three major bureaus provide a credit report and TransUnion provides two different types. No two reports are identical. Equifax and TransUnion offer FICO scores, which are used in more than 75 percent of all loans. Mortgage companies review both FICO reports in their lending decisions, but other creditors (credit card, auto loans, retailers etc.) usually prefer one or the other and tend to rely almost exclusively on that particular one.

Experian and TransUnion each have a separate internal report and score. They aggressively try to market their own internal products, presumably because there is more profit in it. Equifax has no such alternative report.

Auto dealers have their own secret scoring system. They use a FICO Auto Industry Option Score. Once again, the scoring is similar to that of the standard FICO score, but the system looks more closely at how you handled previous auto loans. If you have had other financial problems, but always handled your debts regarding your auto loans properly, you might actually get a lower rate on an auto loan than you would have expected. On the other hand, there is nothing stopping a dealer from reviewing one of your other reports and then using other bad credit against you anyway.

Certain other industries have their own alternatives to the FICO system for their types of loans. They are called Non-auto Installment Industry Options. They include bank cards and installment loans (furniture, electronics, etc.). These lenders' scoring systems operate similarly to those of the auto dealers, with extra weight given to the items on your report that relate to their particular products.

Call to Action

You are entitled to one free consumer report from each of the major bureau every 12 months. You can get them at www.AnnualCreditReport.com. However, those reports do not provide the FICO score, which is what you really want because so many creditors use those particular scores.

You can also purchase three-in-one or "merged" reports, but I don't recommend them either for several reasons: Too few creditors use them; they are expensive; and they are more difficult to read.

That brings us back to the FICO reports. The only way to obtain your FICO reports is to purchase them, so I strongly recommend that you purchase copies of your TransUnion and

Equifax FICO scores. They cost less than $20 each. You can get them at www.MyFICO.com/12.

As stated earlier, Experian no longer offers FICO scores so they only have a non-FICO report. However, you might want to get their free report anyway, just to be certain it does not have any damaging information that you should know about.

Important: Regardless of your financial condition, I suggest you stop everything else and go order your exact FICO scores RIGHT NOW! You will have them online within minutes and you can print them out if you wish. Then you will be able to begin improving your credit score by implementing the recommendations in the next chapters. But do not put it off. There is no benefit in waiting. Go ahead, I promise to wait for you.

Remember, you want the FICO scores from TransUnion and Equifax (here is the Web site again (www.MyFICO.com/12). As stated, once per year you can get the non-FICO score from Experian for free so you might as well get it too: www.freecreditreport.com.

Once you obtain your FICO reports, you can determine who has been checking you out. You will also look for errors you can correct and what areas need improvement. You will find out if you have been a victim of identity theft. You can verify if your lenders have been reporting your good behavior. Be sure to check all current accounts and verify accuracy. You will probably notice that the reports do not all have the same accounts listed. You will want to notify all bureaus of any good accounts you have that might be missing on their reports. On the other hand, if you have some damning information that does not show up on one of the reports, I would leave that sleeping dog alone.

The Payoff

Now that you have gotten your scores, you can look for specific areas you can improve. If you will look along the top of your reports you will observe several rows of tabs. Notice the row with tabs numbered one through nine (1-9). You should review all of these sections and pay special attention to the ones mentioned below.

Negative Reason Scores

Click the tab marked "Understanding Your Score" (Number 2). This could easily be the most critical section of your reports. You will have up to four very specific things you can work on to improve your own particular credit score. They are listed in order of how important they are to your score, and they will tell you what to do about it. Begin fixing them, in order of importance. For example, if you have too much debt for the credit you have available (too high a balance on your cards), you know to pay down your cards or increase your available credit.

Inquiries

Click the tab marked "Inquiries" (Number 6). Here you will discover who has been checking you out. If you do not recognize their names, you may need to perform a Web search. For instance, my life insurance company does their investigating under a name I did not know.

In many, but not all, cases, these inquiries can pull down your score, so keep an eye on this section. Generally, an inquiry by anybody who just wants to learn if you are responsible or not (insurance companies, employers, the military, etc.), will not hurt your score. But, when you have applied for credit or somebody is looking to extend credit to you, your score is vulnerable.

If you see inquiries in that latter group that you did not authorize, you should send each of them a letter and demand that they either prove they had a "permissible purpose" to investigate your report or remove their inquiry.

Accounts

Click tab number five (5) to see if there are any "Accounts" you can improve or upgrade. For instance, one of my credit card accounts showed my unpaid balance, but it did not show how much available credit I had, so, it appeared I was using all of my available credit, even though I was only using 5 percent of it. I sent them a letter and my score bumped up.

Verify the information for all of your accounts. If you find negatives on your report, you can dispute them for any reason. If you had an unfair bill that you refused to pay, but now it shows up as a collection account, you can write a letter to the bureau involved and dispute the charge as "not yours." They are obligated to verify with the creditor that the entry is legit. Sometimes they are unsuccessful in contacting the creditor or getting a timely response, in which case, they are required by law to remove the negative comment from your report. If the creditor reaffirms the information, the bureaus will not modify your report unless they made some error of their own. They will notify you within 30 days of their findings and make changes where appropriate.

Your next step, and best bet, is to go directly to the source of the problem. That means the lender or creditor (not a collection agency) who submitted the negative comment. Send a certified letter to whoever is authorized to review such matters. Do your homework and provide any documents that support your case. Remain civilized. Be sure to tell them exactly what you are asking for. For example, "I would like you to withdraw the account from the collection agency and correct all three credit reports."

Many lenders/creditors will grant one such correction per year as a gesture of goodwill. Sometimes they will even erase several old blemishes if you have a solid year of on-time payments. If they agree to your request, be sure to verify with all of the bureaus that they made the corrections.

"No" does not always mean no. Just because you get turned down is no reason to give up. Wait a few months and try again. There are all sorts of examples of creditors removing bad marks after repeated requests. Sometimes they find that small accounts, old accounts and the ones with similar names are just not worth fighting over. Sometimes they simply change their minds, or put a new person in charge, or just don't care enough to keep fighting. So stick with it. If you are still unsuccessful after several attempts, you can hire a credit repairing expert or an attorney to take up the battle. If you are serious about cleaning up your credit reports, this is worth the time and money.

Collections and Public Records

Collections are accounts that have been turned over to collection agencies. I suggest you discuss these accounts with the lenders themselves and not the collection agencies. If you get an inheritance or a nice raise, and if you are willing to pay a substantial portion of what you owe, they may be willing to remove the accounts from collection status. If so you should see a good improvement in your score.

Public Records indicate any relevant legal proceedings. This includes judgments, bankruptcy, foreclosures, repossessions, tax liens or garnishments. Most of them will stay on your report for 5-10 years, but a tax lien will remain as long as it is unpaid.

Other Tabs

Be sure to check out the remainder of the numbered tabs. There may be specific issues you can work on to improve your score.

Is It Worth the Battle?

When it comes to your final FICO score, some of the errors on your reports matter much more than others do. In fact, some of them don't matter at all. Generally, your time is well spent if you are disputing things like late payments, collections, credit limits that are reported as lower than they should be, charge-offs, negative accounts that are not yours, negative comments that are more than ten years old, accounts that were paid off or written off in a bankruptcy but still show up as unpaid, and accounts listed as anything other than "Current" or "Paid as agreed."

Most inquiries are relatively harmless unless there are unfamiliar creditors snooping around. If you see inquiries like that or accounts that don't make sense, you may be the victim of identity theft. In that case, notify the fraud departments of the credit bureaus and they will tell you what to do from there.

Most other mistakes such as an incorrect spelling of your middle name or the address of your employer or who closed an old account should be updated, but they don't usually play any role in your score.

Remember, your score will be constantly changing so you should regularly obtain updated copies of your TransUnion and Equifax FICO scores. If you discover more than a handful of mistakes on your initial report, you may need to get an updated report once every quarter for the first year. Once you have things cleaned up, I suggest once every six months after that. Get the free Experian score once per year.

I suggest you establish a tradition or HABIT of an annual review on your birthday or New Year's Day or tax time or some other trigger-date that will be easy for you to remember. I get my reports on January 1 and July 1.

So far, we have been discussing the typical, established credit reports, but for those of you who have more serious financial problems or very little credit, you will find the next chapter to be particularly helpful.

STARTING OUT OR STARTING OVER

Two categories of people will find this chapter to be especially useful: those who have little or no credit and, those who have rather serious credit problems. First we shall talk about repairing credit, and then we will discuss how anybody can build credit effectively.

Repairing Bad Credit

Perhaps you are struggling financially, but not as badly as a person who would file for bankruptcy. If so, here are the basic steps to clean up your credit reports.

First things first. If you have not already gotten a copy of your FICO credit reports, you should do that (www.myFICO.com/12). Examine the report in detail. Dispute anything that you think you can improve such as debts that are inaccurate or not yours. Pay special attention to the four reasons your credit is suffering. Take any immediate steps that you can to address those issues and especially whichever items are listed first in the section for that purpose. Write a quick letter to the credit bureaus to clean up any inaccurate personal information such as marital status, address, and employer.

It is better to spread your credit card debt out so that no one card is overly burdened. For example, if you have three cards, each with a thousand dollars in available credit, and one card is maxed out while the other two cards have a zero balance, it would be better to shift the debt so that each card is carrying one-third of the debt. Generally, you do not want your balance on any particular card to exceed 30 percent of the available credit. If you are still over the 30 percent balance, contact your lenders to see if they will raise your credit limit. This will usually increase your score.

If you have equity in your home or other property, consider refinancing to consolidate your debts into one larger loan. There are several benefits: You should get a lower rate; you can probably make lower payments; and the interest is probably deductible on your income taxes.

Before you employ this tactic, be forewarned. I have seen MANY people abuse the concept. The ink is barely dry on their loan documents and they go out to dinner to celebrate. When the bill comes they pull out their credit cards . . . again! Before long they have the same problem, only this time they also have a new, bigger debt on their home to go along with it. Therefore, refinancing is very dangerous if you do not modify your spending habits because sooner or later real estate values won't be able to bail you out. Then you might lose everything you own.

If you have any fees such as over-limit fees or late payment fees, call your creditors and ask them to waive the fees. If you have been a customer for several years, and you have a decent long-term record, you have a good chance of getting these fees waived.

Cash out other accounts. If you have an IRA or a stock portfolio or other path to cash, consider tapping those accounts to pay off your debts. It makes no sense to have one account paying you a small interest rate (which is taxed) while you have your own debt at an even higher rate elsewhere.

Modify your behavior. If you cannot pay your cards in full every month stop using them, and make other sacrifices. Keep modest amounts of cash on hand instead of credit cards. That way you will guard your cash carefully (Note: This technique will not do you any good if you constantly run to the ATM to make up the difference).

Depending on how serious your problem is, you may need to get rid of a car that has payments and drive a clunker with no payments. Sell any frivolities such as a boat, an unnecessary vehicle or raw land that you might have. Use the money to pay down your debts.

Lenders are eager to overcharge anybody who is willing to pay a higher interest rate than the lender is willing to accept. Be certain you are not among that group. Regularly contact your creditors and ask them to lower your interest rate. They will frequently do so right on the spot, simply because you asked. This exercise will lower your payments. Repeat this procedure every 90 days or until you are certain they will not lower your rates further.

If you fall behind on your payments you can call your creditors and ask them to restructure your debt and payments. When a customer is in that situation the lender knows the circumstances are serious. They will frequently try to work something out because it can be cheaper for them than the alternatives. In cases like this, they will likely post a derogatory comment to your credit reports indicating what happened. That negative remark will stick with you for a long time, but you can usually recover within a year or so.

Adopt a new philosophy about credit and debt. Do not use your cards to buy anything if you cannot pay off 100 percent of the purchase when you get your next statement. Never, ever carry a balance on your cards.

Monitor your accounts forever. Paying attention and keeping score will keep you from getting into this problem again. But more importantly, it will free up money you can use in much smarter ways, namely, to save consistently and invest wisely.

Bankruptcy

Nobody wants to go through this process, and it should be avoided if possible, but if you find yourself in a credit hole that you cannot realistically expect to resolve for three years or longer, it may be your best choice. The first thing to do is consult with a credit counselor or a qualified bankruptcy attorney. If you do elect to go this route, do not make things worse by beating yourself up.

It does not benefit society to punish people who have struggled financially, so laws are in place to give people a second chance at productivity. Lots of good people have had to go this route, including four past U.S. presidents and this author. But take it from somebody who's "been there, done that," it can be a priceless second chance. Had I not had that option, I might never have dug out of my hole. Since then I've employed dozens of people, subsidized countless business, donated many thousands of dollars to charities and paid enormous amounts of new taxes. None of that would have been possible without a second chance. In fact, there are all sorts of wealthy people who tried and failed, only to try again, and hit it big. So don't let a bankruptcy scar you for life. Everybody makes mistakes. Forgive yourself, find out what you did incorrectly, fix it, and start over. Chances are things will work out just fine.

Once the bankruptcy is over, it is not overly difficult to establish new credit. With prudent action, a person in this situation can usually obtain new credit to buy a home and car in one to two years. Thereafter, responsible behavior will pay dividends, just like it does for everybody else.

Oddly, it may be better to file for bankruptcy than take the slow path to recovery, as previously spelled out. Creditors sometimes consider people who have filed for bankruptcy to be less risky because the process leaves them with fewer debts, and they cannot repeat the procedure for quite a while.

If you determine that restructuring your debt or filing for bankruptcy is your best option, you need to deal with that before you do much of anything else. The sooner you get this mess behind you, the sooner you can get back on your feet. Before you know it you will have new credit cards and be able to qualify for a home loan again.

The Starting Gate

If you need to start over or if you have never had much credit, there are certain actions you can take that will make your journey more fruitful. The first thing to do is recognize that credit cards are not for incurring or accumulating debt. They are for emergencies, convenience and record keeping only. Do not charge things unless you already have the money to pay for them. Then make your payments on time and in full every month.

If you have not already done so, obtain a copy of your FICO credit reports (www.myFICO.com/12) to find out your starting point. If your score is under 600 or so, you probably need to begin by getting a gas card or retail store card.

In order to qualify, you will ordinarily need the following: 1) you must be at least 18 years old; 2) you need a telephone that is in your own name; 3) you should have a social security number; 4) you must have some sort of verifiable income; and 5) you should have some sort of checking account.

Step One

I recommend that you apply for either a gas card or a retail card, but not both. Multiple inquiries on your credit report and young accounts will temporarily bring your score down, which is counterproductive.

The easiest card to obtain is usually a gasoline card. They frequently have low limits, around $250 or so. If you have a station with which you like to trade, they should have an application onsite. Before submitting your application, be certain they will report your performance to the credit bureaus. Also, verify that there are no annual fees. Finally, discern if you are applying directly to the oil company itself or if they have retained a bank to assist them with credit matters. It is easier to get your credit directly from the oil company.

If you would prefer to obtain a card from a retail store rather than an oil company, they are almost as easy to acquire. Once again, you should verify that they report to the credit bureaus and that there are no annual fees.

Once you receive these cards, use them a little bit each month but do not run up a lot of debt. Pay the bill on time and in full every month for at least six months. Then get an updated FICO credit report to see if you are making progress. If so it is time to go to step two, getting a secured VISA or MasterCard.

Step Two

Set up a meeting with one of the officers at a local and relatively small bank (not one of the big chains). The reason for a small local bank vs. a branch of a major chain is that the people can get to know you on a personal level and they frequently have some flexibility regarding terms, which the bigger banks do not.

Take a recent copy of your FICO credit report. Explain your situation and tell them you would like to open a checking account and obtain a credit card. Show them your FICO credit reports and tell them you are being very protective of your score. Make it clear that before they obtain their own copy of your credit report, you would like them to approve your account, subject to their verification that the report you show them is accurate. By approaching it this way, you don't get an inquiry on your report unless you know you will get the account and card that you want.

They will probably want to put a hold on some of your funds to assure they get paid. That is referred to as a "secured card." It is fine for your purposes. Therefore, you may need to buy a

$1,000 CD or maintain a minimum balance of that amount in order to qualify for your card with a $1,000 credit limit. Ask the banker how long the bank customarily waits before it is willing to release the collateral. Expect 1-2 years.

Be sure you have a credit card, not a debit card. A debit card is nothing more than plastic checks. If they give you a choice, I suggest you get an account with no annual fee, even if the interest rate is higher. The interest rate is not relevant because you are going to pay the card in full every month and thereby avoid paying any interest. Furthermore, once you have this new account you will want to keep it for a long time because aged accounts raise your score. Therefore, you do not want annual fees to come up again and again. You should not have to pay start-up fees but if they want to charge you a one-time fee of $20 or so, that would probably be okay.

Find out about their ATM services and what fees are attached. If you do plan on using an ATM, do not keep your PIN numbers anywhere near your card. However, if your schedule is such that you can get to the bank during office hours, I suggest you do not use ATM at all. There are two primary reasons:

If you get accustomed to the convenience of instant cash for unnecessary purchases, it is too easy to gather up $20 here and $40 there. Then when you get your statement, you are shocked to find out how much money you actually spent. I think it is much better to set up a budget that allows for a reasonable amount of spending money; then, use cash for those purchases. When you are out of cash, you don't make any additional unnecessary purchases until your next payday. If you are using cash this way, you will tend to preserve it for things that really matter.

Remember that your broader goal is to build your credit. We specifically aligned you with a smaller bank for this very purpose. Therefore, it is better to go inside the bank to transact your business. That way they get to know you. I take in a box of cookies about once every six months. Chat with the tellers a little bit. Stick your head in the manager's door occasionally and say hello. Developing relationships in this way will be useful when you come back for a car loan or ask to increase your credit limit.

Before you finalize the relationship and open your accounts, be sure to read all of the boring fine print regarding bank fees and policies. Ask questions if you don't understand what all of the rules are. You should have a working knowledge of what happens if you pay late, or get cash advances or go over your limit and such matters. If you understand it all, and are satisfied with it, remind them that you want loan approval based on their verifying that the credit report you give them is accurate. This is called a "conditional approval."

This way, if the loan committee has any reason to decline your account, you will find out before they log a formal inquiry to your credit report. If they are not willing to proceed without first obtaining their own copy of your credit report, or at least give you a very strong indication that you will indeed be approved, then I suggest that you seek another bank.

Once you have your new credit card, you can discontinue using your gas card or retail card, but you do not need to. Be certain you do not close those accounts out, even if you never intend to use them again. Older accounts and unused credit serve to raise your scores.

Begin charging any and all items that you must buy anyway, such as gasoline and groceries, to your new VISA or MasterCard. Remember to keep the balance on each and every card below 30 percent of the available credit. In other words, if you have a $1,000 limit on any particular card, do not allow your balance on that card to exceed $300. If need be, keep your receipts in your purse or wallet so you will always know where you stand.

If you have not reached the spending limit it is okay to put additional purchases on your card, provided you already have the money on hand to pay for those items when the bill comes due. Remember, you should only be spending money that you already have, not some theoretical money that you hope to have in the future.

When your monthly bill comes in, be sure to pay it before the due date. This does not mean the last day before late fees kick in. It means the real due date. If it is convenient to hand-deliver the payment, do so for reasons previously mentioned. I like automatic withdrawal plans if you can be absolutely certain you will always have funds in your account to pay the bill when needed. However, if you cannot be that certain, then auto-pay plans can cause you aggravation, late fees, and damage to your credit score if the timing does not work out.

If a payment comes due, but you don't have enough money to pay the bill in full, you are at a critical crossroads. It is much worse to make a minimum payment than it is to borrow money from a friend or family member to pay the account in full. When you do not make the full payment, high interest rates automatically kick in on the unpaid balance and you are not painting the best possible financial picture for the bank. As your unpaid balance grows, so does the required monthly payment, and that is the exact opposite of what you are trying to do. Don't allow yourself to establish a bad habit in this way. It is a lot easier to resolve this relatively small, one-time matter now than it is to dig out of a big hole after you have compounded your problem month after month. So, work a little overtime or tighten your belt to pay your friend back and don't repeat this mistake.

Stay on this course for approximately 12 months and it will be time to take your next step. If you have done the things mentioned you will have built up some points on your credit score. Any points you lost from previous inquiries should be restored. In addition your good behavior will be paying dividends. Obtain a new copy of your FICO credit scores to be certain (www.myFICO.com/12).

If your score is over 650 you should approach your friendly banker and ask him or her to release the collateral you have pledged. The bank may authorize a partial release, or wish to wait another six to twelve months, but you are on track and doing very well. Eventually, you will get your collateral released.

After That

Every 12 months or so, you will do something new to steadily improve your score. Do not move much faster than that because it makes lenders nervous. However, slow and deliberate progress is heavily rewarded. I suggest you acquire at least one other major card but not more than two extra ones. You do not need any other minor cards such as the gas card you acquired in the first place.

Avoid accepting exciting offers at retail stores, and other places to sign up for their cards. It can be tempting to get a 20 percent discount on a flashy new computer, but you will probably be better off with cards that you can use in a wider variety of places.

You should shop carefully for your next major card. Avoid introductory offers and opportunities to transfer balances to new cards unless you like the long-term benefits of that particular card. There are excellent opportunities to acquire fantastic rewards such as free dining or air travel and there are cards that pay you a cash refund on all of your purchases. Those are both very exciting additions to your credit packages. An excellent place to shop for such cards and get other information about credit is www.creditcards.com.

It is easy to get carried away with credit. The unpaid balance has a way of sneaking up on people. From there, the problems gain momentum like a freight train headed downhill. However, the people who learn how to use this awesome tool effectively have other incredible opportunities. Now you know the basics to get started on the right track.

Remember these fundamental philosophies: Credit can be a best friend or a worst enemy; credit cards are not for incurring or accumulating debt—they are for emergencies, convenience and record keeping only; you should use your credit cards to pay for the things you already buy anyway, like gasoline, insurance, and groceries; finally, do not charge things unless you can pay your statement "on time and in full" when the bill comes due.

ADVANCED CREDIT STRATEGIES

Managing your credit is a lot like taking a shower. You will function better if you make it an ongoing practice. Before we leave the ever-important topic of credit, I suggest you review the following list of 32 additional items, in alphabetical order, which will assist you to build and protect your score. The worse your score is the more these things will help you. Once your score gets to 750 or so, your efforts and improvements will be of only minor benefit, but you should still employ them. The stronger your report, the better it can withstand problems like inquiries or an accidental late payment. Be patient but persistent. With consistent effort you should be able to join the exclusive "800 club" and find your score among the top 5 percent of all consumers.

Adopt a New Attitude

You should only allow creditors that you interview and approve to have access to your report. Here are the things you should ask potential creditors BEFORE you make formal application and allow access to your information:

Which credit bureau report(s) do you use?
Do you use FICO scores to determine my risk?
What is the minimum FICO score needed for approval?
What is the minimum FICO score needed to get the best rate?

Do you report my high limit and my current balance?
Do you report my activity to all three credit bureaus?
How does negative credit (bankruptcy, repossession) affect your
decisions?
If I give you a copy of my current FICO score and credit report,
will you get me a conditional approval subject to verifying
that the score is accurate? (Note: This assures your loan is
approved prior to any inquiries being entered on your report.)

Closing Older or Inactive Accounts

It is usually not a good idea to close old accounts or other accounts that you do not intend to use any longer. The credit reports tend to average the age of your accounts, and the older the better. However, if you have such an account that has an annual fee and you have a score above 750, you might contact the lender to find out if it would restructure the account to exclude the annual fee. If not, the damage from closing the account may be minor.

Co-Signing

Do not get in the habit of co-signing for other people. It is very risky, no matter who you are trying to help. If they default, you are responsible for the debt. You also expose your score to any of their actions or inactions such as late payments. Even if they pay on time, they pull your score down because they lower your debt-to-income ratio. If your score comes down, your own ability to qualify for later credit might be in jeopardy. Furthermore, if your insurance company gets wind of your FICO credit score dropping they might raise your insurance premiums. In my opinion it would be better to lend people your cash than your credit.

Credit Cards vs. Cash (and Checks)

Paying with cash can actually hurt your credit scores because your creditors have no way of knowing that you pay back your debts. Whenever you have an option, you should pay with credit cards instead of cash or checks because paying back those debts builds your credit score. This is especially true if your card offers cash-back or other bonuses. You can even build your credit or accumulate freebies by paying somebody else's bill with your card and collecting cash or a check from them.

Credit Unions

Credit unions tend to be more liberal in their lending guidelines, but the majority of them do not report to any bureaus. So use them if you will have trouble qualifying for a traditional loan or if you wish to hide a debt from your credit reports, but if you want your good habits to be reported, do not use credit unions for loans. Obviously you should verify their philosophy before you decide if they are right for you.

Debit Cards

Debit cards are not the same as credit cards. They are just plastic checks.

Department Store and Other Retail Cards

These stores can be good places to get a credit history going, but after that, do not apply for these cards. They frequently come with annual fees. Their interest rates are high and you cannot use them for other purchases. If you apply to several of them on one weekend, each inquiry counts against your credit score (the 45 day rule does not apply). These stores will try to offer you a one-time 20 percent discount to get their card but resist the temptation and use your VISA or MasterCard instead.

Divorce

Do not be cavalier about who pays what. In most cases you are both responsible for any debts you took on jointly, even if just one person agrees to take over the debt. If a court orders your spouse to pay a joint debt, that does not remove your obligation as far as the lender and credit bureau are concerned. Try to get the lender to release you, in writing, or refinance the accounts into the proper person's name. It may even be better to take on all of the debts yourself, rather than expose yourself to years of bad credit because your ex does not look upon your score with the same seriousness that you do.

Explanation Letters

You have the right to explain anything on your credit report and it might make you feel better, but such explanations do not affect your score. Very few lenders read them anyway. If you feel a need to dispute something, your time will be better spent by going directly to the creditor that reported the activity in the first place. If needed, you can hire an attorney or a credit repairing company to help you.

Finance Companies

Your FICO score likes banks a lot more than finance companies. Finance companies usually (but not always) include the word "financial" in their name. Having any loan at a finance company can actually lower your score. Avoid them.

How Income Affects Credit Ratings

Ordinarily, your income has nothing to do with your credit score. High income, raises, bonuses, etc. will not overcome poor credit. It illustrates your capability for making payments, but it does not indicate whether you will pay your bills on time or at all.

Inquiries

There are two basic types of inquiries to your credit scores. One type is relatively harmless but the other one poses more risk to you. If someone is checking you out just to find out if you are a responsible person, like a potential employer or an insurance company, there is little or no effect on your credit score.

But if you knowingly give a lender or anybody else your social security number or actually apply for credit, their inquiry can bring down your score. People with scores above 750 do not have to worry about this very much because they will only lose a few points, but people who are just starting to build their scores or pose other risks might see drops in their score of 10 points or more. Credit-related inquiries remain on your report for two years and count against your score for one year.

Ordinarily, all similar inquiries within a 45-day window count as one inquiry. The system understands that a person might be "rate shopping," so you should bunch similar inquiries together to prevent unnecessary damage to your score.

To reduce or avoid unnecessary inquiries, obtain your own current copy of your credit report and FICO score, and then provide that to lenders yourself for review prior to formal application. Your inquiry of your own score does not count against you.

Lag Time

In the worst case, it may take up to 60 days for changes to show up on your report after they are received.

Late Payments

Know what constitutes a late payment with your creditors. Sometimes you have a grace period but sometimes not. It is not just a matter of when late fees kick in. You want to know about their reporting practices.

Recent late payments or a pattern of late payments will be more damaging to your report than a late payment in the past. When a lender reviews your payment patterns it can recognize that one late payment is an exception to your usual good habits.

Limit Reporting

Some lenders do not report your "limit," or even worse, they report your current balance as your limit. This implies that you are stretched financially and brings down your score. You should avoid these lenders.

Negative Comments

Do not allow negative comments to invade your credit report. These include collection accounts, judgments, deed in lieu of foreclosure, write-offs, repossession, negotiated settlement, accounts included in wage earner plan, bankruptcy, negotiated settlement, and FED actions (financial arrangements for tenants facing eviction). These comments lower your score and paying them off will not raise the score back up. If you pay such an account after it shows up on your report you are still stuck with it as negative information on your report for seven years. Work with lenders to remove such comments or hire an attorney or credit repairing company to help you remove these types of comments ASAP.

Negotiated Settlements

If you settle an account such as a deed in lieu of foreclosure for a real estate loan, or an account that was sent to collections, try to get the lender, as part of the settlement, to report the account as "paid as agreed" instead of "settled" or some similar damaging term.

Old Accounts

Dormant accounts might get closed by the lender/creditor, which neither helps nor hurts, but using those old accounts enough to keep them active serves to help your score. You get the best impact on your report if you use the credit you have and pay it off each month. I suggest you use each account at least twice per year and pay them off in full and on time when the bill comes in.

On-Time Payments

This is the single most important thing you can do to build your score. If it looks like you may not be able to make your payment on time, try to borrow some money from somebody else so that you can fulfill your obligation. Set up auto pay if it fits your lifestyle. It is painless and it makes you smell like a rose.

If you want the best possible credit habits, observe that paying "on time" means no later than the due date. For example, there are ordinarily four time frames in which you might pay a mortgage payment: 1) it is due on the first of the month; 2) on the second of the month it is "late without penalty" and a grace period takes effect; 3) somewhere around the tenth, a late fee kicks in; 4) on the thirtieth, it is late for credit purposes. Therefore, any payment that is not made before the first of the month is late, even if there is a grace period. The best practice is to pay such bills on or before the first of the month. This may be the one thing that gets you favorable treatment the next time you apply for new credit.

Plan Ahead

If you are planning on getting both a home mortgage and a new car loan (or other personal property) in the near future, it is much better to get the home loan first. When it comes to qualifying, auto dealers and banks are much easier to work with than mortgage companies.

Preapproved Credit

Ignore notices that you are "preapproved" for a credit card or home loan. If the letter suggests that they still have to check your credit score, then they are no different than any other lender. This is not the best way to determine who deserves your business. A much better alternative is to check out www.creditcards.com.

Protection Programs

Somewhere along the way, your credit card company will probably offer you a "protection program," which is nothing more than insurance wherein they propose to make payments for you if you get hurt or lose your job. I do not recommend these programs unless you have more of this type of risk than the average person.

Refinancing Real Estate

Avoid perpetual refinancing of your home to get cash out. It creates inquiries, it adds to your debt ratios and it cuts down on long-term reporting.

Reward Credit Cards

Certain banks offer frequent flier miles, cash back or other perks each time you use your card. Sometimes they will even give you a huge upfront bonus for opening an account. My wife and I each obtained such a card just because they offered us a free round-trip ticket to San Diego with a popular airline. The interest rate they charge for these cards tends to be higher than some other cards, but if you expect to pay off your card each month the interest rate is not relevant.

If you acquire cards that pay you cash back or bonuses, you can dig deeper for ways to use your card. For instance, many car dealers will let you pay the first $2,500 of your purchase with your credit card. You can also pay for most insurance (health, life, auto, home owners) this way. Similar opportunities might be available at your utility companies. My sister-in-law has been known to pay bills for her adult-age children with her card and then get reimbursed from them.

Security Issues

Do not ever give out your card numbers to anybody you do not know, especially over the phone. If someone wants your information, you should acquire the phone number of their company from an alternate and reliable source, and then call them back to be certain they are who they say they are.

One way to cut down risk when you want to make online payments with your card is to set up an account with PayPal. You give them your credit card number and they process the transactions for you. They are a reputable company, owned by eBay. This approach protects your card information from online businesses with which you might like to do business.

I am not a fan of signing the back of my cards because I do not want bad guys to know what my signature looks like if my cards get lost or stolen. Sometimes, merchants will make me show an ID when they notice my card is not signed, but that is fine with me.

It is possible that someday, somebody will gain access to your card and charge purchases that you do not authorize. You will not ordinarily have to pay for those expenses, provided you report the matter to your credit card company within 60 days. They will usually close down your account and issue a new card with new numbers. Obviously, this is an important example of why you need to pay close attention to the details of your statements.

If you receive a new card, remember to update your credit card information for any automatic bill paying arrangements you have set up.

Split Accounts

A married couple may find it useful to apply for some separate credit. That way, certain debts don't count against both of you. Also, each individual is better off if there is a divorce or death.

The 45-Day Rule

Use this dynamic rule to your benefit. If there are multiple inquiries on your report for a similar-looking loan, within a 45-day window, the credit report believes you are rate shopping, not buying multiple items; therefore all of those similar-looking inquiries combined only count as one inquiry against your score. You can apply to several lenders for an auto loan or a new VISA card to see who might give you the best rate. You might even elect to take on two or more MasterCard accounts at the same time. If so, the damage from inquiries will be minimal. Furthermore, your utilization rate (see below) could improve substantially because you have more unused credit. On the down side, the average age of your accounts will drop, which usually lowers scores. However, a year later you would still be better off than the person who gets one such account now and another one after the year passes. Therefore, we are back to the original point: The 45-day rule can be an effective tool.

Transferring Balances

Pay debt rather than shifting it to new accounts. It seems smart to transfer debt to loans or cards with lower rates, but it can actually hurt you. New lenders will perform a new inquiry and may ask you to close an old account before they extend credit to you. You could end up with a closed account or an unwanted inquiry and both of those reduce your credit scores.

Tweak Older Accounts

From time to time, review your older established accounts and seek to improve them. For instance, you might be able to get the annual fee eliminated or the interest rate lowered. Sometimes lenders will update a comment from 30 days late to "paid as agreed" as a courtesy. It is fairly easy to get credit limits raised, which is usually an immediate improvement to your score.

Types of Accounts

It is considered prudent to have a variety of accounts. A good balance would be two to three major credit cards, one installment loan (car), one home loan, and a retail card or gas card.

Utilization Rate

Lenders compare your total debt to your available credit to get a measure of how much risk you present. Assume you have two cards, each with a $2,000 limit. One card is maxed out but the other card has a zero balance. Your revolving utilization is 50 percent. If you close the account with no balance, then your revolving utilization jumps to 100 percent, which is horrible. It is far better to have a low percentage, say 30 percent.

Verify

Whenever you open a new account, wait for 60 days and then verify that the lender is indeed reporting your good behavior to all three credit reporting agencies.

By implementing the concepts of the last four chapters about the various aspects of credit, you will be well on your way to joining the elite "800 Club," a group of people with outstanding credit scores. In addition, you will have filled in a significant portion of your financial puzzle. Congratulations are in order.

Now, we can reward ourselves by taking a trip to a virtual bakery. I can smell it already.

RAISING YOUR DOUGH

"Dough" and "bread" became popular slang words for money in the mid-1800s. "Dough" became especially accepted in the 1920s and 1930s. In those years, criminals in the underworld referred to counterfeit money as "sourdough."

One of the fascinating facts about dough is it will double in size all by itself, and that is exactly what we want your "dough" to do . . . grow all by itself.

Extra Money for You

How would you like to have an extra income earner in your family who donates money to you each and every month? I bet you will be enthusiastic if I tell you the earner does not take up space, does not eat your food, does not spend your money, does not make demands, and does not take vacations. No matter what you do, that reliable and invisible friend does its job and brings you knew income every month, like a faithful dog that retrieves your slippers. That loyal earner has a name; it is called "passive income."

By learning how to use money as a tool, you can put it to work for you. You don't have to be rich. You just have to find some money to invest. It doesn't even have to be your money. If you think about it, isn't that what most businesses do?

Banks take money from one group of customers and lend it to another group of customers at a higher rate, and the bank keeps the profits. Insurance companies take money from one group and give some of it to another group and they keep what is left over. The same goes for a grocery store or an apartment building owner or any other business. You can do it too.

Three-Step Plan

In my previous book, I introduced Realtors to a three-step plan I have been employing for years. It was a big part of my path to financial success. It is very simple and consists of ideas I developed myself with the assistance of two of my pals, Rocky and Bob. They each have their own version of the plan but the results are very similar. We were all financially secure at a relatively young age.

Upon reaching that plateau, our lives were enriched in ways we had not imagined. For one thing we discovered that our work took on a brand-new meaning. You might be surprised how much you can enjoy your job when you don't "have to" do it. If you genuinely dislike your employment you can pursue activities that bring you pleasure in lieu of money.

There are other similar plans out there, but I have not seen one that is as succinct as mine. By keeping it simple, nearly anybody can understand it and implement it. The three phases to the plan are:

Hate Debt

Save Consistently

Invest Wisely

I have devoted a chapter to each of them. Together, they complete a very significant part of your financial puzzle. Let's check 'em out.

HATE DEBT

The title of this chapter might suggest that I think all debt is bad, but that is not the case. In fact I have millions of dollars in debt, so technically I am not opposed to all debt, just certain types of it. The determining factor lies in who has to pay back the debt.

Bad Debt

Bad debt is any debt you have to pay back with your own money, and which you cannot pay in full, within a month. It is often referred to as consumer debt. Generally speaking it includes installment credit, like car loans, and items people commonly buy with a credit card.

In a perfect world, we would never take on bad debt at all, but this is far from a perfect world. Unfortunately, most consumers are drowning in bad debt. An MSN study revealed that Americans have about two trillion dollars in consumer debt. That includes car loans, credit cards, student loans or similar debts, but not home loans.

The average household has slightly more than four people, so the average family's share of the debt is $27,000, of which $9,000 is just in credit cards. If we arbitrarily assign a 14 percent interest rate to their credit card debt and 6 percent to the remainder of their consumer debt (usually for cars), they lose $195 per month, just in interest.

Earlier in this book we learned that wasting $4 per day, compounded at 7 percent, for 40 years grows to nearly a half million dollars in buying power. So, if the adults in this family were to buy the exact same items with cash, they could use their interest savings to assemble an incredible legacy to hand to their heirs someday. I am not talking about living without those items; I am simply focused on paying for them in a different way.

We could be talking about any purchases, but let us suppose we are considering buying a car. In one case the consumer borrows the money and makes monthly payments, including interest; in the other situation, he or she makes similar monthly deposits into a savings account that generates some interest income and then buys the car with cash. In both cases the consumer is making payments, but in one case there is an interest expense FROM the consumer and in the other situation there is interest income TO the consumer. If the average consumer in the study would approach all of his consumer purchases this way, the cost-difference is way more than $6 per day.

So the question becomes, "Would you like to accumulate an extra half million dollars throughout your lifetime, or would you prefer to buy the exact same things and forgo the half million dollars? The average family in this study has elected to take the latter route. Can you say "mega-flush"?

In another study, it was observed that half of all American families have no such debt, so that means that somebody else has to carry twice as much. Those poor souls forfeit the chance to accumulate more than one million dollars in buying power.

When we look at debt in this way we can recognize just how damning it is and why it is referred to as bad debt. Bad debt is as destructive to your financial wellbeing as any disease is to your physical or emotional wellbeing.

So bad debt is usually hurting consumers on multiple levels. It steals away other spending opportunities, it flushes resources on interest, it reduces investments, it diminishes quality of life, it delays retirement and it denies the likelihood of empowering your heirs. That is a very, very costly package!

It is much better to avoid the purchases that lead to bad debt and use today's money more wisely so that there will be more of it tomorrow. It does not take long before the assets start providing new income all by itself (raising your dough).

Good Debt

I like to refer to good debt as "controlled debt." It is controlled because the consumer is using it as a dynamic tool. For example, if you borrow money to buy a tool like a passenger bus or a quilting machine, and you can keep the item working until it pays for itself, you will end up with a valuable asset for free. In a situation like that, the debt was controlled and used to accumulate something of value. Anything that can pay for itself, including a turnkey business or a rental property, might be a worthy candidate for controlled debt. The underlying issue is somebody else is buying it for you.

Housing also falls in the category of good debt. You must live somewhere and most of us cannot start out with a free and clear home so we must lease a place to live. If you think about it for a moment, your rent payment is a fee you pay to the landlord in exchange for the money he has spent to buy a property in which you live. In other words, he loans you his property in exchange for your paying off his debt. Therefore, it is good debt for both of you. You get an essential product and he gets somebody else to pay if off for him.

But renting is only good debt in a few situations. When you first move out of your parents' home you will probably have to rent something until you can save up a down payment to buy a property of your own. Similar allowances are made for college years or any situation that demands temporary housing. Some possibilities include: you think you are likely to be transferred, or get married, or get some other job, or you are new in town and want to get used to the neighborhood before you decide where to buy. Also, if you are in an area where home prices are falling, it can be prudent to rent until prices bottom out (which could take several years) and the housing market turns around.

I have even known a few people who got such incredible deals from landlords that it made sense to keep renting forever. That is because the rent savings they enjoyed was more than the sum of the benefits of owning a property of their own. Naturally, I would recommend that people in that latter situation actually budget for a realistic housing payment and stockpile the monthly savings until they can buy a property anyway, and then turn that newly purchased property into a rental until the sweetheart deal runs out.

So we can conclude that under certain conditions, renting an apartment or home justifies the related debt, but ordinarily owning a home is even better. We will discuss housing a lot more in a later chapter, but for now we will acknowledge that both renting and home ownership can be good debt.

Surprisingly, the final type of good debt involves certain credit card purchases. There are certain items you must buy such as groceries, insurance and gasoline. If you use a credit card that awards benefits based on the dollar amount of your purchases, then it can be wise to pay for these items with your cards. Some such cards simply offer cash back and others offer deep discounts on products and services.

My wife and I each have cards for this purpose. Every year we accumulate enough points to fly round-trip to a nearby state for free just because we charge the items we were going to buy anyway. This is a nice way to visit family or go on inexpensive vacations. The caveat is you must be able to pay off the card, in full, when the bill comes in.

In addition to the fact that you can convert points into something useful, you also get the bank to lend you their money, interest-free, until you make the payments. That enables you to collect additional interest on your money for a brief period. So, under these conditions credit cards and their related debts can make positive contributions to your overall financial condition and that is an excellent example of controlled debt.

As I write this, there are millions of unemployed Americans. Many of them made a great living for a long time. Of those, some spent everything they made along the way, and financed most of their purchases. Now they are losing their homes, their fancy cars and their self-esteem, and filing for bankruptcy. Their relationships are strained. They are moving into humble properties. Their current situation is sad and their future is no better. Bad debt has destroyed them.

But a few of those unemployed people used their money more wisely. They don't have car loans or credit card payments haunting them. They accumulated passive income over the years and they can live on that until their circumstances improve. They already have all the money they will ever need. Good debt has enriched them.

Finally, I would like to tell you how this played out for our family. There is a lake in our community in which residents sail and swim. It is optional to join the Home Owners Association that manages it all. As our kids grew up, they wanted us to join the association so they could go to the lake whenever they wanted. But the annual fee was $1,000 and the summer was barely 10 weeks long. Considering vacations and other summer activities, there were only about 20 days or so that they could actually use the lake. On those days, they could go as guests of their friends so this was a no-brainer to me. I said, "Go with your friends, as their guests, and I will invest the savings."

Now, 20 years later, we are retired and live in the same home. We also own a log home on 40 acres that overlooks a fabulous mountain lake. We mostly use it on weekends. We have our own boats and canoes as well as a hot tub and gobs of fishing gear. The boys are grown and they take their friends up there a lot. They have both told me they are glad we used that HOA money and other money like it to build such a legacy.

Those old summers are gone now, but the log home will be around for generations.

I love going to our log home, but that would not have been possible if I wasted my money on frivolous spending, especially bad debt. That is why I hate bad debt. What about you?

SAVE CONSISTENTLY

When we think in terms of ten-year blocks of time, it seems like the past has flashed by, but the future will never get here. The point is few of us really give proper consideration to the importance of time, especially as it relates to the future.

In our everyday lives we tend to think of instant gratification rather than the long run. But the people who prepare for their futures can accumulate some incredibly impressive sums without making big sacrifices. I am fortunate to have instinctively figured that out as a young adult, but more importantly, I decided to do something about it, and that critical extra step has enabled this otherwise normal fellow to achieve financial security and retirement while still in his forties. One of my sources for inspiration came from anecdotes about compound interest. Here are a few of my favorite yarns on the topic of compounding.

If you put $100 per month into a savings account or investment for ten years, and if that investment always pays 7 percent interest, you can pull out $100 per month for all eternity. WOW and double WOW! If our grandparents did that when we were babies, we all would have had more money when we needed it.

If Christopher Columbus was your great, great, great granddaddy and he placed one single penny in an account bearing 6 percent interest and you stumbled upon that account now, it would be worth an astounding 110 billion dollars, or over sixteen million dollars PER DAY. That would make you nearly as rich as Bill Gates and Warren Buffet, combined.

In the early 1600s, the American Indians sold Manhattan Island, in New York, for beads and trinkets worth about $24. Now, that real estate is among the most expensive anywhere in the world. That would suggest the American Indians got the worst end of the deal. However, if they had invested their $24 and received 8 percent compounded interest, they would now have way more than a QUADRILLION dollars. That is enough money to buy back the island and get all of the buildings free and clear, and still have billions of dollars left over. OMG!

Obviously, neither you nor I have the time to enjoy these levels of success, but on the other hand, we don't have to start out with trinkets. These examples show us why even the smallest sums can grow into enormous stockpiles of money through the power of compounding. We also know that we can convert $4 per day into nearly a half-million dollars by compounding. We have already discussed lots of ways to find even more money than that to invest, just from money we are wasting now.

The Bad News

This would be a good time to remind you that compounding also works against you. As we noted earlier, there is FOREVER interest debt attached to wasted money. This is such an important concept it needs to be repeated for anybody who did not grasp it the first time.

For example, if you get an income tax refund of $500 and blow the money rather than pay off debt somewhere, then the interest on that debt lives on and demands perpetual payments from you. If we suppose you have a mortgage payment on your home demanding 6 percent interest, then you will save $2.70 in interest every month, for all eternity, if you simply apply the $500 toward your loan. If you can pay off credit card debt that carries 15 percent interest, you will avoid paying $6.25 per month, forever.

Furthermore, you have the loss even if you have no debt, because you could have invested the wasted money and earned an interest income, which is no longer possible. Therefore, there is a Forever Interest Expense whenever you waste money, regardless of whether you have debt or not.

If we are only talking about a one-time mistake, it may not be all that relevant, but people who do not understand this concept tend to duplicate the pattern over and over again. They do things like buy a dozen lattes per month, spend too much on cars, pick up some nice jewelry, carry credit card balances, get pizza delivered and have the wrong deductible on their home owners insurance. Throw in a few pets, a couple nights a week to go out to dinner and an extravagant vacation here and there. Before long, these people are losing a ton of money that they could be investing instead. Then they could use the passive income off of those investments to buy most of the things they like anyway. The difference is, the quality of their lives gets better and better whether they work or not.

My son has heard me make this point a few times but he never really understood it as well as he did the other day. He happens to like professional basketball and he stumbled upon four tickets that were available, just a couple rows behind the visitor's bench. He was offered the tickets for $300, which was half their face value. By the time he arrived at the ticket broker's office, the broker sold them to somebody else. When my son told me the story, I reminded him that those tickets would have cost him $15 per year for every year of the remainder of his life and beyond.

I guess he was more receptive to the concept this time, so he asked what I meant. I went on to tell him that his interest rate on his home loan is 5 percent. If he pays the same $300 that he was willing to *flush* for tickets (not to mention parking fees, a hot dog and a beer for everybody) to his mortgage, he will save $15 per year in interest because he will be carrying less debt. To my surprise, he said, "Well, I am willing to pay $300 now, but I am not willing to pay $15 next year and EVERY YEAR for those tickets." I could tell by his tone that this was the first time he REALLY got it! That night I went to his house and we watched the game on TV. Since he will never have to pay for those tickets the money will be saved . . . consistently. Then the interest savings will compound itself over and over again, just like it did for Christopher Columbus or the American Indians mentioned earlier.

I hope by now you understand how damning it is to carry consistent debt and how important it is to save consistently. Every dollar you can put to work can grow into its own little gold mine via compounding. But simply "knowing" these things is not enough. There are all sorts of people, even grade school kids, who can understand it intellectually, but only a select few do much of anything about it.

Follow Through

In order to save consistently, there are two simple but necessary follow-up steps needed: commitment and action.

Commitment

Commitment is a thought process, a decision. Let's suppose you are thinking about visiting your Aunt Bertha on your vacation. You can imagine what it would be like. You can dream of her homemade cookies and all of the great times you might have. You can entertain your mind for hours, but somewhere along the line, you have to "decide" that indeed you are going to do it. Thinking about it is not enough. You have to actually make a commitment or nothing is going to happen.

Action

Once you make a commitment, you still have to take action. This progression is not automatic. It is possible to make a commitment and not take action. For example, have you ever gone to a family reunion and seen a cousin whom you have always liked and before the evening was over you agreed (commitment) that "we are going to get together sometime for dinner," but you just never do? That is an example of commitment but no action.

My same son whom we just discussed has a constant problem with the bridge between commitment and action. We have a log home in the mountains and his friends regularly talk about going there for a weekend. He calls me to reserve it "in two weeks" for people who have said they want to go, but when the designated weekend rolls around, they sometimes change their minds. So, they made a commitment, but they did not take action.

Putting It All Together

Saving consistently is no different from visiting Aunt Bertha, or going to dinner with your cousin or spending a weekend at a cabin in the mountains, or anything else you want to accomplish. Once you are inspired, you have to make a commitment; and then you have to take action.

I have tried to provide you with the inspiration you need, but inspiration without these follow-up steps is nothing more than fleeting fantasy. Fantasy is okay in many situations, but preparing for your monetary future requires more than fleeting fantasies. You have to make the commitment and take action on your own.

As we discussed, a commitment is just a decision, so it is time to ask you a question. Are you willing to take the next step and make that commitment? The decision is yours. So what is it? Do you want to build a prosperous future or are you content to join the countless millions of people who have to rely on the government or others in retirement? If you are willing to live off of Social Security and Medicare, then you don't have to do much of anything, just *flush* your money away and take your chances.

But, if you are ready to take control of your future, this is your chance to do something about it. I hope you are sufficiently inspired to save consistently and put compounding to work for you. Assuming that is the case, let's see what kind of action is required.

Make it conscious – Start out by writing down a few basic philosophies that you intend to adopt. For example, "I am going to keep track of my money. I will make a 'realistic' budget and stick to it." Then include some specific plans to get started: "I am going to call my insurance company and review all of my policies and then really 'save' any money I have been wasting" or "I am going to forget that idea I had about going to Hawaii and begin saving the $8 per month that trip would have cost me in FOREVER interest."

Pay yourself first – You must now treat yourself as your most important creditor. Put an envelope in your bill drawer and put at least 5 percent of your take-home pay in this envelope each month (10 percent is better). Whenever you get $100 in it, take it to the bank and put it in savings and begin earning interest (more on this in the next chapter).

Remember the long term – This is not a get-rich-quick strategy. It is a long-term plan. It is more important to develop good habits than it is to accumulate money quickly. Therefore do not put big blocks of money into this account if you are going to be tempted to take it back out as soon as some emergency or whim visits you. It is wise to allow for those items, but do it in a separate account, not your long-term savings account.

Trailing Points

There are a few other concepts to share with you regarding compounding and saving consistently. Consider these:

The single biggest mistake you can make is "not starting." It is much better to get going, even with very modest amounts, than to put it off. Develop a reliable habit of saving. Remember the key word in all of this is "consistent."

The sooner the better. If you have access to a computer, you can pull up some graphs about this concept. You will discover that you will accumulate more savings if you save consistently for ten years and then let the profits grow than if you wait ten years and then save for 45 years after that.

Finally, keep it realistic. If you put too much pressure on yourself in the beginning, it may be difficult to stick with it. I suggest you make a modest plan and stick to it for six months or a year and then adjust accordingly.

In the next chapter we will discuss what to do with your "dough" as it grows and grows.

INVEST WISELY

I recently visited a bank with my elderly mother-in-law and discovered that her bank was paying a measly 1.1% for CDs. Furthermore, she has to pay income tax on the interest she receives, and in the meantime, inflation is stealing away some of her buying power. Based on all of those forces, it is obvious that a person has to look for a more profitable place to put his or her savings. Fortunately, that is the final critical section of your financial puzzle.

It is fun to imagine all of the potential profit an investment might generate, but the prudent investor also considers the evil twins: management and risk.

As far as management is concerned, if you buy a carwash, you can do all of the work yourself, or you have to pay somebody else to attend to all of the details. All of that can be a management nightmare.

Risk has a lot to do with "control." If you buy stock in an exciting new company, you have very little control of how they handle their business.

So you see, some investments require your time and attention and others subject you to more risk because you have to trust people and circumstances over which you have little or no control. Somewhere along the way you have got to come to grips with your tolerance for risk and your desired level of involvement. Generally, but not always, the less risk, the lower the return.

We must also keep in mind that we are investing money for the long term, and along the way we are bound to have temporary setbacks and short-term windfalls. The stock market and the real estate market are good examples. They have both suffered lately, but they each had a very long run prior to that. And they also have a fairly good record over the last 60 years. So the question is, should we pursue those options, with all of their volatility, or look for something else? And, what are some of the other choices?

Big Payoff, Low Risk

At the risk of chasing you off by beating the same old drum, please indulge me as I suggest that the first investment you should look at is your debt, especially consumer debt, which is essentially any non-real estate debt. If you have credit cards and car loans, you can usually enjoy a fantastic rate of return by simply paying those off and saving the interest. Now before you yawn, let me tell you why saving is so much more important than other types of investing.

Beating Ben Franklin To Death

You probably recall the familiar quote of good ol' Ben Franklin, "A penny saved is a penny earned." That may have been true 230 years ago, but things have changed so drastically that now it would be more correct to say, "A penny saved is much, much better than a penny earned." It all has to do with the income tax system.

When you earn a dollar, you have to pay 35 cents or so in taxes (depending on your tax bracket), leaving you with only 65 cents in buying power. But, whenever you save a dollar, you get the full benefit of that dollar without a new tax consequence.

The same holds true with your credit card debt and the interest that goes along with it. For instance, if you owe $10,000 on a Visa card that carries a 15 percent interest rate, you will have to pay $125 every month just for interest. Therefore, you will have to earn approximately $170 somewhere else (work or investment) and pay the IRS out of that money before you will have enough money left over to pay the interest you owe on your Visa card. You can avoid all of that simply by directing your investment dollars toward the credit card debt in the first place. In this example, if you invest $10,000 to pay off your Visa card, you will save the $170 per month, which amounts to a greater than 20 percent return on your investment. That rate of return would make ol' Ben and your stockbroker drool.

The benefits for paying off a car loan are not usually as significant because the interest rate is usually lower. Nevertheless, we should get rid of that loan next because now we know that the income tax system makes all interest expenses more draconian than they seem.

Home Loans

Once you have your consumer debt out of the way, you need to consider any real estate debt you might have. In most cases I do not recommend paying off your home loan unless the interest rate is 7 percent or higher. Some second mortgages and some non-owner occupied loans carry rates that high, or higher.

One exception that justifies paying off a home loan apples to people with a very low tolerance for risk. For these people, I see no harm in paying off your home in 15-20 years rather than the more typical 30-year plan. If you do that, you will save a great deal of money in your lifetime and enhance your retirement substantially. Overall, you may not get returns as substantial as somebody who takes bigger risks, but please believe me when I tell you there are many millions of people who would love to have a home paid off.

Eventually, you will have your loans paid down to the preferred level and any additional funds need to be put to work somewhere else. What do you do then?

Asset Classes

The most common investment vehicles for beginning investors are the stock market and rental real estate so I will have information about each of them in a moment, but before we do that, you should have a brief introduction to some of other investment options. A thorough overview of them is not necessary because they are generally beyond the scope of this book. But still, I thought you might like to know some of the games that the big boys like to play.

Cash - There are times when it is wise to accumulate cash, such as in deflationary times. When prices are dropping you will find folks trying to attract your cash. They will offer you higher rates of return or more goods for your money. He who has cash wins.

Foreign Stocks and Bonds - I included this category to remind you that the U.S. is not the only place that has a stock market. There are times when an informed investor can enjoy nice returns in these markets.

Natural Resources - Generally, these are items of value found on or in the land: oil, lumber, granite, coal, wild lobsters, water, etc.

Precious Metals - The most well-known are gold and silver, but there are many others, including platinum and palladium.

Commodities - If you happen to have a farm, you might be able to raise green beans or corn. Or, if you know how to raise cattle, you might be well suited to investing in such endeavors.

Personal Property - A person can accumulate classic cars, antique furniture, art, guns, baseball cards or any number of other potential investments.

Businesses - Sometimes people wish to sell a successful business such as a photography studio or a restaurant. Their cash flow has value. Certain investors have a knack for buying these companies and either holding them for cash flow or reselling them for lump-sum profits.

Stocks

I recently performed a quick Web-search of the word "investment." I checked out the first 100 offerings and only a handful of them discussed any investment other than stocks. Stocks and mutual funds are appealing to entry-level investors because the investor can buy small quantities, and there is practically no management necessary.

Perhaps the biggest incentive is that brokers, mutual fund managers and financial planners are all willing to help investors, and it seems like they are working for free. Generally the professionals will try to help you make a profit without exposing you to high risk. That is certainly a worthwhile strategy. But they have no way of controlling the market or any of the stocks they pick for you, so their ability to avoid risk is limited.

As far as making profits is concerned, very few of these professionals beat the averages of the various indexes with which they work. Furthermore, just because one of them did well last year is no guarantee he or she will maintain the momentum.

The bottom line is this: You might be using the wrong broker, buying the wrong products or getting bad advice. Therefore, there is still a fair amount of gambling involved.

As far as the common mantras of "diversify" and "stay in it for the long run" are concerned, here is my basic philosophy.

Diversify - As far as I am concerned, diversification is a poor strategy. Whenever I diversify it diminishes my successes and exposes me to more opportunities to lose. If I have 100 stocks in a mutual fund and one of them increases in value, the benefit is diluted by the ineffectiveness of the other 99 stocks. I would have been better off with all my money in that one good company, if by some miracle I could have identified it; but how do I do that without inside information?

I also believe I have plenty more risk when I diversify. In the above example I have 100 different chances that somebody in that group is going to screw up and cost me money. When I am exposed to so many opportunities to lose my money, the laws of probability work against me. If just one of those stocks drops in value, and it probably will, that one bad actor can easily wipe out the small benefit I enjoy on my already diluted successes.

Stay in It for the Long Run - Once again, I have my own rebuttal: "Any plan to stay in it for the long run is the wrong one." The long-run philosophy is used to discourage investors from selling when the market goes against them. The theory is that there is no actual loss until you "recognize" it by selling, but that assumption is also flawed. The truth is you already lost the money, whether you recognize it or not. Unless you have some compelling reason to believe that the company that just lost your money is somehow poised for a remarkable recovery, it could easily be wiser to take the loss now, enjoy a tax deduction and put your money somewhere that offers some genuine promise.

It would be foolish to ignore the true beneficiary of the "stay in it for the long run" philosophy. If investors were cashing in their investments whenever things went against them, financial advisers would soon be out of customers. As long as the expert has control of my dollars, he or she is the one who has the greatest benefit for keeping me in it for the long run.

Contrary to appearances, I am not hostile to the stock market. I will admit that it is fairly easy to understand and it has had a respectable long-term run. What I am trying to do is point out the negatives, which nobody else tells you about until it is too late.

Considering the above, if I was interested in buying stock, I would be more inclined to see what Warren Buffet is up to than follow the advice of a random financial planner. Not too long ago Buffet invested billions of dollars in the railroads. I would consider buying the same stocks he does whenever their price dips a bit.

Real Estate

This option is my favorite investment for most people,

although it is not for everybody. The biggest drawbacks are: 1) it takes a fair amount of money to invest; 2) it is not very liquid; and 3) there is a fair amount of management required. However, all is not lost. If an investor has the money needed and can get by without the liquidity factor, then the management problem can be solved by hiring professional property managers. Whenever I buy an investment property it is expected to pay for this service.

There are several other benefits to investing in real estate. For instance, there are four different ways to make a profit: cash flow, principal reduction, appreciation and tax benefits. Want more?

- As rents go up, there is passive income, which can replace or supplement your ordinary income.
- You can get the tenants to pay off your debt, so you eventually end up with property that is free and clear.
- Most or all of your profits can be free of taxes if you know about trading and estate planning.
- Inside tips about good deals are not illegal.
- Sometimes you can buy property well below the market and start off with a nice profit.
- The federal government implements policies that practically guarantee a modest amount of inflation, which increases the value of most properties, over time.
- You can actually do things yourself to create or add value to your property: fix them up, put on additions, finish attics or basements, rezone them, convert apartments into condos or develop land.
- You can get to your equity (new investment dollars) by refinancing, and there are no immediate tax consequences.
- You can control a $100,000 investment with a fraction of that amount.
- You get to control the investment yourself rather than relying on people you do not know.

Finally, did you know that you can buy a property, keep it for many years and make a profit even if its value drops in half? Here's why. If you buy a townhome for $100,000 and pay 20 percent down you will have $80,000 in debt. Over time the rents will pay off all of the debt. So even if the property drops in value to $50,000 (half its original price) the investor still has a $30,000 profit.

Considering the points mentioned here, I think real estate is a much better investment than stocks. Only a select few people make big money because of their stock portfolio, while more people become millionaires as a result of investing in real estate than any other asset.

Wrapping It Up

Here are a few other facts to think about.

There is a difference between investing and gambling. Try not to get them confused. Once you save a dollar I think you should protect it. This money should never be used for penny stocks and wild ventures.

The younger you are, the more risk you can accept because you have more time to recover from your losses.

Generally, I recommend you always keep an amount of equity in your portfolio that is equal to your age, give or take 10 percent. In other words, if you have a million-dollar real estate portfolio and you are 30 years old, try to keep 30 percent equity. If you have a high tolerance for risk, or you are in the business, then you might get by with only 20 percent equity. If you are 55 with the same portfolio then you would want 55 percent equity (your age) but if you wanted to be especially careful you would want an additional 10 percent equity, or 65 percent total.

You don't have to buy at the bottom or sell at the top. You will do very well if you will just buy near the bottom and sell near the top.

Do not look upon your home's equity as an income source unless you are going to use that money for smart investments.

Do not refinance to subsidize other purchases—past, present or future.

As Polonius said, "Neither a borrower nor a lender be." Be very careful about taking on partners, lending money or co-signing for friends or family. If other people are having financial problems you don't want to jump into the fire with them.

This was a very important chapter because all of your other smart moves can be wiped out if you don't know what to do with your money once you get it. Now you have quite a few choices. And you know the benefits and pitfalls of the most common ones.

Obviously, it is difficult for me to make any specific recommendations to you. I do not know what your local real estate market is like, what business opportunities might be available to you or what special circumstances might offer you unique options. But if you held my feet to the fire, I would put real estate at the top of the list, then mutual funds and then business opportunities for people who can play an active role managing their investments.

Finally, you should read more books and seek expert advice before you start throwing your money around, but at least now you should have a good foundation.

SECTION TWO CONCLUSION

Your puzzle is finally finished. Way to go! Each piece is in its place and together they form a great financial picture.

Before we move on, let's review what you have learned in this section. The second major segment of the book focused on the things that can be done NOW to fix and improve your financial status.

You started out by observing that we all make mistakes. You decided to forgive yourself for past errors and to simply move forward. You took a Mulligan.

From there, you began putting your financial life back together, as you would do with a puzzle. You began with four corners: self-honesty; establish realistic goals; get organized; and take action.

Then you added the framework to the puzzle: clean up messes; make a budget; employ discipline; and keep score.

In Chapters Four through Seven you assembled the first major section of the puzzle, which was all about credit. You adopted some new philosophies about what credit should be and what it should not be. Next you actually got a copy of your credit report. You observed how it is constructed and that it could be a dynamic tool as you rebuild. From there you learned how to put together a good credit score from scratch. The final chapter about credit introduced 32 advanced strategies that will enable you to raise your credit score to a level your banker will envy.

In the next major section of your puzzle you took a quick trip to a bakery and learned a bit about raising your dough. You observed the importance of generating new income in the form of passive income. You discovered a wonderful and simple three-step system that will guide your approach to money from this day forward.

There have probably not been many times in your life when you have been encouraged to hate anything, but Chapter Nine did exactly that. You learned to hate debt and you found out why things cost more than they seem to.

Once you understood why debt is so destructive, you learned how and why you should save consistently. Examples of compound interest were used to illustrate why ordinary people, like you, can accumulate massive amounts of money.

The final chapter was about investing wisely. It revealed the various asset classes and provided a few details regarding the more common investment vehicles of stocks and real estate.

By this point, you should be able to see that it is very realistic for you to govern your finances in a responsible and rewarding way.

Now that you have observed most of the things that have gotten you in trouble in the past and explored what to do now to get the ball rolling in a positive, downhill direction, there is one more important section for you. It will provide some monetary pointers about dealing with the kinds of things that life might throw at you in the future.

SECTION THREE

CREATING A BRIGHT FUTURE

MAKING SMART CHOICES

Section One of this book focused on the financial problems of the PAST. Section Two was about the financial strategies you should implement now, in the PRESENT. Therefore, it follows that Section Three will address the kinds of things that are likely to come up from time to time, in the FUTURE.

If you are already into a profession that you like, the first few chapters may not apply to you, in which case it will not hurt my feelings if you wish to skip over them and jump to the one about Food, Clothing and Other Goods and Services. However, if you know other people who are going to pursue new careers, you may want to read the noted chapters anyway so that you can pass along the information to them.

For the rest of you, in any conversation about wasting money, we must recognize that failing to fulfill our income potential is a major shortcoming. There are certain things one can do to enhance his or her value, such as seek training, go to school or gather experience. Thus, we will identify some of the pathways one can take to ascend the rungs of society's ladder.

Let's get going.

COLLEGE

Is the high cost of higher education really worth it? You might be surprised to learn that I believe that the value of a college education is overrated. Furthermore, I predict that if you will stick with me, you will come to the same conclusion.

I will freely admit that if you want to become an accountant, a lawyer, a rocket scientist or some other white collar professional, then college is essential. However, there are millions of college students who are duped into spending tens of thousands of dollars for a degree they do not need or use. Many of those graduates soon find out they were victims of an overly zealous system, whose gate keepers are more interested in the checkbooks of those students, and their deeper pocketed parents, than anything else.

There is a strong likelihood that you know college graduates who are holding all sorts of jobs less glamorous than they expected. In a great number of these cases the workers could have gotten those same jobs without the old sheepskin. I know several Realtors who have Masters degrees. When I ask them what good their degrees are to them, they have a difficult time coming up with a significant answer. All of these people (or their parents) paid an incredible amount of money for their diplomas, which might as well be lining the bottom of birdcages.

And then there are the jobs that require the diploma but still don't pay all that much. In our area, an entry-level teacher earns around $30,000/year, which is less than it costs to get the degree. At the same time, an entry-level plumber makes $34,000 and does not need to invest four years and tens of thousands of dollars in schooling.

Of those who do indeed get jobs as a direct result of their education, there are still plenty of problems. For example, how would you feel if you spent four to five years studying to become an engineer only to discover that you really don't care for the work after all? This is a common occurrence because high school graduates rarely know what they really want to do "for the rest of their lives." After a few years on the job, they discover they do not like it as much as they thought they would.

Another problem for nearly every college graduate is that the employer establishes the compensation package. For example, a particular position may offer a salary range of $37,000-$42,000. The employer has set the range, not the graduate. So the diploma may get you in the door, but it is only as valuable as the boss says it is.

There is another misconception about college degrees. Many people believe that a diploma is a sign of leadership, but most of the time the opposite is true. A sheepskin does indeed tell an employer that the student can complete certain challenges. But the broader message is that the student has successfully performed tasks that others assigned him or her. That indicates a good follower, not a good leader. In the end, that stick-to-it quality may prove to be a curse as the grad is doomed to become a company servant rather than a real leader.

Another drawback to college degrees was observed by the famous author and motivator, Zig Ziglar, when he noted that more than 80 percent of college grads end up working in fields unrelated to what they studied in school. As an example, Caroline worked at a major grocery chain to help pay for her degree in graphic design. As soon as she graduated, the grocer started throwing opportunities at her. Five years later, and while still in her twenties, she is one step away from a position as store manager. Caroline has plenty of fine qualities that would have served her well in any field, so it is difficult to determine exactly what role, if any, college played in her success.

Caroline's brother, Matt, is another example. He majored in mathematics at a very expensive university. A few years after he graduated, he secured a fine job running a machine shop for an agency of our state. That particular job did indeed require a degree of some sort, but his mathematics background is nearly irrelevant.

I am not suggesting that a college education is a waste of time because that would be untrue in the majority of cases. I suspect that only a small percentage of college-educated adults would trade their college years for additional work experience. Furthermore, we should all be able to agree that a diploma will open certain doors that would not open at all without the sheepskin. Therefore, we can conclude that there is indeed a worthwhile purpose to advanced schooling in certain cases, but you can understand why I maintain that it is over-hyped.

I don't wish to cast doubt on the motives of the admissions department or high school counselors or any other professional educators because I think they really do believe that college is a worthwhile endeavor. Why wouldn't they? They have spent years of their own lives walking the hallways of academia in the same pursuit. It would be contrary to their core beliefs to do one thing for so many years and then recommend a contrary endeavor. Besides, how the heck are they going to figure out which students will actually use their diplomas and which ones will not? These educators are smart, but they are not clairvoyant. So they rely upon a nebulous fallback position: Almost everybody would benefit from college in one way or another.

In spite of the good intentions of the majority of educators, there is a lot of necessary and unseemly money grabbing going on. It costs a lot of money to wrangle up a good faculty and to maintain all of those buildings. So educational institutions have a huge incentive to promote their product, regardless of whether it is really in the best interest of a particular student or not.

The Economics

A good way to decide if college is really worth it for you is to break down the costs and benefits that a high school graduate might expect. Naturally, the costs vary around the country based on cost of living, but you should be able to follow the reasoning in a "typical" situation.

For starters, let's suppose the student could have joined the workforce right out of school. Perhaps he or she would work in a grocery store or as a carpenter's assistant, making $12 per hour. In that case our student would make $25,000 per year.

As an alternative, he or she elects to go to college. The price for this education ranges from a low of about $5,000 per year for local colleges, to $40,000 per year or more for top-tier universities. For our purposes, we will pick out a college near the lower end and say it will cost our student $15,000 per year for each of four years of education, including room and board—even though many students take five years to graduate.

Once the student has the diploma in hand, we can measure his or her income. The typical jobs for these graduates would be teacher, loan officer in a bank, an apprentice accountant, administrator in a government job or an engineer. The starting pay range would be between the low thirties and the middle forties. For our purposes we shall assume the new employee starts out at $38,000 per year.

From there it is not difficult to do the math. The diploma cost our student a total of $160,000. There was $25,000 per year in lost wages, and there was $60,000 in actual costs.

The new job, with the diploma, pays $13,000 more that what this person could have earned from the job he or she got right out of high school, which we said was $25,000. Since our graduate makes an extra $13,000 per year and has to make up $160,000 in costs, it will take this person approximately 12 years to reach the break-even point.

You could plug in all sorts of other variables such as inflation, interest on the money, raises, what if a mom drops out of the work force for a few years to raise a child, what if you end up with a job that does not require the diploma, etc., and you will probably get a more relevant picture, but in most cases the conclusion will be similar—namely, it takes a long time to recover the losses.

Putting It All into Perspective

Many of life's important decisions come with a mixed bag of information. I think whether or not to attend college is such a case. Just to be sure you know what to consider, the following is an overview of where all this has taken us.

Benefits of Going To College

Very few high school students have the wisdom to know what they want to do in life, so college provides an excellent weaning process wherein they acquire exposure to a variety of options while doing something productive in the process.

There are many jobs you cannot acquire without a degree, whether it is relevant to that work or not.

There are situations in which a degree will help you, even if it is not officially required to land the position.

The skill-set a student develops (persistence, learning how to learn, task management, living on one's own, etc.) is valuable in life regardless of whether it is used for employment purposes or not.

The social life of college students is appealing. Some of those parties are priceless. Then there are all of the vacations, including spring break and long summers. You only get one chance to be young. It would be a shame to miss out on these opportunities.

Drawbacks of College

A college degree is not essential to securing all worthwhile jobs.

Certain jobs that require a diploma may not compensate you any better than jobs that do not require a degree.

Since somebody else sets the monetary value of a diploma, the graduate's paydays have limits.

It is possible to spend all that time and money to acquire a diploma and then land a job that you do not like.

College is very expensive, regardless of who pays for it, and it takes a long time to recapture that money.

An objective overview of the above lists would suggest that the importance of a degree varies widely. In some industries it is priceless; in others it is nearly irrelevant. A degree might help you to get off the bottom rung of the employment ladder; nonetheless, those who don't really want to spend their lives as somebody else's follower could easily gain more fulfillment by becoming an entrepreneur.

At the beginning of this chapter, I suggested that a college education is overrated. Now you know why. The institutions need your funds so they tend to oversell the value of their products. Some people do indeed gain some measurable and immeasurable benefits from their advanced schooling, but many others go through all of that time, money and effort and cannot really justify the high cost. I hope that now you will be better able to decide if higher education is really a prudent financial choice for you.

Before we leave this topic, there is one other matter I would like to share with you. I suggest you also consider the "real" importance of grades. As you would expect, I am going to rain on the picnic somewhat. In my opinion the grade-thing is also overrated. There are certain employers who will indeed want your transcripts and in those situations the grades certainly matter. But with those exceptions, your transcripts will probably never be reviewed. Therefore Cs are just as good as As. Consider the two examples I cited earlier. The lady in the grocery store was already working for her employer before she got her degree. They loved her character and work habits. It was unimportant if she got a D in volleyball or a C in Algebra. The math student's grades were also of little concern. All that really mattered was that he majored in math and he graduated.

The point of all of this is, don't drive yourself nuts trying to get somebody else's approval. It just doesn't matter that much. If you really are a C student and you want to go to school, do not deny yourself the opportunity just because an irrelevant grade might show up on a piece of paper. On the other hand, if you are an A student, very few people will ever give a darn, so don't obsess over the grades themselves, unless they really matter to you.

EMPLOYMENT

If this book were about the employment process in general, we might discuss topics such as how to make an effective resume, or employment trends and such things. But this book is focused on how to stop wasting money, so we will remain focused on the "economic factors" of the job.

If you are in some sort of a union, there is a good chance there is a contract that determines your compensation package, including your pay scale, benefits, and when you will get your raises. In a situation like this it is difficult to climb the ladder, except as you accumulate seniority, because the workers tend to know what the minimum expectations are, and most of them see no benefit in producing above that level. Therefore, if you come in and work harder or smarter, there is a risk you make the others look bad and their resentment toward you will create some uncomfortable dynamics.

Union workers can benefit from the information that follows, but people who are not subject to the restraints and advantages of union contracts should benefit even more.

Jobs and Careers

Technically speaking, a person who is studying to become an engineer and working nights as a bartender to pay for schooling might consider the former to be a career and the latter to be "just a job," but I look at it differently. Each and every job that you hold represents part of "your" working career, and you can use nearly any position to advance your earning power. Here is how it happened to me.

I was barely in my twenties and wanted to work in the produce department for the local grocery chain. At the time, Safeway was the only major company that had an opening. I applied for a job with Safeway and treated it as if it was the only job on the planet. I was punctual, courteous and devoted. I learned as much as I could about the produce department and the entire retail operation. In the meantime, I kept going back to the local chain and reminding anybody who would listen that I preferred to join them. About fourteen months later, the preferred company called me and I was hired. Several months later I got a merit raise. I later found out that they had been sending spies to the Safeway store to observe my work. If I had not taken the Safeway job seriously, I probably never would have gotten the job I really wanted. But that wasn't the end of it.

I ended up working in the retail field for about six years; then I obtained my real estate license. By that time, I knew so many grocery people I ended up representing quite a few of them in their real estate transactions. All of that was possible, or at least easier, because I took that very first job, at Safeway, seriously.

In another example, Dan applied for an entry-level job in a machine shop. The work was hot and boring. There were a fair number of welders there and it was Dan's job to hand-grind the welded spots into a more appealing semi-flat appearance. Dan took his non-glamorous job seriously. He showed up on time. He was well groomed. He had a good attitude. Day after day he ground down those boring welds. All along he watched for something that paid better or was more interesting.

Within six months, a competing machine shop in the area had an opening. It involved a different task and required some basic tools, which meant it paid a little more. Dan secured the position even though he had no experience with the particular machine to which he was assigned. It was his work habits at the first shop that made the difference. But Dan wanted more.

By that time, he had amassed a nice collection of tools. He always kept his work area clean and safe. He showed up on time. He was turning out great work on lathes, drill presses and other sophisticated equipment. Each time he proved himself, he was given more challenging machines to operate. After a couple years, he was an accomplished machinist with a broad range of skills.

Then a large aerospace company came to town in search of some people to help build rockets and satellites in another state. Dan was hired on the spot. After a few years in the aerospace field, he proved his mettle again. His new company paid for him to go to Cal Tech to get an engineering degree. Finally, Dan moved off of "the floor" of the shop and into the offices. That was more than twenty years ago. His very impressive career is the sum of a series of jobs, all made possible by developing good work habits, even in the most humble situations.

These are examples of why your reputation is your most valuable asset. Employers are always starving for responsible workers and they are willing to pay for good work habits. So no matter how mundane the job seems, keep the broader perspective in mind and act like a professional.

Profiting from the Interview

An interview has the potential to affect your income for years to come. Therefore, it is vitally important that you maximize your salary right from the beginning. The additional funds you secure from an effective interview offer precious resources to save consistently and invest wisely, but any money you leave behind is *flushed* down the drain and we already decided to stop doing that.

If the salary for a particular job is clearly established in advance, there is not much you can do during you interview to increase your income. But in most situations, the employers are thinking of a salary range, so the interview leads to a negotiation process. In those circumstances the employer will usually try to uncover your financial expectations by asking you how much money you need.

If you blurt out a number that is too high, you may not get the job because you appear uninformed or unrealistic. On the other hand, if you offer to accept a low amount, and hope the employer will reward you later for your sense of fair play, you have three problems: 1) you may have started out at a figure lower than necessary, and any money you leave on the table is money you *flush* down the drain; 2) it appears you do not have a very high opinion of your value, so the employer will probably take your word for your value; and 3) the employer has very little incentive to reward you later, as you hoped.

It is obvious from the above that it is very important to get the most compensation you can in the first place. Here are some pointers to help you control the salary discussions during the interview.

Who Goes First

When it comes to negotiating the salary, there are two contrary schools of thought. The first one suggests that whoever puts the first number on the table is at a disadvantage because that person has less bargaining room after the starting point is established.

The other idea is that you have the best chance of getting the most money if you identify your expectations right from the beginning. That is because you can eliminate the lower end of any salary range the employer has in mind. I like this approach better, but we shall look at each.

Try to Delay- If you are asked how much money you expect to earn, you may prefer to delay the discussion because you don't want to hand the interviewer an easy reason to eliminate you. So, say something respectful like, "I was hoping we could delay that conversation until I find out what you need, and you get more familiar with me. Then I hope we can find a fair number."

You Go First – If you prefer to go first or the interviewer seems determined to get a number out of you, you can cut down on your risk by discovering what range they had in mind. The exact words go something like this, "I am sure you have already discussed the possibilities with the department manager. What kind of a salary range did you decide was appropriate for this position?" Then, consider your qualifications and give an objective answer near the upper end of the range.

Responding to an Offer - Very few employers are going to give you their best offer right away. So a good way to find out if they have left some room for negotiating is to ask, "Quite frankly, I was thinking of a number that is a little higher than that. Do you suppose we could meet somewhere in between?" If they ask you what you have in mind, there is a very good chance the door is still open. Your follow-up comment is, "I am at X and you are at Y, so what is the closest you can come to my number?" Most people will have a tendency to try and split the difference. It usually won't take very long before they tell you they have made their final and best offer; then you have a fairly good idea of where you stand.

Benefits - During the negotiation process you may determine that the employer cannot offer you more money but you suspect she would be willing to sweeten the offer in some other ways. In such cases it is possible to enhance your benefits package. For example you might get flex-time, personal days, travel pay, a dental plan or more paid vacation. When I held one of my traditional jobs, they only allowed one week of vacation, after a year. I would have valued a little more time off, even if it was without pay.

You Still Want More - There are many occasions when the employer indicates they would like to start off paying you a particular salary and see how things work out before they consider a raise. You should not allow that sentiment to go undocumented. Their comment could be very sincere, or it could be just a brush-off. Either way, it lends you a specific opportunity to improve your position in the future. Ask the employer if you can thrash out exactly what needs to be accomplished for you to get the money you think you deserve. Establish a specific timeline for getting back together. Take notes as you discuss the matter. Once you have determined precisely what is required, and when, offer to put it all in writing so both of you can sign it. Then, from time to time remind the employer of your progress, and ask for feedback.

How to Get a Raise

I suspect there are countless numbers of men and women going to work every day and feeling bitter because nobody has given them a raise. In some cases, they have worked for the same salary for years. Over time, they have gotten better at what they do and inflation has eaten away the buying power of their paychecks. So the net result is they have become more valuable, but nobody seems to care.

When employers are asked why they did not give raises to their employees, the most common answer is, "because they never asked." What a tragic and unnecessary situation. The employee is a victim of his or her own fear of rejection. But you can overcome apprehension about asking for a raise if you plan ahead.

Enhance Your Value

Once you land a job, you should at least get raises equal to the inflation rate. So keep track of both your hire date and the inflation rate, so that you can incorporate those factors into any conversation about a raise. Beyond that, there are certain things you can do on a day-to-day basis to enhance your value and increase your ability to get raises in the future. Make these things a regular part of your workday and the employer cannot deny your value.

Attitude, attitude, attitude. Everybody likes to be around happy and positive people. Remain upbeat so that you are a constructive and pleasant influence on others. Be just as pleasant with your subordinates as you are to your superiors.

Good enough is not good enough when you want a raise. Perform your primary job better than an average person would do.

Let your supervisor know you are trying to earn a raise, so she will pay attention. Keep her posted of your accomplishments and seek feedback on what you can do better.

Put in some harmless extra effort. Show that you care about the work environment by picking up that lone piece of trash that everybody else steps over on the way to and from the parking lot (this habit has become so normal for me, I even do it in other places like the grocery store or gas station); wipe off the counter top in the break room; keep your desk clean; put your dirty coffee cups in the dishwasher rather than leaving them in the sink.

Punctuality. Get to work at least ten minutes early. Use those few minutes to say good morning to your co-workers. When it is time to go home, do not lend the impression that you can't wait to get out of there. It is better to take a moment to hold the door for somebody than it is to get home three minutes earlier.

Grooming. Dress at the upper end of what is expected for the job-class. If blue jeans are okay, wear nice ones with no holes or stains. If dresses are common, be sure that your dresses say "success" all by themselves. Pay special attention to your shoes. Keep them clean and polished. If you have tattoos and piercings, don't flaunt them unless you happen to be a bartender in a biker bar.

Do not call in sick unless you really are sick. If you are constantly sneaking days off, it screams out that you don't really want to be there. The boss needs people who are reliable, not people who are disinterested.

A leader doesn't have to diminish others in order to succeed. Avoid back-stabbing, gossip and hate speech. In fact, you should do the opposite. You are trying to build good relationships, not tear them down. Speak well of your fellow workers even when they are not there. It is much better to build bridges than burn them.

Keep criticisms to a minimum unless you are the supervisor of the person in question. If it is necessary to reprimand somebody, reserve your discussions for private meetings. People do not want to be disciplined or corrected in public.

Always give plenty of notice before terminating your employment. Departing may be your final act with that group and you want the lasting impression to be a positive one. You may need references or become involved with these people again, so make sure you leave on a positive note.

Be patient. You cannot expect to get a lifetime of rewards by being good for a couple of days. You must establish that these things are regular long-term habits that make you more valuable than an average employee.

Regardless of where you work, these things will help you maximize your opportunity for advancement. It may come in the form of a raise or a new job classification that pays more money or just in earning a good reference for the next job. In any case, you win. Besides, even if you do all of these things for an entire lifetime and never derive one single monetary benefit, you will enjoy your work a lot more. There is a lot of personal satisfaction in being good at important things, and our work plays such a major role in our lives it is certainly worth the extra effort.

Do Your Homework

You still have some more work to do before you go ask for that raise. You need to do some research so that you are armed with information to justify your request. Before you throw the bosses doors open and attack like a predator, here are some prudent steps to take:

You will be more successful if you broach the topic when the company's needs are the greatest: just before the busy season or when a new project has been funded. Another good time is immediately after you have accomplished a major task or received some sort of formal recognition. It is not usually a good idea to ask for raises when the work is calming down or the company is struggling.

Try to schedule an appointment with the boss at a time and place that is not distracting. Perhaps you can grab a lunch together or meet before work starts. If she wants to know what you want to discuss, tell her it is about money matters.

Remember, your boss may be caught off-guard, so you may get some initial resistance. Remain calm. It will not serve your purposes to get irritated.

Do some behind-the-scenes investigating. Find out what similar jobs are paying in your company and in the broader market. If the market supports your request, your chances are very good. The boss will not want to risk losing you. On the other hand, if you are already at the top of the pay scale, you might have to wait or seek a different position.

Do not talk in terms of your feelings or needs: "I need this raise because my car is falling apart." Instead focus on the "value" you bring to the company. If you are a salesman, a dental hygienist or a plumber your value is fairly easy to quantify, but if you make the boss's job easier remind her that you take your job seriously so that she can focus on other matters. The point is your spotlight should be on your contribution and your value, not how much you need the money. Your comments should sound more like this: "I have become much more efficient and valuable than when I first accepted this position, and now my salary is not in line with my skill-set."

Present records of all your accomplishments. Make an eye appealing list or presentation emphasizing anything that is above and beyond what is customarily expected from the position. Dwell on the money they made or saved, not the long hours you worked. They want to know how you helped them, not how tired you were.

If you employ these guidelines your chances are very good.

Your attitude, performance and all of the evidence support your request. It would be risky for them to say "no" to such a high-quality employee.

Ask

As stated earlier, bosses say the primary reason that employees do not get raises is they do not ask for them. Therefore, the employee must take the responsibility for securing his/her own raises. The only way to do that is to ASK! Common sense says the worst thing that happens is you end up right where you started, but there are several more favorable possibilities. Here are the most likely ones:

If the boss wants to "think about it" ask her when you can expect her answer. If you don't tie this down she may forget and you will drive yourself nuts, wondering if she forgot you.

If the answer is "no," ask if the boss will reconsider at a later time. It is a lot easier for people to make commitments when there is no immediate pressure. If they agree to reconsider at a later date, ask them what they need from you and put it in writing for them. Make a clear signature-line and ask them to sign the "understanding."

If you strike out completely, and end up with no gain and no potential for one, you have four options: 1) you can graciously learn to live with it; 2) you can stay there and try to change the boss's mind, which may not even be possible; 3) you can look for something else; and 4) you can stay there and become bitter (unfortunately there are millions of people wasting their lives in this type of situation).

If you do get the raise, be grateful, but not gushy. Try to do even better to begin earning your next one.

It does not take a brain surgeon to figure out that one of the best ways to get ahead financially is to get a raise, but it is foolish to expect somebody to hand it to you. Therefore, it is your responsibility to earn it and ask for it.

In the end, any job is worth a sincere effort because it might assist you to climb employment ladders. Anything less is *flushing* money down the drain, which is exactly what we want to avoid.

SELF-EMPLOYMENT

"Formal education will make you a living;
self-education will make you a fortune."
—Jim Rohn

In 1975, Bill Gates didn't know he was destined to become "the" Bill Gates. The same concept holds true for Ted Turner, Carrie Underwood, Donald Trump, Oprah and me. Furthermore, there are many millions of other people just like the ones mentioned. Each one of them started out on a fantastic journey without really knowing where they would end up. All of them were essentially self-employed.

Self-employed people would rather rely upon themselves than outsiders. They are more interested in accomplishments than comfort and they are well rewarded for their successes. There are very few employees who can match that level of financial fulfillment. Fortunately, you don't have to be Bill Gates to gain substantial benefits from self-employment.

Just about anybody can be successful at self-employment. In my own neighborhood there have been plenty of kids who have set up shop in one way or the other. Some of them shovel snow, mow lawns, paint houses and baby sit. One time, I paid two young girls $5 for a glass of warm and sticky lemonade, just because I wanted to reward their effort of setting up a stand.

Our own kids were sure to get in on the action. One year, when they were about 16 years old, a massive and heavy snowstorm hit our community in late spring. Monster trees and limbs were all over the ground. They joined forces with some classmates and borrowed a large hauling trailer; then they went door-to-door getting jobs hauling off the branches and cleaning up the messes. Each one of them made several hundred dollars a day, fully six times as much as their peers who held jobs delivering pizzas and flipping burgers.

I share all of this with you to illustrate that the tent of self-employment includes many possibilities, even for children. We will discuss a few other worthy examples that might be better suited to you in a moment, but before we do that, let's first examine why this topic is so important in the first place. Here are some of the primary reasons:

Taxes - In an earlier chapter of this book, we identified taxes as one of the worst ways we flush money down the drain. You may recall that it is not uncommon for half of a person's income to go to taxes. Self-employment affords you all sorts of tax deductions so that you can use the money you are currently giving to the IRS for your own endeavors. For example, if you set up a maintenance company, you will probably need a pick-up truck. Everything you do in that truck, in the line of work, provides tax deductions. Anytime you acquire new tax deductions, you have the potential to get back a tax refund of 30-40 percent of every dollar you write off. That is a huge wad of cash for the side pocket in your purse.

Fulfillment - You can work on something you like to do. For example you might like traveling or photography or riding horses. Since you already enjoy these things anyway, why not figure out a way to get paid for your knowledge?

Planning - You can take income or claim expenses at times that matter the most to you.

Flexibility - You set your own hours. If you enjoy what you do, it even gets to the point that what you do does not even seem like "work." Take off as much time as you want. Work overtime if you want to take advantage of your momentum.

Compensation -You can hire your spouse or kids and provide them with nice financial rewards, such as group health insurance, retirement plans or paid vacations. You can also shift the income to people in a lower tax bracket.

Achieve Potential - Under ordinary employment conditions, your advancement opportunities are limited, but the people above are fine examples of how much potential there is for those who remove the traditional shackles of working for others.

Decision Making - If you are tired of working for people who can't seem to tell one foot from the other, self-employment will enable you to do things your way.

If you are a risk/reward type of person, then self-employment might be the best situation for you, but before you jump in with both feet, be certain to think it through. Just because you can make good tacos is no assurance you can run a Mexican restaurant. Then there is the overhead—rent, utilities, health insurance and so forth. And if you lack the people skills to deal with employees or the public, you might just be setting yourself up for frustration.

So you see, running your own business is not a guarantee of success. It can be a major and risky undertaking. Furthermore, it is frequently suggested that 90 percent of all new businesses fail within the first year. The key here is to figure out what you can do to get the benefits of self-employment without all of the risks, and there are lots of ways to do that.

To begin with you don't really have to make an enormous commitment to get the advantages of self-employment. Perhaps you can start out smaller and build a steady clientele. You might be able to set up a home-based Internet business and avoid a lot of overhead. You might simply write a book or make a DVD to sell online.

Here are some of the simple, low-cost things that people I know have done:

Chris has set up a door-to-door dry-cleaning service in the downtown area. He has taught his clients to keep more than one set of clothes at work; then he saves them trips to the dry cleaners. He does not even own a dry-cleaning business. He just provides a delivery service. He has quite a few regulars and all he needs is a van.

Several people have written books (What I Learned, Where I Traveled, How To, etc.) and have self-published those books or converted them to electronic versions and sold them online.

Kim gives online seminars to women who want to run their own businesses. Among other things, she teaches them how and why they should carve out a niche.

David set up a business that hosts Web sites.

One company packages candy and trail-mixes and other munchies. They have routes where they visit businesses in the late mornings and late afternoons offering their goodies to hungry office workers.

Three fellows set up an apartment painting business. They call exclusively on property managers who routinely have many places that need to be painted.

Matt is mechanical, so he buys his own used soda pop machines as well as washers and dryers and puts them in apartment communities.

Pam is a professional photographer. She enjoys those online networking sites like Facebook and a lot of people see samples of her work and call her when their needs arise.

Smart people buy items from surplus dealers or on eBay, then resell them in smaller quantities.

Bob sells specialty information to Realtors. He visits real estate chat rooms to promote his products.

I have known people who have sold pottery, Christmas trees, fireworks, houseplants and vegetables along the side of the road.

I once met a fellow who bought leftovers from garage sales for pennies on the dollar and then resold those items at a flea market.

Mark has played guitar in rock bands.

Dan has an incredible logging company.

I have also known dozens of people who have taken up more industrious endeavors such as running restaurants, sign painting shops, a packaging store, real estate offices, law firms, plumbing companies, property management companies, landscaping companies and the like. They did not all work out but most of them made a very good living, while several became millionaires.

So you see, self-employment can be very profitable. But if you ask these people for other reasons why they like self-employment, you would hear a lot about their lifestyle. Self-employed people are their own bosses. They have much more freedom. They decide for themselves how much vacation they want.

In my own case, I have never in my life gotten a job out of the newspaper or made up a resume. Those are the types of things perpetual employees and college graduates do. On the few occasions when I worked for somebody else, I even created those jobs. I went to companies when they did not have openings and convinced them they ought to hire me. I kept calling them back and insisting that they needed me because I could make them more profit. When a job showed up, I got the call because of my spunk. People with great resumes never even heard about those jobs.

Regardless of whether I held a traditional job or not, I have almost always had some sort of self-employment gig going on, at least "on the side." I have started a painting company, run a property management company, sold soap products for an Amway-type organization, opened several tropical plant stores, worked full-time as a Realtor for nearly 25 years, been a real estate investor, designed toys, written ads for *The National Enquirer* to sell informational brochures, hosted a radio call-in program, sold firewood, sold, owned and operated vending machines, and written books. I have purchased all sorts of things on eBay and from surplus dealers, just to resell them. I have bought and sold coins, silver, foreign money, baseball cards and penny stocks, all with the intent of making a profit. I sell products and information on the Internet. I also have helped many other people to pursue similar dreams of their own.

When I opened my own painting company or obtained a real estate license or any of these other things, I didn't seek anybody else's approval. I acquired hundreds of rental properties and nobody cared what my employment history was. Sometimes I made a lot of money, sometimes not. But I always had a lot of freedom and great tax benefits and retired before my 50th birthday.

A Closer Look at the Tax Angle

I keep bringing up the tax matter because it is so important. If you can take the money you are giving to the IRS and redirect that money into the pursuit of a profit, you have a wonderful opportunity that employees do not have.

Let's take a look at two people to observe how this works out. Earlier I mentioned a maintenance person who needs a pick-up truck. Let's compare him to somebody else who buys a similar truck just because he wants one, but is not self-employed. To keep numbers simple, we will suppose they both pay $10,000 for their trucks. Let's examine just how substantial the tax benefits might be.

To begin with, the fellow who is not self-employed has to earn roughly $15,000 on his job to buy his truck. That is because he is faced with income tax, FICA and other expenses before he has any take-home pay with which to buy the vehicle. But the self-employed person does not pay income tax and FICA on earnings until after all of his deductions are taken into consideration, including the truck.

As far as actual costs are concerned, there was some sales tax when those trucks were purchased, say $600. The self-employed fellow gets to write off the sales tax (and gets 30-45 percent of it back, in income tax savings), but the other guy does not. The same holds true for new tires, license plates, oil changes, gasoline, insurance and all of the other expenses necessary to keep that truck in working order.

Then there is the fact that the self-employed fellow gets to take a depreciation allowance for his truck. In many cases, that amounts to 50 cents per mile, or more. If both drivers put 15,000 miles per year on their trucks, the self-employed guy deducts $7,500 from his taxable income (15,000 miles times 50 cents each) and ends up paying less income tax. If he is only in the 33 percent tax bracket, he pays $2,500 less in income taxes than the fellow who gets no such income tax savings.

All of these deductions are limited to the actual time the truck was in use for business purposes. For example, the maintenance man does not get mileage deductions for trips to church or camping in his truck. But that still leaves a bunch of room for write-offs.

In the end, the maintenance fellow may get back 75 percent of his $10,000 in income tax savings, leaving him with a net cost of $2,500 for his truck. The other buyer paid an extra $5,000 in the first place because he had to earn $15,000 and pay his income taxes out of that, before he had enough money left over to buy the same truck.

The bottom line is one guy has to earn $15,000 to buy the truck, but the self-employed person only has to earn $2,500 to get the same truck. That leaves him with a ton of money that he would have otherwise given to the IRS. He can then save and invest that same money in other ways.

Pick-up trucks are not the only expenses to write off. Perhaps you want to write a book about rest stops on the interstate highway system. Some of your travel may be deductible and send you a nice refund at income tax time. What if you set up an in-home, online business selling hand-made pottery? A great deal of your pottery tools, the computer, your printer and office space can provide deductions, which in turn let you keep and use a lot of money you would have otherwise sent to the tax man. You might even be able to write off such things as health insurance premiums or some of your entertainment expenses.

You do not need to be a big business to get these benefits. You just have to be sincerely trying to make a profit. It all boils down to "intent." Naturally, I am not trying to tell you to cheat on your taxes. I am just suggesting that you use self-employment as a means to cut your taxes whenever possible. Obviously, you should have a discussion with your own tax expert before you embark on this journey, but I am certain you can find a way to keep some of your dollars through one endeavor or another if you just do a little homework.

As we discussed in previous chapters, employees and college graduates have limited upside potential, but for the self-employed person, the potential earnings are unlimited. College graduates work for entrepreneurs, not the other way around.

Our country owes a great deal of its success to people who believe in themselves. Do you have the temperament and the discipline necessary to be self-employed? Are you tired of *flushing* away your tax dollars and opportunities? Do you want your own little piece of the greatness that America offers? If so, I wholeheartedly recommend that you always have some sort of self-employment endeavor in your life. Who knows, you might even become the next Bill Gates.

OTHER CAREER PATHS

We know that one of the worst ways to *flush* money down the drain is to work for less money than we are worth. It can be a waste of funds to go to college and then accept some job that does not require or acknowledge that schooling. It can be just as wasteful to pursue jobs that require college diplomas if they don't pay any more than other jobs that are easier to obtain. Likewise, it is not financially smart to flip burgers if you are qualified to be the manager of a McDonald's franchise.

Do not misunderstand me. There is nothing wrong with earning beneath your potential if you are doing something that brings you genuine happiness or peace, or if it is really what you want to do. So happiness trumps dollars, but that does not mean we should be oblivious to our earning power.

There are many people who want some advanced training but don't think traditional college is well suited to them because of the cost or time involved. Here are some other options for those folks to consider:

Trade Schools - Trade schools offer high quality, concentrated training, which can usually be completed in 18-24 months. In addition, the cost is much lower than a 4- to 5-year degree at a college, and students know exactly what field they are going into when they complete their training. There are literally hundreds of options, but a few examples include Aviation Mechanics, Computer Science, Visual Arts, Beauty College, Truck Driving, Culinary Arts, Health Industry, Home Inspectors and Veterinarian

Assistant. You can get a complete list of options with a quick Internet search of "types of trade schools." Lots of these schools have financial aid programs that make this an affordable option. Before you enroll in one of these programs, be sure you verify the job opportunities that are available, as well as the pay scale. Don't forget that these schools are in the business of selling information, just like traditional colleges and universities, so they need students and tend to oversell their products. Anyway, trade schools can offer a nice shortcut to some higher-paying jobs if you do your homework.

Apprenticeships - You might be amazed at how much money a good plumber, sign painter, furnace repairman or a carpet installer can make. Most of these professions, and many others like them, have an apprenticeship program wherein the new workers enjoy advancement as they gain experience and knowledge. Most of the time the experience gained is "on the job" rather than in the classroom. They are frequently entangled with unions, which can be a blessing or a curse. For example, union workers tend to have scheduled pay raises and fairly good benefits, but individual members usually cannot advance any faster than anybody else, even if they are better workers. If you want to learn a trade and get paid while you are doing it, an apprenticeship program could be a good fit. Once again you should do a quick online search of the possibilities. But before you embark on this journey, consider that some professions tend to go through peaks and valleys. A good example would be the construction trades, so a furnace repairman might have more steady work than a furnace installer.

Internships - Internships are "tweeners." There are some "on the job" qualities to them and they are similar to schooling because the intern is learning the ins and outs of the business. Students frequently hold these positions in the summer. They are fairly common in the legal profession, as well as in the medical, political, technology, accounting and engineering fields. They usually only last a few months and they sometimes offer a small paycheck, called a stipend. They are a good way to gain some experience and find out if you like a profession without making a costly, life-long commitment to it. As in the previous examples, the Internet is your friend for finding a full range of possibilities.

The Third Sector - There are three primary sectors to the work force: the business or private sector, the government sector, and the nonprofit sector, also known as the community sector, voluntary sector, or civic sector.

For our purposes, the first two sectors are fairly similar in that they offer traditional jobs, but nonprofit organizations are different. They offer good jobs, excellent training and other compensation in the form of personal gratification. One of my pals went into the Peace Corps for a couple of years. When he got out he knew so much about two other countries he put together a life-long career bringing the blessings of America to people there and all over the globe. Third sector organizations include Vista (a domestic Peace Corps), AmeriCorps, Mormon missions, Boys and Girls clubs, The United Way, Make a Wish Foundation, Haiti Relief Fund, Habitat for Humanity, The Franciscans, The International Rescue Committee and The Red Cross. There can be lots of travel if that appeals to you. There is always a need for fundraisers and they can make a very handsome living. There are also trade journals that need to be assembled, and plenty of office jobs. If you want to serve humanity in this way, it is very honorable and gratifying work.

Military - Depending on the circumstances, this can be an excellent career option. But before you go throwing yourself at an enlistment officer, you had better understand a few things. For example, the military is not the private sector. They do not have to play fair. There is no obligation to accept anybody. If a recruiter offers you a specific position, I suggest you get it in writing. In addition, some people are surprised to learn that the military will not usually overlook other social woes. For example, enlistees may not be single parents and they may not have too many dependents, a criminal record or severe credit problems. The military is not a path to citizenship. Furthermore, there are plenty of qualifications to get in, including age, schooling and citizenship requirements. There are height and weight requirements and each enlistee must pass a physical. If all of that is acceptable to you, then this could be a good way to get you on your feet and establish some basic discipline in your life, both of which can help your financial situation throughout your life.

For our purposes (maximizing your income over a lifetime), I suggest you seek some sort of military duty (your job) that is also useful in society, for example, law enforcement, computer science, construction, working on air fields, operating heavy equipment, transportation, mechanics, medicine, maintenance, and any kind of management, such as kitchens, offices, or warehouses. Your local recruitment office will have many more choices for you to consider. The bottom line is this can be a good way to spend a few years, learn some valuable skills and habits and serve your country at the same time.

People who languish in employment that is beneath their capabilities are *flushing* enormous amounts of money down the drain. Most people have plenty of options to improve their financial situation if they just know where to look. It does not matter whether you are coming out of high school or are already employed. We have covered the ways that you can rise to higher levels. It is my goal to show you how you can maximize monetary compensation and thereby improve other phases of life.

There are so many fulfilling opportunities in America it is a major shame to languish beneath our potential, just because we never really know what the options are.

FOOD, CLOTHING
AND OTHER GOODS

Here is a little brain teaser for you: Why is a coupon for one dollar worth more than a real dollar that you earn? The answer is at end of this chapter.

I hate paying retail price for almost anything. I guess I owe that stingy attitude to my mother. She was the queen of good deals. She frequented all sorts of stores, clipped coupons and gathered goodies like a magnet attracts steel filings. It was a sort of game to her. When it came to bargain hunting, Shirley surely would have been declared an "all-pro" if there was such a designation. By the time she passed away, she had socked away a surprising amount of money to pass on to my six sisters and me, all because she did not *flush* her resources down the drain.

In this day of computers, eBay and affordable shipping rates, there are even more opportunities for bargain hunting than there were in years gone by. By taking smart buying seriously, you can save thousands of dollars every year, and sometimes even tens of thousands. You can even learn how to get a fair amount of your food and clothing for FREE! Here are some areas in which we can routinely save a lot of money, and thereby stop *flushing* precious resources down the drain.

Clothing

Shortly after my friend Heather had her first baby, she

219

figured out a great idea for buying baby clothes. By that time, she had already become aware of two undeniable facts: 1) her daughter, Abbie, was growing quickly; and 2) children's clothes are expensive. Those ideas led her to check out the category of children's clothing on eBay. Some people bought close-out items and were reselling brand-new individual articles and outfits. Others had so many clothes (probably gifts from Grandma) that the kids just never wore them all. So moms were selling the unused items to pick up a few dollars. But Heather quickly discovered that the biggest bargains of all were in the used clothing section, where she found some designer brands for a fraction of what they cost new. Before long she also stumbled upon some larger lots which various sellers packaged up after their children outgrew them.

Heather ended up buying her daughter a fantastic wardrobe of designer clothing, and nobody could ever tell that the clothes had already been worn a few times. Heather had her second and final child, a son, about two years later. By that time, Baby Abbie had outgrown her early clothes so Heather put them back on eBay and recovered nearly all of her money. Naturally she repeated the pattern for her son.

This smart mom figured out how to dress her children in designer wardrobes for nearly nothing. Some of the lessons from Heather's story are: 1) new clothes are only new until somebody wears them once and used clothes are a lot cheaper, so buy used clothes in the first place; 2) buy clothes out of season; 3) buy in bulk for extra discounts; 4) buy high-quality used clothes; and 5) you can recover most or all of your money on eBay or at garage sales.

Heather's kids aren't the only ones who enjoy designer clothes at discount prices. Sharon loves to shop at secondhand stores for pricey attire. She tells me she gets all sorts of great deals and a couple times a year the retailers have a close-out sale (why don't they call it "clothes out" sale?) that she especially likes. I agree with these astute women. As mentioned earlier, when people wear an outfit, just once, it is used anyway. Therefore, everybody is wearing used clothes practically all of the time. Heather and Sharon are smart consumers who simply figured how to dress extremely well for pennies on the dollar. Way to go, ladies.

Food

The chances are high that I pay less for nearly everything in a grocery store than you do. When I was a young man, I worked for several years in various retail food stores, mostly in the produce departments. It did not take long to figure out that there were always some incredible deals to be had in those stores. For example, if there was a substantial snowstorm on one day, many people could not get to the store. The next day, the meat department would have to grind their steaks into high-quality burger and mark it 30 percent off, just to get it out of there. Once in a while they would even have a side-of-beef sale. Then there were the Thanksgiving turkeys, St. Patrick's Day corned beef, Easter hams, 4th of July hot dogs and countless other bargains. My mother's fine example taught me how to seize these situations. Whenever the deal was good enough, I would simply find out how long an item would hold in a freezer and buy enough of that item to last me throughout that length of time.

To this day, I still buy 6-8 small turkeys at Thanksgiving when they are just a few dollars each. Likewise I stock up on the other items when the time is right. As a result, we have turkey several times a year and never pay retail price for them or other meat items. The same holds true for produce items, frozen foods, canned goods and toiletries. When the opportunity presents itself, I strike big.

One time I got disposable razors for a few cents each because the retailer was reworking its shelves. The usual price is about 40 cents per blade. I bought a 15-year supply for myself and several additional cases for the homeless shelter.

There are other ways to get incredible bargains from stores. They usually have mark-down sections for the produce, bakery or meat items that they want to move that day. These items are of good quality if eaten within 24 hours or frozen for future use. In the case of produce, most fruits are actually at their very best when they no longer pass the eye test. That is usually the very day of the mark-down.

I also recommend that you watch the weekly newspaper or online store ads. One of my favorite techniques revolves around the timing of the weekly ads. If the ads come out on Wednesday, I like to go on that day and buy enough of the featured items to last us through the week, but when they have especially appealing sales, I also go back on the last day of the ad cycle to stock up for several months. Lots of times, they run out of the better items and give out rain checks that can be used at a later time, which enables me to extend the ad well into the future. As a matter of fact, that very thing happened this week when large boxes of strawberries were one dollar each. They ran out on the last day and I got three different rain checks for 10 boxes each. We will be munching on fantastic low-cost strawberries for the next couple months.

Retail stores sometimes sell items at a modest loss, just to get people to come visit them. Soda pop and fresh produce are among the possibilities. Finally, be sure to watch for coupons in newspapers, magazines and mailings. Many manufacturers often have coupons on their Web sites. You can even buy them on eBay if you want to. If you pay attention, some of the stores will double or triple the coupons on selected days.

Heather, whom I mentioned earlier, just came to grips with the bargains that can be found at grocery stores. Here is a recent email she sent me regarding her observations:

"I feel like an idiot for paying retail for groceries all those years. Anyone can very easily chop 20 to 30 percent off of their grocery budget by simply shopping the sales and being willing to go to 2 or 3 stores per week. You can easily save 50 percent or more if you do that and clip coupons, and 70 percent or more if you combine the coupon with the sale. It's not rocket science, but it is time consuming and I can see why some people wouldn't want to bother with it but it's worth it to me. And after 2 months of doing it, I find it kind of fun."

A person can also get food bargains when going out to dinner. You can obtain coupon books or watch for special promotions. Some places have discounts for seniors or children or simply offer reduced prices on certain days of the week. You can also get some good coupons from Restaurant.com. As of this writing they do all of their marketing on eBay. But they frequently sell a ten dollar coupon for just three bucks. Finally, if you want to take this food-savings concept seriously, I suggest you get a freezer (look for a used one on Craigslist or in the newspaper) and a vacuum sealer.

The other day we found in the back of our freezer a package of high-quality hamburger that I sealed and froze more than three years ago. It was 99 cents a pound. We cooked it up, added some fresh sliced pineapple (one dollar each) and sprinkled it all with teriyaki sauce. We enjoyed fabulous Hawaiian burgers at bargain basement prices. There was no hint of freezer burn or any other imperfections in the burger. By buying things in bulk, you will recover your money for freezers and vacuum sealers very quickly.

Other Products and Services

There are many other bargains to be had at your local retail outlets. For example, if you visit places like Wal-Mart or Target immediately after Christmas they practically give away wrapping papers, tree lights, decorations, ornaments and the like. By buying them then for the next season, you will pay no more than half as much for these items as what other shoppers pay. Similar savings can be enjoyed after other holidays, such as Valentine's Day, Easter and Halloween.

One September I bought a half-dozen picnic tables from

Home Depot for 67 percent off of the retail price. The next spring, Home Depot raised the price of picnic tables back to the full price. That is when I took my cheaper tables to our apartment buildings for the tenants to enjoy.

Speaking of Home Depot, my nephew once bought a bunch of very large snow-covered deciduous trees there in December. He picked up more than fifty trees for $5 each to landscape his yard. Earlier that season, other people paid up to $100 each for the exact same inventory. My nephew planted all of those trees when there was three inches of snow on the ground. The next spring, his yard came to life for a tiny fraction of what less-prudent consumers had to pay.

The point of the two previous paragraphs is to shop out of season. In these cases we hit the garden department when everybody else was done with summer and buying snow shovels instead (guess when we buy snow shovels and winter clothes?). Naturally, I recommend you get in the habit of checking out eBay and Craigslist, especially in the off-season. I also find garage sales and trips to the flea market to be entertaining and productive. When it comes to buying items out of season, you should buy sweatshirts in the early summer, swim suits in the early winter, garden seeds in the fall and most other items when nobody else wants them. The savings can be phenomenal.

Once you become an effective bargain hunter at the retail outlets, it just spills over into other areas of your life. For example, a few years back, my wife and I built a small log home in the mountains. To furnish it, we attended several auctions. We ended up buying some very nice large area rugs, plus two complete bedroom sets, two very nice large display cabinets and lots of really cool decorative items. I suppose somebody else would never buy used furniture, but as soon as they take their brand-new furniture home, it also becomes "used," so there really isn't much difference. By the time we finished decorating that property we saved at least $5,000 just for learning to enjoy auctions.

In other situations you can get good discounts just for bothering to ask. I recently made a phone call to my cable company. I explained to the service representative that I had been noticing quite a few TV commercials promoting satellite dishes. I told the nice lady that it just makes sense for me to look into getting a dish. I then asked her if there was anything they could do to lower my bill. She quickly advised me that she could drop our rates by $9 per month for the next six months, after which time the monthly fee would return to the current level. Before we hung up she apologized because she could not reduce it more.

Another friend of mine employed the same tactic and got six months of free premium movie channels. The same opportunities are all over the place. Many merchants will lower the price right on the spot. All we have to do is ask. Here is a good non-offensive question you can ask of the people with whom you do business, "What is the best price you can give me if I buy this item right now?" You will be surprised how many times you get an unexpected discount.

As I said at the beginning of this chapter, I hate to pay retail price for almost anything, and now you know why: It usually is just not necessary. The routine items like food and clothing offer all sorts of bargains and the occasional big-ticket items that we acquire offer even better opportunities. Now let me share with you why this is even more important that you might first think. The answer can be found it the trivia question I asked you at the very beginning of this chapter. Here it is again.

Question:

Why is a coupon for one dollar (or any other discount) worth more than a real dollar that you earn?

Answer:

When you earn a dollar, the government takes away about one-third of it for taxes, as well as another 7 percent for FICA.

Therefore, your earned dollar only has about 60 cents in buying power. But a one-dollar coupon, or discount, is worth a full dollar in buying power. Therefore, a one-dollar coupon is worth more than any earned dollar.

Furthermore, coupon clipping is the only household chore for which you can get paid. It just makes sense.

It is not difficult to save thousands of dollars a year with coupons and discounts. Failure to take advantage of these tips is simply to *flush* too many valuable dollars away that can be saved and invested for a comfortable retirement. This chapter proves you do not have to earn extra money to get wealthy; you just have to use the money you already make in smarter ways.

RENTING

If you will pardon an obvious understatement, evictions are no picnic for tenants. Sometimes they have genuinely fallen on hard times, but usually they get into the predicament because of poor money management practices.

Regardless of the genesis of the situation, the reader can avoid it (or help others to avoid it) by understanding what a lease is and what it is not. As usual, knowledge is power.

The Basics

A lease is not always in writing. For example, if you are 20 years old and living in your parents' home, you may be considered a guest or you might be on a verbal lease. It all depends on whether you are paying anything of value for your right to live there.

There are other landlords who never do use written leases; however, certain laws still apply to oral leases. Sophisticated owners and most property managers prefer written ones. I also prefer that leases and related documents, such as pet deposits, security agreements and so forth, be in writing.

If a potential landlord does offer you a lease, it is important that you read all of it and all papers to make certain you understand exactly what you are agreeing to. However, do not assume that the lease is cast in stone. Some of the details might be negotiable and you have no way of knowing unless you engage in a conversation about the issues at hand. For example, one of my friends recently asked me to help her when she wanted to rent a condominium. The owner offered either a six-month or a one-year lease, at the tenant's option.

I took my friend aside and explained if she takes the one-year lease, she is locked into a property that she may not like. On the other hand, if she accepted a six-month lease and wanted to stay after that, they could raise her rent at the end of the first six months.

Then I asked the rental agent if the company would let my friend rent for six months, with an option to extend for another six months at the same rate. The showing agent said, "No, they only do one or the other." I asked her to call the owner and ask if they would reconsider. You guessed it. They accepted my friend's proposal and she got the best of both worlds.

Finally, do not walk away from an active lease. There may be dire consequences. Even unwritten month-to-month leases carry certain responsibilities regarding giving notice, maintaining the property, etc. In the most extreme case you might be liable for the rent for many months.

Other Worthy Points

Here are some other things you should know about renting and leases:

With a few exceptions, the fair housing laws forbid landlords from discriminating against persons based on race, color, religion, national origin, sex, age, or family status, as well as mental and physical disabilities. Furthermore, some states recognize additional categories, including, marital status or sexual orientation. Persons with disabilities are usually allowed to keep helper-pets, such as seeing-eye dogs, even if the property has a "no pets" policy. Landlords may not require different damage deposits or deny access to property or treat people differently based on these classifications. If you suspect you have been discriminated against because you belong to one of these categories, immediately contact the appropriate authorities.

Generally speaking, the landlord owes you a place that is habitable. That means the furnace, sewer system, electricity and water are all working as expected. But if your child flushes a doll down the toilet and clogs the drain, that is your responsibility.

The landlord is not ordinarily responsible for telling you about matters that might stigmatize the property. This can include things like the fact that the tenant before you had the HIV AIDS virus, it has been rumored that a ghost lives in the attic, devil worshipers once lived there, the former owner was assaulted in the property, or somebody died in a gunfight. If you have concerns like those mentioned, you should check with the police and ask the neighbors about the history of the unit.

If the property was constructed on or before 1978, the landlord is supposed to give you information about the consequences of living with lead-based paint, but just in case they forget to give you the literature, please take this notice that such paint can be dangerous if accidently consumed. This usually happens if an infant chews on a paint chip.

Verify the property condition when you move in. If the landlord does not provide a "property condition" form, be sure to take DATED pictures of any imperfections or dirty areas in the property when you move in. It may also be useful to have a friend also note any damages, in case you need a witness in court. Once you have such evidence the best thing to do is get the owner/landlord to sign a form of your own, acknowledging any damages so that you are not held responsible for them upon your departure. But if you fail to do this you may get stuck for repair or clean-up costs, even if you leave the property in better condition than you found it.

If something goes wrong with the property after you move in, such as a water faucet starts leaking, contact the manager right away. If you do not and further damage occurs you may be responsible for negligence.

The landlord may have reasonable access to your property. That means with sufficient notice (24-48 hours), or in any emergency, or if they have good reason to believe you have abandoned the property, or if they are instructed to do so by a court.

If there is someone down the hall who is making too much noise or breaking other house rules, contact the manager. If the problem persists they may need to evict the tenant, which might take a month or longer.

If you suspect illegal activities or violence in neighboring properties, contact the police. The landlord may not have any discretion or authority in these matters.

There is a difference between a co-tenant and a guest. If your roommate is not paying rent and you are unhappy with the arrangement, you do not have to evict him or her. You can just ask him or her to leave. If he or she refuses to leave, you can have the police ask him or her to move out. However, if the person helps pay the rent or utilities or any other related expenses and you want him or her out, you may have to evict him or her and abide by the same laws that any other landlord would.

In some states, the landlord must return damage deposits, with interest, upon termination of the lease.

In most cases the landlord has a limited amount of time, such as thirty days, to return your deposit after the lease term has expired. Courts can punish landlords who fail to refund deposits in a timely manner.

If the landlord withholds any part of your damage deposit, he/she must give you written notice of how much money was withheld and for what. You may be charged for unpaid rent, repairs and cleaning beyond normal wear and tear.

If you fall behind in your rent or breach your lease terms, you should have an opportunity to bring your rent current or correct the breach before the landlord can remove your personal property from the rental property.

The landlord's insurance policies do not ordinarily protect your property in the event of some sort of fire or leaking roof or other accident. If you want to protect your furniture and other property, you can obtain renter's insurance for a nominal cost.

When you lease a home or condominium, ask the landlord if they will apply any of your rent payments as option money toward the possibility of eventually buying the property. If so, what are the terms and conditions?

If you do enter into a lease with an option-to-buy arrangement, be certain that you get a neutral real estate agent or appraiser to give you a good indication of the property's value. If the owner sets an unrealistic price for the property and also charges you extra money for the option you might be paying too much money for a hopeless situation.

As you can tell, there are a lot of things a smart tenant needs to know. This is not all of it, but it ought to keep you out of most of the common problems. The most important thing I can tell you is read your lease and related documents before you sign them. It will be a lot easier to stay out of trouble if you actually know what the rules are.

HOME OWNERSHIP

I teach a continuing education course to Realtors about investing in real estate. In that course I make the point that, generally speaking, home prices tend to go up. This is due in large part to the government's basic objective of maintaining a steady and modest inflation rate of around 1 percent.

The Feds like a small inflation rate for a couple of reasons. First, the U.S. government is the largest debtor in the world and if we can pay back our debt, over time, with cheaper dollars it lowers the effective cost of borrowing the money. Second, if the price of everything goes up, then more and more taxpayers will find themselves in higher income-tax brackets (even though they are performing the exact same services). This "bracket creeping" generates more income for the IRS.

State and local governments also like property values to rise. The states charge property taxes based on property values and the local governments benefit when home values increase because many homeowners will refinance their property and spend the money. That creates revenue from sales taxes, stimulates the local economy and creates additional jobs.

The Feds manipulate inflation by determining how many new goods and services are being created and then they release just a tiny bit more new money into circulation than those goods would justify. The excess supply of money tends to move prices upward.

All of this ties directly into real estate because inflation causes building materials to get more expensive, and builders have to raise the price of new homes to recoup their expenses. As those homes get more expensive, existing homes become more appealing, by comparison. The extra attention on the used homes puts upward pressure on their prices.

However, just because the government implements such practices does not assure that the desired result will occur everywhere at the same time or to the same degree. In other words, not all areas are created equal. Some communities have not seen increases in home values for decades. Other areas experience fairly radical swings in value. All of this makes it difficult to tell people if it is a good time or not to buy a home in their particular area. But if you plan on staying in your home for a long time, things should work out, even if you are buying at a relatively high price.

As I write this (2013), it appears to be an excellent time to buy a home in many areas, including Denver, where I am. In fact, I have been increasing my holdings because of our market dynamics. Prices have come down but stabilized, selection is good, interest rates are low and our local economy is improving. I expect this market to stay in a "buy" mode for a couple of years and other markets to follow the same path. Which markets and when depends on local and national factors.

So I do not want to say it is always a good time to buy a home but I would suggest that it usually good enough, and over the long term, it usually works out very well. The bottom line is home prices tend to be like a fellow walking uphill with a yoyo. Sometimes the yoyo (home prices) will be going down, but the trend is generally up.

The Whys of Home Ownership

The investment angle is just one justification for buying a home. Here is a more complete list of reasons why people acquire their own little piece of the American dream.

Freedom from Landlords - When you own your own place,

you are the CDO (Chief Decorating Officer). If you have always wanted a pink and purple kitchen, that is the way it is going to be. If you want to accumulate junk in your back yard or have three giant dogs or leave the windows open, it is all up to you. As long as you live within the laws of the area and the rules of the community in which you live, there will be no interference in your day-to-day decisions.

Pride of Ownership - There is something cool about owning your own home. It is a lot like getting your first car, only better. It implies a sense of responsibility, and a feeling that you have "arrived." It is an adult activity that commands respect.

Lock in Payment - In the early years of home ownership, the monthly payment may be higher than what the same property would command in rent, but given typical inflationary pressures, rents will ordinarily rise. Assuming the homeowner obtains a fixed rate loan, the home payment will eventually be lower than the rent will be for that same property. Finally, the home will ultimately be paid off, leaving only the operating costs as a monthly expense. So the sooner we buy, the less we pay in lifetime housing expenses.

Tax Benefits - Interest and property taxes are deductible. That means that you will pay lower income taxes than people who earn the same amount of money as you, but do not own homes. This is a primary reason why people are willing to accept higher payments in the early years. Furthermore, many people make tax-free profits when they sell their home. A single person can pocket $250,000 in profit with no tax consequences and a married couple can make up to a half-million tax-free dollars without the government taking a share. If you should make even more than that, your profits still get preferential treatment because they are usually taxed as long-term capital gains, not as ordinary income.

Appreciation - In spite of what I told you in the beginning of this chapter, I do not ordinarily consider a home to be an investment. It is primarily a place to live without interference by others. I generally subscribe to the philosophy that any profit from an increase in your home's value ought to be left alone unless you can use it to make other profitable investments (see next point). I think it is a dangerous and bad habit to look upon home equity as an income source. I have watched countless numbers of people refinance their homes again and again to hide from the fact that they are living beyond their means. I hope you won't fall into that dangerous trap.

Valuable Financial Tool - As I just stated, I do not recommend refinancing a home to pay off consumer debt, but once you build up equity you can usually borrow against your home at a lower interest rate than you can get anywhere else. If you can borrow $50,000 from your home equity and use that money to buy a $50,000 rental condominium, you can frequently get more net profit from the condominium than the debt you have taken on; therefore, that is a good investment. Warning: I do not recommend such a strategy if you are using the equity money for riskier endeavors like opening new businesses, lending to friends or investing in speculative stocks.

Stability - As we settle into our homes, over the years, a lot of the buzz that accompanied our youth succumbs to other equally precious qualities, such as stability. There is a certain peace in having your kids in stable schools, growing your own garden, enjoying lasting relationships with good neighbors and knowing where things are kept at the local grocery store.

Extra Tips For You

Now that you know why you should buy a home, here are some other tips I have picked up after thirty years in the real estate business.

Get Tax Savings Monthly - One time I was discussing the benefits of homeownership with a young couple and we came around to the topic of tax benefits. This family was on a very tight budget and the fellow said to me, "I need everything I make now just to pay my bills, but the home payment will be higher than my rent, so I cannot justify the purchase if I have to wait until income-tax time for a tax refund." I told him all he has to do is figure out how much the tax savings will be per year and then convert that number to a monthly amount. After that, he was advised to visit the payroll department of his employer to raise the number of exemptions he claims by a sufficient amount to raise his take-home pay by the amount he needed. Thus he can add that new take-home money to what he is currently paying his landlord and use the sum to pay his mortgage payment. He bought a home for his family just a few weeks later.

Save Tens of Thousands in Interest - If you have ever seen an amortization schedule, you know that in the early months almost all of your payment goes to interest and only a small amount applies to principal (the debt). The good news is any modest amount of additional principal you pay on your loan relieves you of an enormous amount of interest in later years. You could just recompute your loan and make payments based on a shorter term such as a 15-year amortization, but the difference in the payment for the 15-year term and the 30-year term is fairly substantial. For example, the principal and interest payment on a loan of $150,000 at 6% interest and amortized over 30 years is $899 but if that same loan is amortized over 15 years the payment jumps to $1,266, which is a whopping 40 percent increase.

In most cases, new buyers have enough difficulty making ends meet when the payments are spread out over 30 years, so it is effectively impossible for them to make the higher payments of a 15-year loan. However, there's is a technique called, "next month's principal" that will enable a borrower to pay back the loan in 15 years without such a drastic increase in the monthly payment. First obtain an amortization schedule based on your loan. Each month thereafter when you make a payment, take note of the amount necessary to also pay the "next month's principal" as indicated on the amortization schedule. In the example we just cited, that would be about $140. Add that amount to your current payment and you have just chopped off a full month's interest and one payment at the end of your loan. Then scratch off the next two payments from your amortization schedule. That extra principal amount will get higher and higher each new payment cycle, but not by a lot. You should be able to adjust to the gradual increase in your payment and end up mortgage-free in fifteen years.

Prepayment - Do not prepay your loan if you cannot resist the temptation to refinance as soon as there is juicy equity to be had. Refinancing is expensive so any savings you enjoy by prepaying your loan can easily be offset by the high cost of getting the money back. I am also apprehensive about prepaying loans when interest rates seem to be trending upward and are expected to stay that way for two or more years. You may never be able to borrow money so cheaply again. It might be wiser to use your extra money to pay off credit cards or car loans instead.

Refinancing - Most people move every six years or so. If that is likely in your case, do not refinance your loan unless your lower loan payments will recover the loan costs within three years. If you expect to remain in the same property for an extended period, a longer recapture period is acceptable, but generally not more than five years. Be cautious, because a lot can happen in that time. Interest rates might drop even further or you may end up moving quicker than you expected.

There is one situation that justifies refinancing your home to pay off consumer debt. If you are absolutely certain you are not going to go out and max out your credit cards again or upgrade a car, you can use the proceeds from a new home loan to pay off credit cards and car loans. The interest rate from home loans is usually lower and it is usually deductible. Furthermore, paying off consumer debt improves your utilization rate on your credit report, which in turn improves your credit score. Therefore, this concept is acceptable once and only once. If you find yourself repeating the practice, you need to adjust your spending habits.

ARMs - If fixed interest rates are 6 percent or lower, I do not recommend Adjustable Rate Loans (ARMs). Many a good consumer has been financially destroyed by the adjustment cycle of an ARM loan. If your payments go up every six months or so for 2-3 years, you may not be able to handle it. On the other hand it is not overly difficult to budget for a steady 6 percent loan. The exception to this is when we can be fairly certain that rates are trending down and we can expect that trend to continue for a couple years. In that case, it is okay to ride the wave downward. However, as soon as it looks like rates are about as low as they can be expected to go for a few years, I suggest you grab whatever is the best fixed-rate loan at the time.

Right-Sizing - Buy the right size house. If you buy a home that is too big and expensive just because you can afford it or your ego feels gratified, you will be paying unnecessary interest expenses to service the debt and you could use that money for so many other better choices. On the other hand, if you buy too small a home, you may have to resell when your family grows, and that is also costly. However, it can sometimes be an excellent strategy to buy a very modest first home and then convert it to a rental property when you need a bigger property.

Buying for the Wrong Reason - If you are in a tumultuous relationship, do not buy a home with the idea that somehow sharing a dream home will miraculously fix the marriage. I have seen quite a few hasty moves of this nature and the people nearly always ended up calling me back to sell the home. The property usually does not rise in value enough to pay brokerage fees and closing costs, so the couple ends up adding more financial stress to an already unpleasant situation.

I could write several volumes about the importance of buying a home and the "how to's" of it all, but the objective of this book is broader. It is about the many ways that good people *flush* their money down the drain. As we have discussed, failing to own a home and misunderstanding the financial implications of such a situation can be very costly. Hopefully, you now can recognize where the major traps and opportunities are to be found.

AUTOS

Pop. Pop. Pop. Pop. Pop. Pop.

I started driving when I was fourteen years old. My dad helped me get a motor scooter, which was only slightly more glamorous than a motorized bicycle. Any sensible person would say it sounded like a popcorn machine. The gas tank was a shiny pumpkin-orange color. I thought it sounded and looked cool! My mom hated it because she was a champion worrier.

However, my dad was wiser than it first appeared. That particular scooter only ran about half the time and I spent more time tinkering with it than driving it around. On the few occasions when it did run, the engine was so small and underpowered, it did not allow me to go very fast, but that did not matter to me. As far as I was concerned, I was the king of the road.

The excitement of driving in our early years is really special, but our inexperience often leads to some very unwise financial choices. Sadly, many of us never really do learn our lesson and we make the same mistakes over and over again. For the rest of us, we can improve our financial status both in the near term and long term if we understand the automobile industry a little better. Generally speaking, it is easier to get fleeced when buying a car than selling it so this chapter has more information about that phase of a transaction. But it also includes useful particulars about trade-ins, leasing and selling.

Reality Check

Let's face it; if you are not a good negotiator, buying a car is like roughhousing with your big brother. You don't have much of a chance. Dealers know everything you know, and a lot more. There are all sorts of ways they can take advantage of your ignorance. That does not mean that all dealers are crooks, but if your dealer does happen to be a scam artist, at least you should know how to recognize it. We will explore some of their favorite tricks a little later, but first I would like to discuss the shopping experience with you.

General Practices

Regardless of whether you expect to buy a new or used vehicle, here are a few things you should consider.

An automobile should be a means to get where you need to go, not a vanity statement.

Try to approach the transaction from a logical, rather than an emotional, perspective. If you fall in love with a stereo or leather seats (or an orange gas tank), you may end up buying a lot more car than you need, and flush precious dollars down the drain.

Sales tax on a vehicle is usually determined based on where you take possession. Call your local city and state agencies to determine what the sales tax will be if you elect to have a vehicle delivered to your home and/or to your workplace. This can be higher or lower than what it would be if you took possession at the dealership. A two-percent savings on a $25,000 vehicle is $500. That is certainly worth a half-hour or so of your time.

Many urban areas require regular emission tests and the like. But if you have a second home in some other outlying area with less severe requirements, you may be better off to get the vehicle from a dealer in that area and take possession there. Thereafter you may be able to avoid the time, expense and aggravation of those emission procedures. They might also have lower taxes and lower overhead, which could mean a lower price for you.

If you determine that you will take possession at a dealership, it can easily be worth your time to call around to find out which dealers are in areas with lower sales taxes, especially if you live in a large community that has lots of dealerships. For example, I live in the metro Denver area. Boulder and Lakewood have high sales taxes, but Greeley and Brighton are much lower. Would you drive an hour away to a cross-town dealership to save $500 in sales taxes? You can bet I would.

If you expect to obtain financing, get your FICO Auto Industry Option Scores from two credit bureaus. They can be found at www.AutoCreditScores.com. Then contact your own bank or credit union and an online bank such as MyAutoLoan.com to find out what rate they will charge you for a loan based on that score. Also inquire about any and all closing and financing costs they might charge. This will help you get the very best interest rates. That interest savings can mean several hundred dollars EVERY YEAR until you pay off your car.

I recommend you sell your old car yourself or donate it before going to the dealership because dealers make their greatest profit from their trade-in programs. I do not see a need to flush all of that money away. However I realize that some people find the entire selling process to be so unpleasant they would rather take a loss than jump through the necessary hoops of taking calls, meeting strangers, etc. Other times we don't want to stick a private party with that old lemon we have been driving, so the dealer offers an acceptable way out.

If you insist on trading in a vehicle, do some research to discover its wholesale value. You can get a good idea at Kelly Blue Book (kbb.com.) Don't forget to factor in the mileage and extras, such as air-conditioning. If you do complete a transaction, it will be a lot easier to keep the numbers clear if you think in terms of trading your vehicle at wholesale for their vehicle at wholesale, and then add a "reasonable" profit for the dealer on the one he is selling (more on "reasonable" in a moment).

The transaction is more likely to go your way if the dealer is more motivated than you are. One of the worst things you can tell them is, "My old car died, and I have to get something right away." Therefore, if you do not have a vehicle that you can drive for a couple weeks, while you shop try to borrow a car from a friend so that you do not put unnecessary pressure on yourself.

When the salesman probes for some basic information, let him know you are serious about buying, but make it clear that you do not have to buy today. They know that people like that usually buy within a couple weeks and do not ordinarily come back. This motivates the salesman and dealership to lower their price as much as necessary, rather than let you slip away.

New Vehicles

By now you know that I am not a big fan of buying new vehicles because of the expensive depreciation, high sales taxes, high licensing fees, ongoing payments, high cost of insurance and the interest rates that accompany these purchases, but if you decide to buy a new car, here are some good things to know:

All dealers pay the same basic price for the vehicles. You can find out their price by checking online. A few places to check are InvoiceDealers.com, Cars.com and MyRide.com.

Depending upon your point of view, there are several different "prices" for any new car. You should be familiar with all of them. First, the Manufacturers Suggested Retail Price (MSRP) is top retail as indicated on the sticker. Dealers love buyers who actually pay that amount. Next, there is the dealer's "list" price. They may try to tell you this is what they paid for the car, but that is misleading, because there is some "fancy accounting" going on. More on that in a moment. Finally, there is the dealer's "actual cost," which is lower than the list price.

The dealers get to keep a "hold-back" fee of two to three percent of the list price on every vehicle they sell. On cheaper, entry-level cars that will be a few hundred dollars but on top-end luxury vehicles it can be a thousand dollars or more.

The dealer also gets factory kickbacks from the manufacturer. These might include year-end closeouts or other promotions, including highly profitable "loaded" cars. That is why so many of the cars on the lots have expensive extras.

When we take into consideration the hold-back fee and the manufacturer's kickbacks, a dealer can actually sell a car at below the list price and still make a handsome profit. But they will try to get more, a lot more.

Most dealers like to charge $300-600 for "dealer preparation" fees. This is strictly another profit-grab because part of the sticker price is supposed to cover this service. Ask your salesman what the philosophy is before you make any offers. Tell him if the dealer wants $500 for "preparing" a vehicle that he is supposed to prepare anyway, you will lower your offer accordingly. I would not pay more than the list price for any car that carries a dealer prep fee.

There is a similar issue with "destination" charges. Some dealers will put their own sticker on the vehicle and add an entry for transportation or destination charges. This is just another way to increase profits because the transportation fees are already built into the list price. If you pay extra for destination you are paying twice for the same service. Therefore, beware of customized stickers.

When we add the hold-back fee plus any manufacturer's factory incentives, dealer preparation fees and destination charges, the dealer can easily make $2,000 even if he sells the car at his list price. But that does not stop him from marking up the asking price even more, and that is where the MSRP comes in. As far as I am concerned, $1,500 over the dealer's actual cost is plenty of profit for entry-level vehicles (below $20,000) and $2,000 over actual cost is the maximum for any vehicle.

Once you find a model you like, ask the salesperson if the dealership has more of that model from which you can choose. You are going to do that for three reasons: First, you want to see if you like any particular car more than another. Perhaps you like the gold one or the four-door model. Second, you are finding out how much inventory they have because their motivation will vary depending on the circumstances. If they have only one or two of that model, there may be good demand for it and they may be inclined to hold firm on their prices. But if they have plenty of inventory, or if they are closing out a model, you will know not to pay more than a couple hundred dollars over the list price.

The third reason you want to look at a bunch of cars has to do with all of those extras they have on them. Dealers love to sell "loaded" cars because they often get factory incentive kickbacks, but you can actually use that against them. So, get a note pad and look on a bunch of the stickers to determine exactly how much they try to charge for the individual extras like pin stripes, upgraded tires, etc. Write down every item and its cost. Now ask yourself this question with each item, "If I already owned this vehicle and it did not have that item, would I be willing to go out and buy that item for the price on the sticker?" If you are looking at an air-conditioner and you live in Texas or Arizona the answer would most certainly be "yes," but would you pay extra for air-conditioning if you lived in Alaska? What about that fancy $400 stereo? If you already owned that car would you be willing to shell out an extra $400 for that system or would a simple factory-installed CD player or AM/FM radio do just fine? Fifteen minutes on this exercise will reveal a lot.

Once you have a good wish list, you can ask the dealer which vehicle is the closest to what you like. There is a good chance they won't have your ideal car, but you can still get a very deep discount to take one of his loaded cars. Tell the salesperson the dealership's cars are too expensive because they are loaded with things you don't want. Advise him that you intend to contact a fleet manager (these are very common, especially in larger dealerships) to special-order your vehicle. At this point, he knows he has one last chance to make a commission and will probably be inclined to remove nearly all of the profit from the extras if you will take one of his cars off the lot.

If he does not satisfy you, go home and call a fleet manager in that same dealership or a competitor, and special-order your new vehicle with the extras that you want and no others. There is no sales commission. I custom-ordered an SUV this way and saved several thousand dollars on extras that meant nothing to me. It took six weeks to get the vehicle, but there was some extra pleasure in the wait, sort of like looking forward to a vacation.

Eventually you will have to enter the negotiation process, but how much should you offer? There are several approaches:

You can do like most people and just wing it. I bet you can guess how well they do.

Another approach is to gather all of the data you can from this book and other sources and then make your wisdom known and take your chances. At least the salesman will realize that you are not a complete dummy and you will probably do okay.

If you don't have the time or desire to do all of this homework you can use a simple formula to determine how much the dealer will accept. Here is how it works. Put the number "1" in front of the first digit in the MSRP, and that is the percentage you can deduct from the MSRP.

As an example, suppose the vehicle has an MSRP price of $32,500. In that event, the first digit is a "3" so put the number "1" in front of "3" and you get "13." Therefore you can reasonably expect the dealer to accept a 13 percent discount. In this case, that means your target price would be $28,275, provided there are no dealer prep or destination fees. If you have one of those stubborn dealers who will not sell without those fees, then you will lower your target price accordingly.

Let's do another one. If the MSRP for your new luxury SUV is $50,000, the first digit in the MSRP is a "5." So put a "1" in front of the "5" and you get "15." Therefore you can reasonably expect to get about 15 percent off, or an adjusted price of $42,500. Once again, subtract for any dealer prep or destination fees. Naturally, these numbers vary among manufacturers, models, dealers and other circumstances, but they are usually in the ballpark.

My suggestion is that you avoid all of the above and use a professional buyer service. Some of them sell the cars directly to you, but others negotiate for you, as your agent. In the latter case, there really isn't much "negotiating" involved. They know the dealer's actual cost. They add a modest profit for the dealer and a fair fee for their own services (finding the vehicle and knowing what to pay) and that is your price. There are plenty of these companies so the competition forces them to be reasonable. Since there is no other overhead, such as commissions and dealer prep, it is very unlikely you will beat the deal that a professional buyer will get for you. My favorite company is CarsDirect.com. They have been around a long time. You can go to their site at any time and plug in whatever vehicle you like. They instantly show you what it will cost if you decide to use them. You do not have to provide any private information to see how it works. The only information they ask for is your zip code so that they can consider the shipping costs.

Used Vehicles

Once again, you should get your financing lined up before you go shopping. This will keep you in a position of strength and reduce the likelihood that you will fall victim to dealership financing scams.

Now, get this thought imbedded deep in your mind: Dealers do not pay more than wholesale price for any vehicle and they do not even want to pay that. If they have several similar cars, they probably bought them from a fleet of rental cars or some similar situation. They also buy blocks of cars from each other and at dealer auctions. In cases like that, they can usually buy for slightly below wholesale prices so they have plenty of bargaining room with those cars.

The dealers also get inventory from the public. Sometimes they will buy cars outright but it is more common for them to take cars in trade. If they take a private party's car in trade, the dealer's approach is to start at wholesale and deduct for needed repairs. In other words, if they take in a car that has a wholesale value of $8,000 but it needs $400 worth of tires and $600 worth of body work, they will not pay more than $7,000 for it, but they will probably try to pay you less. Expect them to say something like, "We can get cars like yours at the auction for less than you want." Whether it is true or not is debatable.

The only time a dealer will over-pay for a car is when they are taking a trade-in and they have excess profit built into the vehicle they are selling to that same customer. But in a case like that they write off any amount they overpaid to buy one car against the profit they are making on the other one they are selling; therefore, they still consider themselves to be into the trade-in vehicle at the wholesale value.

The point of all of this is the dealer pays wholesale or less for every car on the lot. Therefore it is easy to compute how much to pay, or more importantly, what NOT to pay.

At some point the salesperson may take out a "book" of some type and try to imply that it is the Bible of pricing, but don't fall for that. Those books are just "guidelines" and they do not all agree (otherwise, why have more than one?) Furthermore, they are not as current as online information. Once you have a vehicle picked out, get to a computer and check out kbb.com (Kelly Blue Book). It will give you a great indicator of value. It even takes into consideration local matters. For example a convertible will have more demand in Florida and a 4-wheel drive will be common in Montana. Add $1,000 or 12 percent, whichever is higher, to the wholesale price and it is as simple as that. It will not work every single time but most dealers are going to have a hard time turning down a respectable profit like that.

If you are buying from a private party, you can employ the same basic procedure. First get your financing lined up and then use the kbb.com site to tell you a fair "private party price." It is usually about halfway between wholesale and full retail.

Frequently, the private parties are just as difficult to negotiate with as the dealers. Some private parties need to get retail pricing because they owe so much debt against the vehicle, but that is not your fault so do not overpay them. Others are just greedy and looking for a full retail buyer. Hopefully, you won't be that person.

Furthermore, the dealers will ordinarily give you some sort of warranty, but private parties do not. In addition, the Better Business Bureau and the State Attorney offer some sort of leverage against a dealer, but they are of little value when dealing with Joe Blow.

Finally, when it comes to buying used vehicles, I have a strong preference for federal government auctions. If you are in a large metro area, there is a good possibility they are right in your neighborhood. A common one is the GSA auction. If there are very few private parties at the auction, you can usually get nice vehicles for wholesale prices. That is because your primary competition is car dealers and as we just noted, they do not pay over wholesale. So if you bid $100 higher than wholesale, there is a good chance you will be the high bidder.

You can generally assume that these vehicles are in good shape because the employees who drive them are supposed to be taking them in for regular maintenance.

In our area, most of the vehicles have less than 65,000 miles on them or they have very few miles but they are 6-7 years old. My last purchase was a seven-year old pickup with 4-wheel drive, air conditioning, automatic transmission and only 28,000 miles (it would have still been on warranty if it was younger) for

$4,700. I have been driving it for about four years now and can still get all of my money back if I want to sell it.

I have bought at least two dozen cars and trucks this way. Many were for personal use, others were helping friends and family, still others were work-trucks, and we have even purchased a fair number of them strictly for resale.

Sometimes they have other interesting items at government auctions such as large trailers, buses, ambulances or wrecked cars.

Other government agencies, as well as businesses and private parties, also sell vehicles via the auction process. The state of Colorado uses eBay's auction format to sell a lot of their vehicles.

The City and County of Denver sells all sorts of fascinating "vehicles" every year. In addition to many dozens of vans, pickups, and autos, they always have excavators, bobcats, trash trucks, dump trucks, tractors, pavers and lots of heavy equipment. One year they sold three very large fire trucks for $2,700 – FOR ALL THREE! Two of them still ran. It is a hoot to go to auctions like that, even if you don't buy anything.

One final point regarding auctions: The best bargains usually come at the very beginning and very end of the auction. In the beginning of the day, many customers arrive late and others hold back until they are familiar with the process. At the end of the day, the excitement wears off and most people already have what they came for so you may only have a couple people or dealers who will bid against you.

The bottom line is, I suggest you get online and search for any auctions in your area. At the very least, you will have a good time and you just might find an incredible deal.

Leasing

Do not fall for the "leasing gets lower payments" line. While that may be "technically" true, you will usually lose too much money in your other pockets to justify the transaction. Practically every dollar you pay under a lease is lost money. You are paying interest, depreciation, high insurance rates, and any other add-ons the dealer can get away with. For example, many people do not know to negotiate the purchase price of a leased car. Other consumers are surprised to discover if they put too many miles on the vehicle they may be penalized.

After driving a leased car for four years or so, you may be able to just hand in the keys and walk away from the deal, but you lose the signing fee and all other money you have paid. All of that can easily be tens of thousands of dollars.

Leases usually allow you to buy the vehicle at the end of the lease term, but if you think you might want to do that, I suggest you just buy it in the first place and avoid *flushing* so many dollars down the drain along the way.

Finally, leasing serves a purpose if you want a new vehicle every few years and few or no maintenance problems. You also get fairly low upfront fees and monthly payments, but all of that gratification comes with a very high cost: Namely, you never get out from under payments. Before you jump into a lease, call your tax preparer and determine if you are one of those rare persons who will really benefit from a lease. If not, buy the car or, better yet, look for something cheaper.

Trade-Ins

We have touched on this a little already but there are still a couple more points to be made. I have heard people brag about how much money they got for their old clunker when they traded it in, but those people are naive. I can assure you that the dealer got the best of them anyway.

One dealer in our town specializes in this over-payment approach. They offer $3,500 for any car you can push, pull or tow into their lot. Ask yourself, "Why would they do that?" The answer is they have an enormous profit built into the vehicle they are trying to sell.

Be especially wary of the dealer who says, "We'll pay off

your old car, no matter what you owe." They are just going to transfer the excess debt from your old car, and all of the new loan costs, to your new vehicle, and thereby prolong or worsen your agony.

Remember this: You will NEVER come out financially better off by trading in a vehicle. It may be convenient, and that could be what matters to you the most, in which case it is okay, but at least now you will know what you are doing, and why.

Meet "Shifty"

Eventually, you will settle on a vehicle you like. It would be nice if you could just take it to the cash register and get a good deal, but many dealers want to see how many extra dollars they can get out of your pocket before they complete the transaction. Let's take a look at some of the common "shifty" practices of the bad boys.

Do not surrender your keys to the used car manager or anybody else in the dealership. Some dealerships will use this ploy to keep you from leaving. Once they have your car and the keys safely set aside, it is difficult for you to get out of there. If they want to test your vehicle go with them and get the keys back before you resume negotiating.

One of their many sales techniques involves using a "manager" against you. The sales person first tries to get you to sell your vehicle for wholesale and buy his vehicle for full price, but when he meets any resistance from you, he starts talking about his manager. They want you to make a written offer, which "must be approved" by the manager. Naturally, the manager NEVER accepts your offer. Managers will always attempt to squeeze more out of you, and they are willing to stretch the negotiations out for hours if necessary because they are obligated to be there all day. On the other hand, they expect you to grow impatient because you want to do something else. The dealer will try desperately to get you to pay more by telling you what a one-of-a-kind bargain this car is, or the other buyer who is just about ready to grab up the vehicle, but don't fall for that. They don't usually let real buyers get away and besides, if you lose this particular auto, there are thousands of others just like it.

When the first salesman suspects that he has exhausted your patience, he will call in a substitute. The "T.O. Man" (take-over man) is a master closer. This fellow is a little different than the mystery manager from the above example because you will actually meet him. He will ask you something like, "What do we have to do to put you in this car today?" Regardless of your response the answer is, "I can't do that, but if I can get the boss (we are back to that practice) to agree to (fill in a price), will you go along with him?" What a loaded question! He has made no commitment at all, but has gotten you to establish your "starting point." Tell him you want to know their best deal and you will decide to take it or leave it. Before you answer them be certain there are no additional fees (like dealer preparation). We have already established what to pay.

Once the price is hammered out, they will escort you to the office of the Financing Manager, where there are more sleazy tricks than anywhere else on the dealer's lot, and those with poor or substandard credit are more vulnerable than anybody else. Here is an interesting and common tactic that comes into play whenever the dealer helps customers to obtain loans from banks. The dealer offers to help you get your loan. He obtains up to five of your credit scores. These can include your FICO scores or standard scores or Enhanced Auto Scores from one or more major reporting agencies. Then he gets you approved based on your best score. But when he presents the loan package to you, he pads the numbers any way he can. He writes up your loan based on whatever he can get you to pay above and beyond what the bank would have accepted. Since the bank cannot accept the overpayment, they kick back the "juice" to the good ol' dealer and you get screwed every month thereafter as you make your payments.

Another tactic involves misleading you about your loan approval. They assure you they can get your loan approved and then they "help" you sign all of the paperwork. After those formalities are out of the way, they whisk you out the door with your new vehicle. About a week later they call you back, whether you got approved or not, and tell you your loan was denied because of poor credit. They advise you that your credit score falls into a high-risk category and lenders have to charge higher rates to offset the risk. Naturally, they can save the deal for you if you pay more money down or make higher payments. When you squawk, they show you the "fine print" on their contract that says the deal is contingent upon getting financing. If you demand to undo the deal and get your trade-in back, they tell you they have already wholesaled it out and they do not have it any longer. If you get caught in this scam demand to see the rejection letter from the bank or tell them you will be giving the state attorney a call.

They have a scam they pull involving co-signers. They tell you that you do not qualify and if you can get somebody else to sign for you, such as Grandma, you can still get the car. Then they prey on Grandma's kindness and ignorance. She does not know what you have agreed to or about the fine print so she willingly signs anything they ask her to, and you can imagine where that leaves you. The bottom line is, if you need a co-signer you ought to consider the possibility that you cannot really afford this particular vehicle in the first place.

Beware when they tell you that your bank's checks are not accepted. Sometimes they will say that your particular bank's checks are no good or they take too long to clear, etc. Then they will try to help you get financing from their own bank. You know what happens from there. Once again tell them you would like to call the Attorney General's office in your state to see if they know about any such practices.

The finance manager is going to try to sell you an extended warranty, but I would NEVER ever get one because of my basic philosophies about insurance (see relevant chapter in the first section of this book about the worse things we spend our money on). However, if there is some reason you think your vehicle is more likely to experience severe maintenance problems than an average vehicle, then you can get good extended warranties online, where there is real competition for your business. Never let the finance manager tell you that the lender requires an extended warranty, because lenders do not do that. If the bad boy persists, tell him to write down the fact that the lender requires it so that you can check that with your state's attorney.

Many dealers like to sell service contracts. You pay an upfront fee and then you can bring your vehicle back for free oil changes, tire rotations and other routine jobs. If you do indeed use all of the coupons, you do actually enjoy a modest discount, but after the dealer has your money, a lot can go wrong. You might forget to come back or sell the car or move away or it gets in a wreck. This program is designed to get you into the service department where you will be unlikely to get any great price breaks on other repairs. I suggest you forego this expense and look for bargains as you need them.

Dealers are notorious for add-ons. This mostly applies to new vehicles but there are some of them in the used market as well. One example is they offer to upgrade your tires, then they charge you for the new tires and keep the other tires, whether they are new or not. Be sure to read your invoice well. Make sure they have not charged you for things like dealer preparation, under-carriage rust protection, extra detailing or cleaning, service contracts, fabric guard, or paint sealant unless you already approved it, which I hope you did not.

This is just a partial list of the ways that naïve consumers get mistreated, but I am certain new tricks are popping up all the time. Fortunately, you can avoid falling into any of these traps just by knowing they exist. Now we can look at some smart ways to put your deal together.

Other Issues

Here are a few other items for you to review.

As the relationship develops, the salesperson will want to know how you expect to pay for the vehicle. Tell them you are prepared to pay cash by obtaining a loan from your own bank, but if they can get you a better rate you will consider it. Tell them your credit score but do not tell them your bank's interest rate or they will know they only have to beat that number rather than give you their very best rate. If they do not offer you a rate that beats your bank's rate, then get the financing from your own bank. If they offer you a better rate than your bank or credit union, tell them you want a loan approval "subject to your credit score being as stated." This way there is no inquiry on your credit report unless you are certain you will be approved.

When you find a car you like, be sure to compare the sales tax rate if you take delivery at the dealership or at home or work. If you can save a couple hundred dollars by having them deliver it to your door, I would suggest you do that.

Try to avoid using finance companies because their rates are usually very high.

Do not believe dealers when they tell you a vehicle has never been in an accident. They might be lying or simply unaware of a previous problem. The bad boys will put a sticker on the car that says something like, "all sales are final" or, "as is." If you should later find out the vehicle has been in a wreck, you cannot do anything about it. Therefore do one of the following: 1) demand a vehicle history report such as is available through Carfax; 2) require a WRITTEN warranty of at least 30 days; or 3) take your vehicle to a qualified mechanic for an inspection before you complete the deal.

If you need to upgrade your car, but you also want to buy a home in the near future, you should buy the home first, unless you have a very good credit rating and strong income history. It is much harder to get a home loan when you have car payments than the other way around.

A good place to get financing is from a line of credit loan that is secured by your home. They allow more payment flexibility because you can pay interest only, or add principal anytime you wish. Another benefit is you don't have a new inquiry on your credit report. Next, you might get a lower interest rate. And finally, the interest you pay is probably deductible. If you don't have enough equity in your home, ask if your bank would consider taking your property as primary collateral and the title to the vehicle itself as additional collateral. If so, you may still qualify for lower interest rates and the interest deduction.

Refer back to the concept of "miles per dollar" discussed in the chapter on Depreciating Assets.

Regarding auto repair shops, this can be a hit-or-miss proposition. For routine matters like oil changes and brake jobs, I recommend you ask the people you know if they have had good luck with any particular shop or mechanic. For more serious repairs I prefer experts. For example, take a vehicle with a transmission problem to a transmission repair shop. If you are uncertain about the ethics of these people, call the Better Business Bureau or a consumer protection agency to find out if there have been complaints filed. Be sure to ask what type of warranty they offer and get it in writing. Finally, if you find an honest shop, stick with them.

Selling

If you are going to sell a vehicle yourself, there are only a few pointers for you. First, keep your car clean. People will tend to assume that you have taken very good care of it. Next, do your homework (kbb.com) and know what the market value is. If your vehicle is more than five years old, call around and see if you can find a bank or finance company that will make a loan on it. If your buyer needs this information you will make it easy for him to buy from you.

Next, remember that buyers care about themselves, not you. So, talk in terms of what they can expect out of this car, not what you need or want. For example, say, "Based on the other cars I have seen, this car is a great value for you at $8,000. It will give you lots of loyal service. " Do not say, "I want to get $8,000 out of it."

Once you decide to sell it, I suggest you promote it in as many places as possible all at once. It is better to get several interested parties and get some competition between them than take a "drip, drip, drip" approach. Consider all of the free online sites as well as the auto magazines you see in the racks at grocery stores. Also post notices on bulletin boards and in local newspapers.

Finally, if you have a fairly new vehicle, it might be a good candidate for a consignment sale. If you can get by without the car until it sells, call a dealer of that model and see if they would like to sell it for you. Since they don't have to tie up any of their own money in it, you may get more than wholesale. They are usually fairly picky and may require you to pay for detailing or new tires, but this can be a good way to get a little more money out of it and avoid all of the aggravation of selling it yourself. You can establish a minimum acceptable price if you want to or allow them to wheel and deal on their own and then call you for approval when they get an offer. Don't get freaked out when you see the high price they ask for it because they have to allow for a trade-in. I have sold several vehicles this way and find it to be a worthwhile option.

Whew! That was a long chapter, but nearly everybody buys autos from time to time, so it is worth the effort. I trust that you found some worthwhile ways to recapture the cost of this book. The most important thing to remember is that the dealer needs you, not the other way around. Don't get emotionally involved. Remember, there are thousands of cars out there. As long as you remain on an intellectual, rather than emotional, level, and employ the lessons of this chapter, you should do great.

I hope you will keep this book around so that when you need this information you can review this chapter and make your best deal ever.

INSURANCE

Insurance may be dull, but it keeps coming up because it is so very important. In the first section of this book we observed that we waste a lot of our money on insurance that we do not need. In the second section we noted what to do now to fix the policies we already have. This section is devoted to helping you to make wise choices regarding insurance decisions in the future, as they arise.

Life Insurance

The two most important things to consider are how much and what type. Your insurance agent might tell you to buy a policy that is 3-4 times your annual salary but that is too general. You need to think this through better than that. I believe life insurance ought to be a means to preserve the lifestyle of your loved ones for a "reasonable" period of time after you die. Ask yourself what things your survivors will need if you and your salary are suddenly gone. Then determine what they can provide for themselves and the difference is probably the amount of life insurance you will want to obtain.

Your thinking should go something like this: If you have two kids who will need college, you may want to provide for that. If your spouse is likely to remarry, then you need to replace your income for enough time to allow for that, perhaps five years. Is your spouse going to work, and if so, how much can he/she earn? If your survivors cannot make mortgage payments, perhaps you want to allow for that. On the other hand, it may be very reasonable for them to move to a more modest home and pay their own way.

If your kids have grown and moved out, and you have enough money in investments to preserve your spouse's lifestyle, you may not need any life insurance at all. If you are a single person and all you have to consider is your final expenses, a modest savings account or a small burial policy is probably all you need. After you analyze these things you should be able to settle on the correct amount of life insurance. Now let's talk about the type of insurance you should consider.

There are two primary choices, whole life and term. Term insurance is life insurance in its purest form. There are no extras and the premiums are the lowest. Since that is all you want in the first place, this is usually what I recommend.

Whole life insurance has more bells and whistles. The insurance company will add on some benefits and charge a higher premium to cover their risk and make additional profit. One of their favorite gimmicks is a policy that returns all of your premiums after 20 years or so. It sounds good but when you think about it they are doing that because they will be able to invest your money and compound their return many times. If you drop the policy early, which most folks do, the company will never have to refund your money. I think the better strategy is to buy term insurance and invest the savings yourself. I am sure there are folks who are glad they bought whole life insurance but I have never met them.

After reviewing the above information, you may determine you have the wrong amount or wrong type of insurance. If so, call your agent and make the adjustments you deem appropriate. Be prepared for the agent to try and talk you out of downsizing, but once you have made your decision, stick to your guns.

Finally, let me repeat that life insurance should not be treated as a way to make your heirs wealthy or to prove that you love them. There are usually better ways to do that. I suggest plenty of hugs while you are still alive.

Auto Insurance

Every driver is required to have liability insurance, which is the basic type. This is intended to protect other people and property that you might damage in an accident. Each state sets its own minimum levels. They are expressed in a series of three numbers, something like 25/50/25. The first number is how much the insurance company will pay for injuries to any one person; the second number is the total they will pay for injuries to multiple persons in one accident; and the last number is what they will pay for property damage. If you cause more damage than that (which is very easy to do), you are obligated for the remainder.

You can also get comprehensive insurance, which protects you if your vehicle is damaged by things like hail storms or theft. In addition, you can obtain collision insurance in case you wreck your own car. If you have all three types (liability, comprehensive and collision) it is called "full coverage." Ordinarily, this is what is required by your bank if you have a car loan.

There are several other options for you. For instance, what if you are hit by someone who has no insurance or too little? There is uninsured motorist coverage and underinsured coverage for those situations. Another choice is extra medical insurance, but if you have health insurance, it would probably be a waste of money to pay for both.

You should become familiar with the term "deductible." This is the amount you must first shell out before the insurance company pays for any of the loss in the event of a covered claim. For example if you have a $500 deductible with a full coverage policy and smash your new truck into a light post, causing $3,000 in damages to your truck, you will have to pay the first $500 and then the insurance company pays the remainder. The higher the deductible amount, the more risk you take on, so the lower your premiums. The important point here is to be certain you are not paying for insurance that you don't need or want.

Regardless of your special circumstances, I highly recommend that you take the time to discuss your policy, in detail, with your carrier. Once you have an accident it is too late. It does not take long to be certain you are only paying for what you need. But be forewarned, the agents usually have a strong bias toward over-insuring their clients. When you talk with an agent, discuss the amount of insurance and the deductible. Here are some good questions and the answers I got from my carrier, but do not assume your policy provides the same protection. Call your own agent to be certain.

Question: *Can I get different coverage for different vehicles?*
Answer: *Yes, you can obtain basic liability insurance for your old truck and full coverage insurance for your new Rolls Royce, if you have one.*

Question: *What happens to my rates if I get a ticket or I am in an accident?*
Answer: *One such incident does not ordinarily raise your rates but any two of them probably will, depending on how much time has elapsed between the incidents.*

Question: *What if I get a speeding ticket in another state?*
Answer: *Other states do not usually report to your home state, so rates are not likely to be affected.*

Question: *What if I pull a boat or rent a hauling trailer?*
Answer: *Ordinarily your auto policy will provide the same coverage if you damage or injure somebody else, but any damage to your boat or trailer is not covered without specifically obtaining extra insurance for that risk.*

Question: *What if I have a specialty car or a work truck that I only drive a couple hundred miles per year?*

Answer: *You do not need year-round coverage. You can obtain insurance on an "as needed" basis.*

Question: *If I only have liability coverage, are the other people covered in my car when I am at fault?*
Answer: *Yes.*

Question: *If I am involved in an accident that is the fault of the other driver, and my passenger's injuries exceed the coverage provided by the other driver's insurance, who pays for the additional medical expenses?*
Answer: *The injured party's health insurance policy can be used, or they may have to sue the other driver to recover their losses.*

Question: *If I let someone else drive my vehicle, are they covered to the same extent as if I was the driver? Even if they are a worse driver?*
Answer: *Yes. Yes.*

Question: *What happens to my rates if I let someone else drive my vehicle and they have an accident?*
Answer: *This is a grey area. The insurance company will want to know if the other driver is going to continue driving your vehicle and other facts before they decide what to do.*

Question: *Will my rates go up if I am hit by an uninsured motorist and your company has to pay to fix my car?*
Answer: *No.*

Question: *Will your company pay to patch chips or repair cracks in my windshield?*
Answer: *We will cover the full amount with no reduction for your deductible, provided you have full coverage. But*

windshields are not covered if you only have liability insurance.

Question: *If my driver's license or license plates should expire, does my insurance stay in force?*
Answer: *Yes.*

Question: *Can I obtain additional medical coverage in case I injure myself or someone else beyond the standard coverage of my policy?*
Answer: *Yes, and if you have a substantial net worth, this might be a good idea because of the high cost of health care these days, but if you already have health insurance, that policy may satisfy this issue.*

Question: *What, if anything, can I do or drop from my policy to reduce my premiums?*
Answer: *It varies.*

Each year when your policy renews you should call or go meet with your agent and review the details to make certain you still have what you need. You may find that your vehicle has depreciated sufficiently to lower the coverage or increase the deductible. Tell your agent you intend to compare his/her policy and quotes with another company and then do it. I would not change agents for a small savings because I place a high value on good relationships, but I want my agent to know he/she always has to earn my business.

I cannot tell you exactly how much insurance to get or what type is best for you because each situation is different, but here are some general recommendations.

If you are young with a relatively low net worth, then the minimum amount of insurance is probably good enough. If you cause a serious accident you may not have enough insurance to pay for all of the expenses but the other person in the accident probably has uninsured or under-insured motorist protection or health insurance of his/her own to pick up the difference.

Depending on your risk tolerance and your net worth, I would recommend full coverage for any vehicle that is worth more than $15,000 and only basic liability insurance if you drive a vehicle that is worth less than $5,000. The range in between those numbers is a grey area. You can decide for yourself how much risk to take. You can probably guess what I do.

You may have a terrific driving record, or a high tolerance for risk. If so, you should consider a higher deductible with lower premiums. On the other hand, if you are going to let your newly licensed teenager drive your vehicle, you may need a lot more coverage with a lower deductible because you have more risk.

One popular auto insurance company claims, "It is so easy a caveman can do it." But, the caveman is extinct for a reason. Consumers who don't want to be similarly destroyed will spend the modest amount of effort it takes to understand auto insurance and use their money wisely.

Hazard Insurance

Hazard insurance is the insurance on your home that covers losses caused by fire, wind, rain, hail, water, earthquake, vandalism or other misfortunes. Do not assume you have coverage for all of these disasters because many policies exclude some of them.

Unless you experience a very serious fire in your lifetime, there is a strong likelihood that you will pay a lot more in premiums than you will ever receive in claims, but in this case it is better to take the medicine than have the disease of risk. Most people are wiped out financially if they have insufficient insurance and their homes are destroyed, so insuring against that is justifiable.

If you have a large loan relative to the home's value, your lender may require you to carry more insurance than you would like. You won't be surprised to learn that lenders are more concerned with their risk than how much your premiums are. Naturally, the insurance company also likes over-insuring you. If your decisions are not governed by your lender, there are some important things to know:

Generally, you should have enough insurance to pay off your loan in the event of a major loss, or 80 percent of the home's value, whichever is more. You don't ordinarily need to insure 100 percent of the property's value because the land will usually have some value. In this case, I assumed it was about 20 percent of the total value of the home.

Ask your agent how the company pays out in the event of a loss. Some companies pay the first dollar after the deductible is met, and then they cover every dollar up to the full amount of the policy; other companies approach it differently. Suppose the replacement cost of your home is $300,000 and you have one loan for $200,000. If you are only carrying sufficient coverage to pay the loan, and no more, then you have 67 percent coverage. If there was damage in the amount of $100,000, they only pay their "proportionate share" (67 percent) of the loss and you have to soak up the difference. In other words, you have to pay $33,000. That may be acceptable to you, but make sure you know what your coverage is before you have a claim.

Once again, I cannot tell you exactly how much insurance to obtain, or what deductible is right for you or what riders might be appropriate. As with your auto insurance, you should take the time to visit with your insurance company and have the agent explain, in common language, exactly what protection you are buying, and why.

Remain mindful of insurance agents' biases. They tend to focus on the potential loss and not the likelihood of your actually experiencing a loss. Also remember that you can take on certain risks, provided a loss is not catastrophic.

Since you are probably going to pay a lot more to these companies than you will ever collect from them, it is just as bad to pay them premiums for insurance you don't need or want as it is to be deeply disappointed if a serious problem should befall you and you are not sufficiently covered.

However, don't bury your head in the sand and take the philosophy you can cross that bridge when you come to it. At that point, it is simply too late.

Health Insurance

So far, we have discussed auto, life and hazard insurance. In all three situations the annual premiums are modest compared to health insurance, which can easily cost more than all three of them combined.

Some people have group insurance at their work. Many of them believe that pooling their money somehow assures them they are getting better rates than they might get on their own, but that is not always true. For instance, if you are fairly young you are less likely to come down with life-threatening illnesses like heart attacks or cancer. However, the older people in your group have greater risk for these problems. If they don't pay any extra money to offset that extra risk, then the expense is spread among everybody else in the group, thereby forcing the healthier people to accept a disproportionate share of the premium. Contrariwise, if you are one of the elder people in your group you may very well enjoy a better deal with a group policy than you might expect from an individual policy.

Not long ago, I was one of the older people in a group and I was paying handsomely for my share of the group policy. One day, I got notice that my rates were going up again, so I decided it was time to investigate further. A few weeks later I had a new policy in place, and successfully cut my premiums in half. My savings amounts to several thousand dollars every year, which is enough to pay for all of my auto, hazard and life insurance policies combined. Interestingly, the other members in the group also started sniffing around and all of them were able to reduce their premiums by getting out of that group. Obviously, the group was disbanded.

When you obtain an individual policy, you can control a lot more than you can as a member of a large group. For example, you can drop the stuff you aren't likely to need (I don't need maternity coverage) or anything that is so insignificant you can cover the cost if an expense occurs. For example, you might lower the premiums if you agree to pay higher deductible, or a higher co-pay arrangement.

Other

Occasionally you will find yourself forced to obtain some other form of insurance. For instance, if you don't have a sufficient down payment when you buy a home, you may need to obtain mortgage insurance before the lender will make you a loan. Or, if you want to be an attorney, you might be required to secure errors and omissions insurance. Or, if you run your own business, you may need to provide workers' compensation insurance.

Generally speaking, avoid buying insurance you do not need and avoid any insurance that is not protecting you from major losses. That means don't buy insurance on your blackjack hands in Las Vegas and don't buy extended "warranties" on anything.

Do not buy credit card "protection" which pays your payments in the event you lose your job or become too ill to work unless you have some reason to believe you might lose your job. Do not buy insurance that pays off your mortgage upon your death. You will get a better deal and more flexibility by buying true term life insurance. I do not recommend travel insurance.

It is true that people have occasional claims from the above group, but overall those claims are much less than the sum of the premiums that people pay for those policies. That is why insurance companies make a lot of money.

Whenever you are faced with a new decision regarding insurance, I hope you will remember that consumers waste a lot of money in this category. Be sure to review this section and do a little extra homework. It will mean a lot to your long-term financial health. I am glad to know you will be using your money wisely.

TRAVEL AND VACATIONS

Nearly all of us fantasize about traveling in one way or another. Even the people who are afraid of flying, or cannot afford it, seem to find alternate ways to explore. So whether you are interested in spending weekends and vacations just snooping around your own state, or traveling the four corners of the globe (an odd phrase), travel is bound to be in the mix.

One of my life-long buddies got the travel bug right out of college and he has never been able to shake it. Mark, a history major, joined the Peace Corps and headed to Guatemala for a year or so. A little later he was sent to Africa. Those journeys brought his history books to life by introducing him to some of the actual people and places he had read about. After that, he just couldn't get enough of it.

Before long, he married a charming and gentle Guatemalan woman named Ligia, and a special family was underway. Their children all enjoy dual citizenship with aunts, uncles, grandmas and grandpas from different countries. They were bilingual before they ever got to school. They not only tolerated people of different backgrounds, but they embraced them. From that seemingly innocent beginning in a few history books, this entire family has been forever enriching the lives of hundreds of people whom they have met.

Mark's early travel successes caused him to wonder what other secrets the world was hiding from him. Who could blame him for wanting to find out? Along the way, he discovered that he could actually make a living doing what he loved. So he and Ligia devoted their lives to propping up people who have so little.

Now, there are African villages that have wells with fresh water and irrigation for crops. There are schools for children that never even knew there was such a thing as a school. Shiploads of life-saving medicine have been delivered to obscure places that most of us have never heard of. Mark has played key roles in all of it.

All of that has required countless hours making plans and working with travel agents. Much of Mark's life has been spent living out of suitcases, eating on the run and parading through scores of unfamiliar airports. But that is the easy part compared to riding donkeys on dirt roads in countries where English-speaking people are few and far between, eating unfamiliar foods for weeks on end, drinking water from unconventional sources, sleeping on the floor or spending weeks at a time without contact with the outside world. But Mark and people like him don't see that stuff as inconveniences; they look upon it as a fascinating classroom wherein they have become both the students and the teachers.

As demanding and exhausting as all of that travel is, you would expect that a fellow like Mark would cherish the time in between his many journeys, and glue himself to a couch, but the opposite is the case. Whenever Mark is not traveling professionally, he is exploring the states or planning a trip to South America or Canada or somewhere else. He loves going back to places he has visited before just as much as he likes discovering new places. Each new trip is met with the enthusiasm the rest of us experience when we embark on a once-in-a-lifetime fantasy vacation.

Over the years I have asked Mark about his insatiable appetite for travel and he has suggested that he has always believed that he should pursue his dreams while he is young enough and healthy enough to do it. He has mentioned some of the older people whom he has met who waited all of their lives for a fancy cruise or other special trip, but when they finally did it they needed walkers to get around. He noticed that they go to bed at nine o'clock because their bodies and minds are worn out. They ride in vans because they cannot walk up old cobblestone roads to 400-year-old churches. They are forced to eat bland foods in easily accessible locations because the years have stolen away any alternatives.

When one hears the conviction in Mark's voice as he suggests that there is a certain urgency to do some traveling while we are capable, it is very compelling.

But talking about all of that travel is cheap and actually doing it is quite another matter. Somebody has to pay the bills, and there are plenty of them. The costs for Mark's professional travels are borne by employers, charities and donors, but he has to pay for most of the personal travels himself. That has certainly amounted to a lot of money over these many years. Let me give you just one example.

A few years ago, my wife and I joined Mark and Ligia on a fantastic 5-day river cruise from Berlin, Germany to Prague in the Czech Republic. Mark made all of the arrangements. Each day our ship would stop at a town or two along the way. We marveled at forts, battlefields, bridges and buildings that had been standing for hundreds of years. We also did a lot of cheap things, away from the tourist traps and gift shops, just to get a taste of the real culture.

After the cruise, we spent several more days in Prague. We stayed in a nice hotel and took a couple of guided tours but mostly we walked from one fascinating site to the next. We took some of our meals at sidewalk cafes and others at fancy places that locals recommended. We enjoyed enough nice activities to capitalize on our splendid opportunity but we were not extravagant or cavalier about the expenses.

The price tag was slightly less than $4,000 per person. Since I had never experienced a trip like that, it was definitely worth it. There were fascinating and historic sites unlike anything I had ever seen in person.

I would not want to suggest that all traveling be that expensive, but it is obvious that someone who loves to travel can spend a small fortune over a lifetime. Whether it is *flushing* too much money down the drain is a matter of perspective.

Mark and Ligia have enjoyed a fabulous lifestyle that very few people would even dream about, but their choices have devoured dollars like a convention of fat people gorging themselves at a Las Vegas buffet. The two are in their early sixties now and they have been taking fabulous trips for all of their adult lives. If we assume they have spent $3,000 a year and that they could have paid off debts which carried 7 percent interest (credit cards, auto loans, mortgage payments etc.), or if they would have simply invested the money at the same 7 percent, they would have accumulated a whopping $930,000 for their retirement. I am certain they would rather have all of their memories and blessings than a stack of money, but their story does illustrate just how important it is for us to be aware of the real long-term costs when we take on such endeavors.

For all of the non-Marks, I would suggest you use your travel dollars to regularly visit your own area of the country. It amuses me that people who live near the East coast like to visit the West coast and vice versa and that those who live near giant redwood trees seek out the sites in the flatlands of the Midwest or Texas.

I am no different. I have lived in the Denver area nearly all of my life. I finally visited Mount Rushmore a few years ago and it is only a six-hour drive. Meanwhile I went to Hawaii, Washington D.C., Europe, Texas and California. What the heck was wrong with me?

In another example, later this year we are planning on visiting Yellowstone National Park and the Grand Tetons in our neighboring state of Wyoming. I am embarrassed to admit that this will be the first time we'll make that nine-hour trip. While I ignored an incredible nearby opportunity, millions of people from all over the globe have dropped by for a peek. This trip is every bit as worthwhile as any of my other trips but it will cost a fraction of what the others did. That is why I say don't overlook the opportunities in your own backyard.

By the way, guess who our travel partners are for the upcoming Yellowstone trip? Yep, you guessed it: our old buddies, Mark and Ligia. He inspired me to finally get off my butt and do what I should have done decades ago.

I do not know what kind of trips you should take, but I can show you the long-term cost of each dollar you spend this way. I can also point out that if you have to pay for these trips with any kind of borrowed money (refinancing your home or credit cards) then you cannot afford it. The interest on those dollars is simply too much money to flush away.

Let's suppose that every year you take a new trip that costs $3,000. Let's also suppose you finance the trip on a credit card that carries 12 percent interest. To pay back that loan within a year you will need to make payments of $266.55/mo., which means that after one year, nearly $200 is flushed for interest. But we are not done measuring the loss.

As an alternative, you could have invested the same amount ($266.55 per month) and gotten some rate of return. If you paid off another credit card, you might have picked up an additional 12 percent in savings ($200/year) because you no longer have to pay interest on that debt. Or, if you just put the money in a certificate of deposit you might have picked up 4 percent ($66/year) in real income. Let's just pick a number somewhere in-between and say you could have received $100 over the year by saving or investing that money instead of paying off a trip that you already charged on a credit card.

When we add the $200 in interest expenses that you have to pay, and the $100 that you could have received in some other pocket, your total loss is $300/year. In that event, you are adding 10 percent to the cost of the entire trip and flush away $25/mo. each and every month for ALL THE REST OF YOUR LIFE! That is an incredible price to pay, just because you finance your trips. As I am sure you realize it would be much wiser to save up the money for your trips and avoid all of those unnecessary losses.

Finally, before you go on any trips, I suggest you spend some time doing research. Sometimes your best deals are in group packages while other times you get great bargains by taking last-minute accommodations that were not sold out. Or you might find that traveling out of season is the best bargain for you.

But, no matter how obscure your destination, there is a good chance that when you finally get there, Mark and Ligia will already be there and waiting for you. Please say, "hi" to them for Patty and me.

Bon voyage!

MARRIAGE

Our federal government has always promoted marriage because of the stability that families offer children and the society as a whole. They have enacted all sorts of laws toward that end.

Once again, I have no intention of telling you to get married or divorced or separated or anything else. I will simply illustrate the financial implications of tying the knot, so you can make your own informed decisions.

One of the most obvious financial benefits of getting married revolves around pooling and sharing expenses. If two single people each own a luxury condo in a nice high-rise building and then get married, they can share the cost of one condo rather than pay for two of them. The thing goes with anything they can share from an automobile to a zebra farm.

Likewise, nearly everything is cheaper with the economy of scale. If you buy the larger size container of cottage cheese, or anything else, you get a better value. If you go out to dinner you can get bargains like "buy one, get one free."

Another financial benefit for married people involves employers that offer health insurance to spouses of employees at little or no additional cost to the employee. Therefore, a single person with no health insurance can really benefit financially by marrying a person with such a plan, and especially if the nonemployee has any serious or preexisting conditions.

Then there are some tax matters. Up until 1969, married people had a clear tax benefit, which two single people did not. Then

Congress tweaked the tax code and created a more progressive system, that is, those with modest earnings pay very little in income taxes, while those who earn more income pay a higher percentage in income taxes. But Congress is never satisfied so they have modified the code again and again.

Still, there are cases where a couple filing jointly pays less than they would pay if filing as two singles. In even rarer cases, the opposite is true. For example, imagine two low-income people who pay no income taxes. By getting married, their combined income could easily be taxable, leaving them with less take-home pay. After all of that, there are still more people who benefit from filing jointly and sharing deductions than those who come out better by filing separately (by a 5 to 4 margin).

There is also the matter of estate taxes. Generally, a person can pass an estate to heirs without much of a consequence, provided it is less than five million dollars; but, if the estate is bigger than that, the taxes can be half of the estate. Ouch! However, married people usually pay no estate taxes when one of them dies.

In another example, Social Security benefits are currently transferable to surviving spouses upon the death of partners or a former spouse, provided they were married for at least ten years. Therefore, a survivor can collect the Social Security income of the deceased spouse if it is greater than that to which the survivor would otherwise be entitled.

Marital status can also play a role in such things as insurance rates. Two married people who drive the same car do not pay twice as much in premiums as a single person who drives the same type of vehicle. They are also more likely to get multiple car discounts than single people.

One other benefit of married people that gets overlooked has to do with implied stability. A single dad or mom may be an extraordinary person, but there is no doubt such a lifestyle can be very demanding. Employers might wonder if he or she can handle it all and still be a reliable employee.

Some landlords also perceive married people as more stable.

While certain federal and state laws prohibit professional rental agencies from discriminating against people based on familial or marital status, private parties are not held to that same standard. In such cases, a single person might be considered a higher risk and charged a greater damage deposit or higher rent or even turned away.

Credit scores are also relevant. Although it is difficult to get the credit reporting agencies to tell us exactly how credit scores are calculated, there is a strong belief that the implied stability of marriage is part of the equation. We have already established that credit scores can play a role in what interest rates one pays for loans and credit cards. So this can easily affect the bottom line.

There's another not-so-official benefit for married folks: synergy. When both people work toward the same goals such as hating debt, saving consistently, and investing wisely, they can be incredibly dynamic. One couple I know has been employing the philosophies of this book for about fifteen years now. They are in their mid-thirties and on track to retire at age 50. They won't need Social Security, pensions, inheritances or anything else to carry them to the end of their days. They'll have enough resources just from accumulating passive income together. If those other income streams happen to drop into their purse, they just serve as gravy (an interesting mixed metaphor—how would you like to have a purse full of gravy?)

I don't know about you, but I think that is a rather impressive list of financial benefits for the married folks. Whether they compete with "love" as a reason to get married is probably a matter of perspective.

CHILDREN

It matters not whether you refer to the little ones as crumb crunchers, rug rats, bundles of joy, tax deductions or simply just kids, the facts are the facts. There are several studies designed to determine how much it costs to raise our children. One of the more thorough ones was done by MSN Money a few years ago. Its study tried to determine the actual costs of raising a child through age seventeen. They studied more than 5,000 families and visited each one four times a year. They also utilized some previous research from the Department of Agriculture (I thought they worried about cows and grasslands).

The MSN group concluded that it takes about a quarter of a million dollars to raise the typical child. It was less in some parts of the country and for families of lower income brackets, but never below $134,000 per child, and the overall cost was higher for children raised in more affluent communities or families.

Even though this appears to be one of the best studies on the topic, I think they missed all sorts of factors and mischaracterized some others. I have massaged their numbers, to determine my own estimate of the actual cost to raise children.

Let's review their categories.

Housing

According to MSN, housing is the biggest expense in raising a youngster, but it left out a lot of significant data.

It begins with a basic assumption that each new family member requires an additional 100-150 square feet of living space. There are several flaws with that conclusion.

When it comes to housing matters, I am an expert on the topic. I have spent 30 years as a Realtor. I have written a book for real estate agents, I teach continuing education courses to licensees. I own nearly 300 rental properties. I have written newspaper articles and hosted a call-in radio program on the topic and a whole bunch more, but you get the point.

They did not break down their data but I suppose they considered facts such as it is impractical to add to a home when a baby arrives so the most logical way for the growing family to fulfill the demand for new space is to move to a larger home.

In a case like that, there are plenty of expenses. For starters, there are the costs and aggravations of selling the old home. Real estate brokers, title companies and buyers are all needed to help complete the move. Then there are the expenses to get a new loan and there will probably be more debt and additional interest charges. The new home also has higher property taxes, higher utility fees and higher insurance rates. The buyer will probably make some immediate remodeling changes.

If we assume that a typical family approaches the matter in that way and they do it several times (once for each new youngster) and if that were all there was to consider, then perhaps the MSN Money figures would have credibility, but I never met a family who approached the matter that way.

Many families buy a home that allows for growth in the first place. When the new family member shows up there is no sale needed.

In another example, two or more children of the same gender can share a room, or the family may only move after two or more new ones join the clan.

Another missed point is that if families add on to their

home or buy a bigger property as their needs change they may not have "spent" the money at all. Money diverted into an asset such as a home carries an element of "investment" with it and it is very likely they can resell the home and recover their money. In fact it is even possible to enjoy a nice profit.

There is yet another issue. The articles suggested that the total cost of raising a child is somewhere around $250,000 and 33-37 percent of that goes to housing expenses, which includes 100-150 square feet of new living space. Well, that does not add up. Thirty-three percent of $250,000 is $83,333, which is approximately 4-6 times what it costs to build a room of that size.

So it appears these studies are way off base. I think the researchers asked people the wrong questions. They asked, "How much did you spend?" But they should have asked, "How much is necessary?"

Just because somebody buys a larger home does not mean that is a net "cost" to them. Ordinarily, they do not lose that money. The newer, bigger home has more value and it can be resold to recapture the expense when the kids leave the nest.

If the family in question never buys its own home, then it would likely have a higher net cost for housing as the family grows because it would have to rent something bigger. But those are mostly lower-income type people and they are more likely to share bedrooms and cut costs wherever they can (I know; I rent homes and apartments to these people).

I will concede there are some modest housing costs associated with having each additional child. There are higher insurance rates, utility fees and maintenance, but all of that combined is a sliver of the costs attributed to this category in the sophisticated studies mentioned.

Considering all of the above, I will make my estimate of real housing costs "necessary" to raise a child to age 17 at somewhere around twelve percent of the amount they indicated, say $10,000, not $83,333.

Food

The same study states that it takes somewhere between $26,490 and $39,470 in food to raise a child through age 17. That averages approximately $165 per month. I doubt that a three-year-old girl needs that much food but it seems in the ballpark for a hungry teenage boy (I raised two of them). Based on my own analysis of the housing costs, I cannot help but think these numbers are also padded. However, money spent on food cannot be recaptured like money "invested" in a bigger home; so, I am going to accept their lower number.

Transportation

The next biggest expense to raise a child through age 17 is transportation. The study said, "Allow $18,660 to $34,860 for this purpose." Although it did not say what was considered, one can assume they accounted for trips to and from soccer practice and similar activities. Wear and tear on the family vehicle also has to count for something but that was not mentioned either.

However, there was an underlying assumption that a parent is somehow obligated to provide a car for each kid once they reach driving age because they focused on the cost of a vehicle plus insurance and maintenance of it. It seems to me like some or most of that cost could be borne by the teenager. Furthermore, the child cannot drive until age 16 so there are only two years to take into consideration.

Even if the parents bought a brand new $30,000 car and gave it to the teenager, it would have residual value after the two years under discussion. That should be deducted from the total cost. This oversight is similar to the one indicated for the housing matters.

When I shuffle all of those cards together I think adolescents can buy their own cars, so I see no reason to assign any more than $5,000 to the parents for this purpose.

Clothing

The study says that it takes somewhere between $8,490 and $12,810 in clothing to raise a child through age 17. That comes to about $600 per year. That seems high for the toddlers but reasonable for teenagers. They did not account for hand-me-downs or other possibilities such as the ones we discussed in an earlier chapter, but for now I will use the lower number of the study, as I did with the food budget.

Healthcare

This expense comes in between $10,680 and $15,870. The study acknowledges that some families have health insurance and no such expense and in more unusual cases the costs can be much higher. Our society keeps moving toward government health services so the out-of-pocket costs to most people is less than the study suggests, let's say $4,000.

Childcare

In this category the study seems right on. It suggests that the cost for childcare is somewhere between $12,090 and $33,870. That is quite a spread, but there are several choices confronting parents.

A popular choice is for one parent to forego working outside the home, given that after paying taxes, travel costs, and the daycare center, there is just not very much "take-home" money left over from a paycheck. In a case like this, it appears the cost for childcare is minimal but there are still lost wages to consider.

A fairly cost-effective way to approach this issue is to drop the kids off at Grandma's home while mom and dad go to work. The thinking goes that both parents can still work outside the home and keep the out-of-pocket cost of childcare to a minimum. If you have this option, count yourself as fortunate.

In other situations, the parents can juggle their work schedules so that they can both get enough time off to share the childcare duties. Caroline and Tom do that. They each work full-time but their employers allow them some flexibility. Caroline works on the weekends and a few evenings during the week at a grocery store, while Tom's job is a typical eight-to-five arrangement. By coordinating their schedules this way, they keep childcare costs to a minimum.

According to a separate survey, nearly two-thirds of moms who have children who are not yet in school actually work outside of the home. A higher percentage of moms work outside of the home once the kids get to school age. Therefore, a significant majority of families have to make daycare arrangements.

In one option, there are uncertified "at home" daycare services. This amounts to adult babysitters. In our area, the fee is about $25 per day per child. The parent drops the children off at the home of the provider, who is supposed to keep a responsible eye on the child. The skill level and sanitation of the property can vary quite a bit from provider to provider.

The more common service is offered by official, certified daycare providers. They charge somewhere around $40 per day unless the child is an infant, in which case the cost is closer to $60 per day.

Matt and Heather have elected to hire an au pair. A young woman from Brazil has been screened and she has moved in with the family. She gets exposed to American culture in exchange for spending 40 hours per week in the family home.

These parents like the concept because the kids stay in their own home and get personalized attention, much like they get when the parents are home. The cost for the au pair is around $18,000 per year for up to three children. This is expensive for one child but an incredible value for three kids. If you have two kids, the cost is roughly the same as you would pay for typical daycare services.

After a child gets to school-age, the costs drop off quite a bit and especially when they reach age ten or so because they can be left alone for an hour or two when they get home from school. In the summer months, working parents can work out special babysitting arrangements with high school students and reduce some of the childcare costs.

Finally, there are certain tax factors that enter into this category. Parents get to deduct up to $5,000 per year for any real out-of-pocket expenses for daycare services. And for those who qualify, due to low income, there is even a tax credit of $1,000 per child. So the parents can get a kick-back on childcare expenses totaling about $2,500 per child.

If we look at all of the relevant options facing parents today, the survey numbers actually make sense.

After considering all of the options, I shall settle in the middle and say that it takes "on average" $23,000 in childcare to raise each child.

Miscellaneous

Once again the survey seems to be pumping up the numbers, presumably for shock value. They say it takes another $13,380 to $32,460 in "other expenses" to raise the average child. Then they say this includes books, personal items and entertainment. I would suggest that most of this can be eliminated. Most kids are more inclined to use the Internet than buy books; they are barely aware of grooming prior to high school and they can pay for most of their own entertainment. Still, the parents may want to provide some financial support for an allowance, birthday gifts, summer camp, prom dresses or other selected items. But, most of that stuff only comes into play after the youngster turns age 8 or so. If we allow $50 per month for all of the items in this category, we get to $10,200.

Other Topics

Before we wrap up, there are a couple of other points worth mentioning. First, parents get tax deductions for their children in addition to any tax refunds for childcare expenses as mentioned earlier.

Second, the study made no allowance for expenses that parents face after the child reaches age 18, such as college or damage deposits for first apartments. They ignored those costs because the study was designed to analyze costs through age 17, but ignoring any such expenses paints an incomplete picture regarding the expense of raising a young person and that is what we are really trying to do.

The Adjusted Cost

Below is an itemization of the costs to raise a kid to the age of 18, both as MSN sees it and as I do. The biggest discrepancy is in housing, where I take a broader and more realistic view. We also look at transportation in a different light. For example they seem to assume the parents are going to buy all kids a car and that the car has no value after two years. I think both of those assumptions are flawed.

Category
Housing
    MSN Projections: $44,580-$100,080
    My Projections: $10,000
Food
    MSN Projections: $26,490-$39,470
    My Projections: $26,490
Transportation
    MSN Projections: $18,660-$34,860
    My Projections: $5,000
Clothing
    MSN Projections: $8,490-$12,810
    My Projections: $8,490

Healthcare
    MSN Projections: $10,680-$15,870
    My Projections: $4,000
Childcare
    MSN Projections: $12,090-$33,870
    My Projections: $23,000
Miscellaneous
    MSN Projections: $13,380-$32,460
    My Projections: $10,200
TOTALS
    MSN Projections: $134,370-$269,420
    My Projections: $87,180

Quite honestly, I think studies like the ones mentioned above tend to exaggerate the numbers to gain readers. A quick review of the MSN numbers reveals a huge spread. I suppose that lends them cover when people like me delve into the specifics. Their high number is three times my number and their lower number is still significantly higher than my number.

Returning to the original point of this chapter, we are trying to determine how much it will cost most people to have each new child. I do not doubt that some families spend the kind of money the studies indicated but the implication was that nearly everybody should expect the kind of overhead they identified, which we proved was not the case.

PETS

Few people would doubt the benefits of including pets in our families, but if we cannot afford to properly care for a dog or cat, we really shouldn't do it at all. Unfortunately, there are hundreds of thousands of pets that suffer through unpleasant lives because their owners don't really take care of them properly. Of those who do a good job in this regard, only a small percentage of them give sufficient consideration to the overall cost of raising a pet until after they bring the innocent ones home.

For our purposes we shall assume that at a minimum, it is necessary to feed your pet and give it all of the shots and medical attention it needs, and avoid exposing it to extreme or dangerous weather conditions. Let's have a look at some of the details.

Purchase Price

First, there is the acquisition of the lovable critter. Some of us take in a stray cat or accept a puppy from the kids down the block or from somebody advertising on Craigslist, but that approach is fraught with risk. Ordinarily, you would not know why a cat is roaming the neighborhood. It could be sick or carrying disease or hate children. That mutt puppy might look particularly cute, but it is difficult to know if it is going to be prone to aggression or have hip problems or other diseases.

If you acquire a professionally bred dog or cat, you have a better chance of knowing what traits your pet may have, but all of that early knowledge and expertise is likely to be accompanied by a stout purchase price. Some such dogs sell for two thousand dollars or more.

Another option is to "rescue" a pet from one of the many shelters. The administrators usually know some details about the particular animal. The pets are usually spayed or neutered and have had their shots. It is also common for them to be checked and treated for customary diseases. There are usually over a quarter of a million pets available via this procedure at any given time. (If you want to check some of them out, simply go to www. PetFinders.com.) Whenever a shelter gives over a pet for adoption it tries to recoup its investment, so expect to pay several hundred dollars for any new family members acquired this way.

Start-Up Costs

Once you bring the new friend home you have some additional start-up fees. Those add up to several hundred dollars and include customary items such as food, collar, bowl, leash, grooming tools, flea control, treats, vaccines, spot remover, sleeping bed, crate and so forth. Some people spend a lot more on grooming, training and better food products. A study by Pet Education says the minimum first-year cost is $511 and it sets the maximum at $6,600, which includes a higher purchase price for the critter plus fancy grooming, advanced training and upgraded fencing.

Ongoing Expenses

As time ticks by, there are additional expenses like, food, medical and occasional boarding. According to the same study, the low end of the range is $287 per year and the higher priced pets require around $2,485 per year in recurring costs.

Other pets have special needs. In a real-life example, my son, Adam, bought a Saint Bernard puppy that proved to have thyroid and pancreas problems. She has cost him $300 per month for meds in addition to all of the normal costs. She is now 11 years old and that adds up to $40,000. Those are real out-of-pocket dollars, not just some theory on a page in a book.

Other

There are other ways that pets dig into the family budget. For example, if you hire somebody to walk your dog or clean up the yard, you will need your checkbook. If you happen to get a digger or a dog that likes to chew on furniture, or a cat that pees in the carpet, you have other losses. If your dog gets out of the yard and gets into a fight with some other dog, you have to deal with all of that.

In our home, we have a recurring expense for pets we don't even own. My wife buys Christmas presents and treats for our kids' dogs.

If we assume your doggie will live for 14 years, and you add all expenses together, you can expect to pay somewhere between $5,000 and $38,000 during its lifetime. A cat costs a little less than that.

Since many families will have two or more pets at a time and acquire new ones whenever the old ones pass away, a family can have eight such pets over several decades, and that can easily add up to $50,000, or a whole bunch more. Add to that the compound interest that we must pay because we did not use that money for paying off debt (or investing for income), and this becomes a very substantial sum.

There is no doubt we derive a lot of pleasure from our pets, but some people really struggle in their golden years because they did not sufficiently understand the consequences of their choices along the way.

CHARITY

We observed in an earlier chapter that half of what we make goes to taxes, in one way or another. In addition, the church wants us to give it 10 percent of whatever we earn. A church uses our money to pay for overhead like insurance, utility fees and salaries as well as maintenance of buildings, printing costs and anything else that it needs. It also helps out its members and other struggling people.

Those are wonderful causes and we want to help as much as we can, but after we pay so much in taxes, plus our 10 percent to the church, we frequently feel like we are those very poor people that the church is trying to help.

In spite of all of that, Americans are the most generous people in the world. Whenever a catastrophe hits some foreign land, our government is the first one to send in aid. But our government's generosity pales compared to the donations made by our corporations and private individuals. I have seen it first-hand.

The infamous Columbine High School is just a mile away from my home. When the gunmen attacked their schoolmates in 1999, the American generosity sprang into action. The split-rail fence that surrounds the school was lined with hundreds and hundreds of bouquets of flowers and posters. Youngsters in classrooms from all around the country donated their pennies to funds that were set up to help family members of the fallen students. Churches and families made substantial donations.

People donated cars and boats to be sold off. Corporations set up scholarship funds in the name of the victims. Millions of dollars were collected without even asking.

Other Americans have favorite causes that they regularly support. Our family is fairly active with a homeless shelter in our community. It feeds 300 people, two meals a day, no questions asked. Anybody who is hungry gets fed. Whenever we take food down there we are amazed at the kindness of others. When we drop off our items, we usually have to wait in line behind other donors. Volunteers meet us and help unload the merchandise. While somebody fills out our receipt, the local grocery store donates bakery products. One family drops off two gallons of milk every day. A small dairy brings butter and eggs. Others bring meat and potatoes. Still others drop by with warm clothes and toiletries. One local merchant sent $10,000 in cash without being asked. That is just one place among dozens in Denver. Other cities enjoy similar blessings.

Americans are amazing, and you are probably one of the kind ones. If you are like me, you enjoy helping others. It feels good. We know we are blessed and we realize that others are not always so lucky. We believe in putting back into a world that has given us so much. Some form of assistance is a regular part of our being.

But at the crossroads of our generosity and our own financial reality lies a challenging enigma, namely, how do we do our part to support the various causes in which we believe when we are constantly wrestling with our own finances? Fortunately, there are some worthwhile options.

First, if you support a specific church or similar institution, I suggest you do some of the work for them instead of donating money. Anytime you can help the church to make its money go farther, you are also making a financial contribution. You might plant the garden, shovel snow off the sidewalk or volunteer for spring cleaning.

Many churches use some of the money they receive from

contributions to assist their members. You can do some of that work so the church can save its money for other causes. For instance if it pays some high school kids to help a neighbor pull weeds or a contractor to paint the trim on an elderly person's home, you can help out or make lemonade. One of my favorite money-stretching activities involves surplus dealers.

One time, the homeless shelter sent out a notice that it needed toothbrushes. Numerous nice people donated money for the cause. Other generous contributors bought packages of toothbrushes. Some of them bought the very best, high-quality, brushes available because they wanted to illustrate their level of compassion. Before long the toothbrushes were piled high and the shelter was set up for another month or so. But there was another opportunity hiding behind all of that kindness.

Buying a high volume of products in that way is not very cost-effective. The average cost of each toothbrush was a little less than one dollar. Furthermore, most of the homeless people had no way of carrying around toothbrushes or similar items, so they had a tendency to throw them away or lose them after one use.

I began to poke around some surplus dealers for a more cost-effective way to acquire toothbrushes. Bingo! Kole Imports had cases of low-quality toothbrushes for less than 3 cents each. One problem was they only lasted through one or two uses before the bristles weakened, but that was fine for this group because they usually throw them out anyway. The second problem was the importer would not sell less than $500 worth at a time. That is more than 16,000 toothbrushes. No problem, we have an ongoing need. I placed my order and the shelter was able to use its funds for other matters.

So you see, if individual toothbrushes are worth nearly a buck each and I was able to round up 16,000 of them, I essentially saved the shelter and its friends $16,000. I could not have made a donation of that size, but that was the value of my effort. The shelter can use the money it did not have to spend on toothbrushes for other things that it cannot obtain at discount prices, like utility fees. I have done similar things with gloves, hats, sweatshirts, plastic forks, razor blades and more.

I have done other variations of surplus deals. One time there was a silk-screener who was going out of business and getting rid of the overruns he had accumulated over the years. We cut a deal and he sent me 2,000 printed t-shirts for 65 cents each, counting shipping. There were all sorts of oddball shirts. Some had bicycles on them; others had jokes or vacation spots, etc. I sold off a bunch of them on eBay in groups of three or four, usually for $10 a group, until I got my money back. It took me several months, but when it was over, I still had about 1,200 shirts left over, essentially for free. I donated 400 identical shirts to a Catholic church that gave them to an Indian tribe (it must have looked like a uniform around there for a while). I gave our maintenance crew about 100 of the shirts and took the rest to the homeless shelter. I have done the same thing with other items like dress shoes, used blue jeans and more. The net result was lots of people got free clothes and I got my money back.

I do similar things at grocery stores. One time Albertsons was reworking their toothpaste section. They filled several buggies with products they pulled from the shelves. They put a half-price sign on the buggies and a week later they still had one buggy full. I offered the manager 25 cents a tube; he was tired of looking at the buggy so he took the deal. I bet you can guess what I did with that toothpaste. I constantly let the stores know I am on the lookout for closeout deals like that. One time they called me with 50 cases of yogurt that had only 5 days left until the expiration date. I bought them all for 15 cents each. It was all gone within two days.

Sometimes the stores just give me stuff. I get lots of the close-out holiday items after the store is tired of looking at them. I have gotten cases of Valentines cards, Halloween candy, Christmas decorations and other items. Recently I got 400 free Easter-egg coloring kits. I put these items in storage and next year I will donate them to a charity that helps out single parents or we will take them to one of the poorer grade schools. By being creative and using our charity dollars this way, we make a big bang in the community without going broke in the process.

You may not want to employ my techniques but you probably have other skills of your own that you can utilize. For example if you like garage sales, you could visit them and ask for donations when their sale is over. Then sell the items on eBay, Craigslist or at the flea market and donate the proceeds to a charity of your choice. Your charity may have some other people who would like to help out by doing the hauling, selling and shipping for you.

Other items can be found in apartment buildings when tenants abandon their belongings. The property managers usually don't want to mess with that stuff so they just throw it away. Every year we accumulate a dozen bicycles that people leave behind in the racks at our buildings. If you asked for them you could fix them up and convert them into nice donations or gifts.

There are many other ways to help out in the community: donate blood; volunteer for causes; mow the lawn for a poor elderly person; visit the veterans hospital; tutor kids at the local grade school; flip pancakes at a fund raiser, join Big Brothers or Big Sisters; coach a little league team; make cookies for the seniors in a nearby community; walk dogs for the pet shelter; serve meals at the homeless shelter; or take disabled kids skiing.

The point is that charity does not always have to mean financial donations. Your time and skills are just as precious as your money. By employing your time and imagination you can do a lot more for the people who need you. At the same time, both you and the charity get to preserve scarce dollars for other critical needs. You might enjoy your life a lot more, too.

To do anything else might be considered *flushing* precious resources down the drain.

TEACH YOUR CHILDREN

In the beginning of this book we noted that a lot of financially challenged people come from parents with similar circumstances. My own parents are good examples. They were fine people, but when it came to finances they could have done much better.

My dad was a good earner, but he spent everything he made and he died broke. He had no concept of saving and investing, which could have enhanced his later years. He moved regularly, and never did build any equity in a home. He died at a young age and had no life insurance. He left behind a dependent who was ill-prepared to care for herself.

My mother was a great saver, but for the wrong reasons: She was a product of the Depression and she was always afraid she would go broke. Therefore, she denied herself simple pleasures even though she could afford them. For example, she wore old tattered clothes even though she had plenty of nice ones. She also bought day-old donuts rather than fresh ones. By the time she passed away she had saved enough money to last her two lifetimes. Meanwhile she had hidden nearly $2,000 in small bills in all sorts of secret places, largely because she had no idea how to invest the money that she saved.

My mom also had control of a rental home that she rented out for half of the market rate because she was afraid of dealing with vacancies. By the time she passed on, her rent-losses amounted to nearly one hundred thousand dollars.

Therefore, my mother was stepping over hundreds of dollars

every month to pick up the pennies she saved on day-old donuts, wearing old clothes and denying herself simple pleasures.

There are plenty of other examples for each of my parents, but you get the point. If you guessed that their parents had similar financial shortcomings, you were correct.

If our own parents are not sufficiently informed to pass on economic wisdom, how is the average youngster supposed to gain the necessary knowledge? That shortcoming creates a great opportunity for our schools to teach these things, at least as an elective, but they never really get around to it either. Furthermore, I know quite a few teachers, and most of them have the same money problems everybody else does. Since neither the parents nor the schools are sufficiently equipped to impart this knowledge, most of us are subject to the whims of fate, usually via trial and error . . . with emphasis on the "error" part.

Fortunately, you can break the chain in your family by sharing with your youngsters the lessons that you have learned from this book. As your children grow older, the combination of your fine example and your wise lessons should inspire them and enhance their opportunities as well as the generations to follow.

It is not necessary for young people to "worship" money. In fact, that can be just as unhealthy as a life of debt and stress. The objective is merely to help them understand how to use their money wisely. We do not need to overwhelm them with data as some college-level course would do. Simply provide the information, in small doses, as they are capable of understanding it. Following are guidelines toward that end.

By Ages

As you review these suggestions, do not fret over the exact age groups as they are laid out. There is plenty of room for overlap. In other words, if your youngster is seven years old and clearly understands the information for that age group, it is acceptable to progress to the lessons of the next older group. Likewise, if your twelve-year-old has never heard any of these things it is fine to start at the beginning. The important thing is to recognize the progression of information and share it with them as soon as they can understand it.

Ages 3-5

Phase into the basics when they are ready to learn where money comes from and why we need it. ("Mommy and Daddy go to work and then our boss pays us money, which we use to buy the things we need.") If they watch educational TV and are learning to count, slip some coins into the discussion. Help them separate pennies, nickels and quarters. ("How many pennies are there on the table?" "Which coin is a nickel?" "What is more, a penny or a quarter?") You can show them that four quarters equal a dollar and five of those equal a five-dollar bill.

Ages 5-8

Introduce them to your paychecks, bills and bank statements. They do not need to know the specifics, they just need to get an idea that money comes in, money goes out and you have to keep score because you might run out. If you have a savings account show them how it works and what you do with the money. ("We use this money for our vacation.") Explain that there is not an infinite amount of money. ("When your money is gone, you cannot buy the things you want unless you work some more. That is why we cannot buy you everything you want.")

This is a good time to introduce them to an allowance and tie it to simple chores. ("You do some chores and you get a reward, just like us.") Whenever you give them money for chores or birthday gifts or their allowance, break it into smaller amounts so it is easy to set some of it aside for savings. For example, if you give them $10 for a birthday gift, split it into a five-dollar bill and five ones. That way, they can easily peel off a couple bucks right away for savings. Have them bring a little of their own money when you go to the store.

Let them buy things and complete their own transactions.

Ages 8-11

By this age, they should know multiplication and division. They can understand day-to-day transactions and how to balance a checkbook.

Make sure they know how much things cost so they have a realistic impression of the value of money. They should be able to decide how many coins of which denominations it takes to complete simple transactions and how much change they should get back.

Have them help clip coupons and shop for bargains. Quiz them at retail stores. ("If the oranges are four for a dollar, how much is one?")

Show them the cost per ounce of items when you buy larger quantities and have them explain how much you saved by buying in bulk. When you get home, review your receipts with them and keep score of the savings over time. At gas stations, ask them questions such as, "If I have $10 and gas is $2.50/gallon, how many gallons will I get?" "If I get 17 miles to a gallon how far can I go on my $10?" "How much gas will we need to drive to California?" "How much money will that cost us?"

Raise their allowance and require more demanding chores. They can do dishes, vacuum, take out the trash, etc. Teach them to save up for some of the things they want.

There are great stories all over the Internet that explain how compound interest grows. They are perfect for this age group. You probably know the one about putting one penny on the first day of a month and doubling it every day. By the last day of the month you will have a million dollars. Expose them to more details about the family budget. When you use a credit card, explain how it works, including interest rates, billing cycles and monthly payments. Have them compute the tip at a restaurant. Teach them to set aside money for charity.

Ages 11-14

Show them that in addition to their allowance, they can earn extra money by taking on more challenging work like baby-sitting, mowing lawns and shoveling snow. Once a month or so have them use their own money to buy food for a family dinner. Then they can prepare the meal and submit a bill to you for the total and make a reasonable profit. If it is acceptable quality, they get full payment plus a tip; if not, they only get their money back for the food but no money for the time they invested. Introduce them to credit reports and stress how financial consistency enhances the score, and why that is important.

Have them keep receipts of all their purchases and review those receipts from time to time to determine if they could spend their money in smarter ways. As they get used to making spending decisions and the limits of their resources, they are ready to make simple but realistic budgets.

Remind them that it is okay to spend some money on a t-shirt or concert now and then, but that the bulk of their money should fit into a financial plan, which includes saving and investing. They should also allow for gifts, vacations, charity, etc.

Have them open their own savings account with some of their own earnings, say $10 per month. Explain that they will be able to buy nice tennis shoes or an iPod or attend a concert. Take them to the bank each month to make their deposit.

Be sure to allow them occasional withdrawals so they get to taste the rewards of saving. Discuss and begin an additional regular long-term savings program for a car and college. Perhaps you can match any additional dollars they set aside from working for this purpose.

Reemphasize the power of compound interest, so they know why they are saving. Introduce them to investing as an adjunct to saving. Tell them about the asset classes including the stock market, bonds and real estate.

Explain the consequences of hasty and risky investments. Discuss why boring, long-term investments (like paying off your home) work out so well. Encourage them to study people like Bill Gates and Warren Buffet.

If you make any larger purchases like an auto or home, include them in the pre-purchase discussions. Tell them what your goals are, how to shop smartly, and what impact the purchase might have on the family budget.

Ages 14-17

Discuss their earning potential and ask them to identify career objectives that they think are worthwhile. Introduce them to credit. Explain that credit can be a worst enemy or a best friend.

Illustrate how compound interest can make them wealthy if they use it as a tool for income, or it can wipe them out if they take on debt and the accompanying interest.

Explain the futility of spending their money on interest expenses for past purchases, therefore why it is critical to pay off credit cards in full and on time every month. Show them that an item that is charged on a credit card with 18 percent interest will cost twice as much if it remains unpaid for four years. Explain "living within your means."

Introduce them to the section of this book on "The Worst Things on Which We Waste our Money." Discuss the items that are likely to lure them into bad choices at this stage of their lives: conveniences, impulse items, smoking, drinking, buying every new techno-toy (such as cell phones), legal matters like traffic tickets, depreciating assets like cars, and the wrong type of auto insurance.

Encourage them to get a job so they can deal with withholding taxes. Have a complete discussion about cars, auto insurance, college and financial demands after that. Explore the idea of student loans, grants and scholarships. Remind them they will be living on their own in a few years. Discuss that renting offers more freedom, but comes with more responsibility.

Ages 17-21

Help them get on some sort of a career path. Help them make a budget and stick to it. Remind them, "If you cannot pay cash, you cannot afford it."

Encourage them to secure the first checking account and credit card, and help them to start building credit, but smartly, with a card at a retail outlet or a gas station. Point out that it is easy to get carried away. Tell them how to obtain a credit report and encourage them to review it at least once every year.

Examine all of the other items in section "The Worst Things on Which We Waste Our Money." Remind them of the responsibilities contained in leases. Discuss the benefits and responsibilities of home ownership.

Emphasize how much it costs to raise children and to keep pets. Introduce them to National Monetary Policies such as foreign aid, deficits and national debt. Make sure they know about taxes, tax deductions and filing income tax returns.

Age 21

They should get a will as soon as they get married or have children. Then they should update it every few years. It is more important than ever to have a budget.

They should buy a condo or home as soon as they have stable income and intend to stay in one place for five years or longer. They should take advantage of retirement plans at work or begin their own plan.

Expose them to good investment choices such as mutual funds and real estate. They should be fully aware of income taxes and how to legally pay the least they can. They should consider maintaining a side business for extra income and tax savings.

They should understand the cost of having children and pets. Remind them that obsessing over material things will steal away what really matters, and that true wealth is being happy, not wearing their money on their sleeves.

Finally, they should expect to teach their own children these things because nobody else will.

None of this is very complicated, but it is amazing how many adults do not know these things or they ignore the knowledge they have. I hope you will freely share this information with your own children so they can get started on the right foot. By helping them to avoid common mistakes, they will have a great opportunity to use their money wisely rather than *flush* it down the drain like so many other citizens do.

SECTION THREE CONCLUSION

The final section of this book was intended to identify most of the important decisions that might come up at some time in your future. You do not need to commit the information to memory, but keep the book close by, so you can review the information as you are confronted with the experiences that we have discussed.

I hope that the chapters of this section will continue to guide and enrich your family for many years to come. Please stay in touch!

Other books by this author

INSTANT EXPERIENCE for REAL ESTATE AGENTS

*Great Lessons, True Stories
and Lots of Fun for Real Estate Agents*

ISBN 978-1-937862-62-6

Copies of this author's books may be ordered from
www.bookcrafters.net
and other online bookstores

This book available in digital format.

CPSIA information can be obtained at www.ICGtesting.com
Printed in the USA
BVOW05s0125220914

367749BV00001B/125/P

9 781937 862633